D1568717

Caribbean**Visions**

Contemporary Painting and Sculpture

Art Services International
Alexandria, Virginia
1995

Participating Museums

Center for the Fine Arts
Miami, Florida

New Orleans Museum of Art
New Orleans, Louisiana

Wadsworth Atheneum
Hartford, Connecticut

and additional sites

This exhibition is organized and circulated by Art Services International, Alexandria, Virginia

Library of Congress Cataloging-in-Publication Data
Lewis, Samella S.
Caribbean visions : contemporary painting and sculpture / Samela Sanders Lewis.
p. cm.
Includes bibliographical references.
ISBN 0–88397–118–6 (alk. paper)
1. Art, Caribbean—Exhibitions. 2. Art, Modern—20th century—Caribbean Area—Exhibitions. I. Title.
N6591.L48 1995
709' .729'07473—dc20 95-30576
CIP

Editor: Nancy Eickel
Designer: Polly Franchine
Printer: South China Printing Co. (1988) Ltd.
Printed and bound in Hong Kong

In the catalogue of works section, (pp. 95–207), artists appear alphabetically according to country of birth.
Also refer to the list of participating artists (p. 9) and the index of artists (p. 227).
All dimensions of works are given in inches, with height preceding width preceding depth.

Cover: Dudley Charles, *Forest Lights,* 1991
Page 1: José Bedia, *Mujer de poder,* 1993
Pages 2 & 3: Annalee Davis, *The Things We Worship,* 1992 (shown open)
Page 4: Arnaldo Roche Rabell, *La sabiduría de la loca,* 1991
Page 10: Philippe Dodard, *Magic Wedding,* n.d. (detail)

Caribbean**Visions**
Contemporary Painting and Sculpture

is made possible through support of the
Lila Wallace-Reader's Digest Fund
and we gratefully appreciate their sponsorship of this exhibition and tour

Additional generous support has been provided by

Metropolitan Life Foundation

and by the Official Caribbean Carrier,

BWIA **BWIA International Airways Limited**
The International Airline of the Caribbean

and the Official United States Carrier,

USAir
USAir begins with you

and also by the Barbados Investment and Development Corporation
and the Puerto Rican Economic Development Commission

The Caribbean

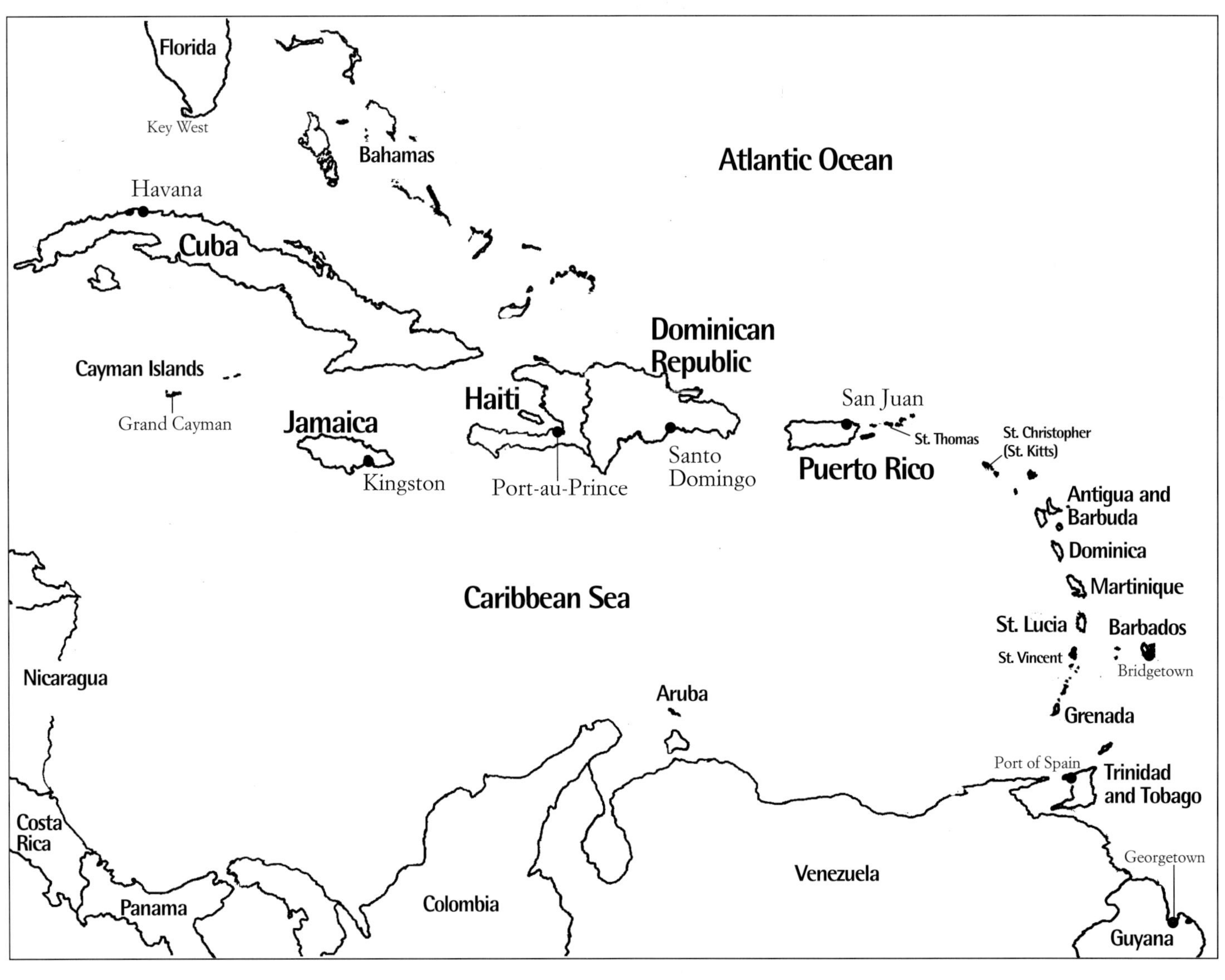
Florida
Key West
Bahamas
Atlantic Ocean
Havana
Cuba
Dominican
Republic
Cayman Islands
Grand Cayman
Jamaica
Kingston
Haiti
Port-au-Prince
Santo
Domingo
San Juan
St. Thomas
Puerto Rico
St. Christopher
(St. Kitts)
Antigua and
Barbuda
Dominica
Martinique
Caribbean Sea
St. Lucia
Barbados
St. Vincent
Bridgetown
Nicaragua
Aruba
Grenada
Port of Spain
Trinidad
and Tobago
Costa
Rica
Georgetown
Venezuela
Panama
Colombia
Guyana

Participating Artists

Barbados
Ras Ishi Butcher
Annalee Davis
David Gall
Gwen Knight
Ras Akyem Ramsay

Cayman Islands
Bendel Hydes

Cuba
Luis Cruz Azaceta
José Bedia
María Magdalena Campos-Pons
Tomás Esson
Lia Galletti
Wifredo Lam

Dominican Republic
José García Cordero
José Perdomo
Genaro Phillips
Inés Tolentino

Guyana
Frank Bowling
Karl Broodhagen
Dudley Charles
Stanley Greaves
Gregory A. Henry

Haiti
Philippe Dodard
Edouard Duval Carrié
Andre Juste
Jean Claude Rigaud
Bernard Séjourné
Luce Turnier

Jamaica
David Boxer
Eric Cadien
Margaret Chen
Albert Chong
Karl "Jerry" Craig
Christopher Gonzalez
Peter Wayne Lewis
Edna Manley
Alvin Marriott
Michael M. Milton
Ronald Moody
Keith Morrison
Stafford Schliefer
Osmond Watson

Puerto Rico
Myrna Báez
Diógenes Ballester
María de Mater O'Neill
Arnaldo Roche Rabell
Nelson Santiago
Juan Carlos Toca

St. Thomas
Ademola Olugebefola

St. Vincent
Claude Fiddler

Trinidad and Tobago
Francisco Cabral
LeRoy Clarke
Christopher Cozier
Kenwyn Crichlow
Shastri Maharaj
Wendy M. Nanan
Shengé Ka Pharaoh

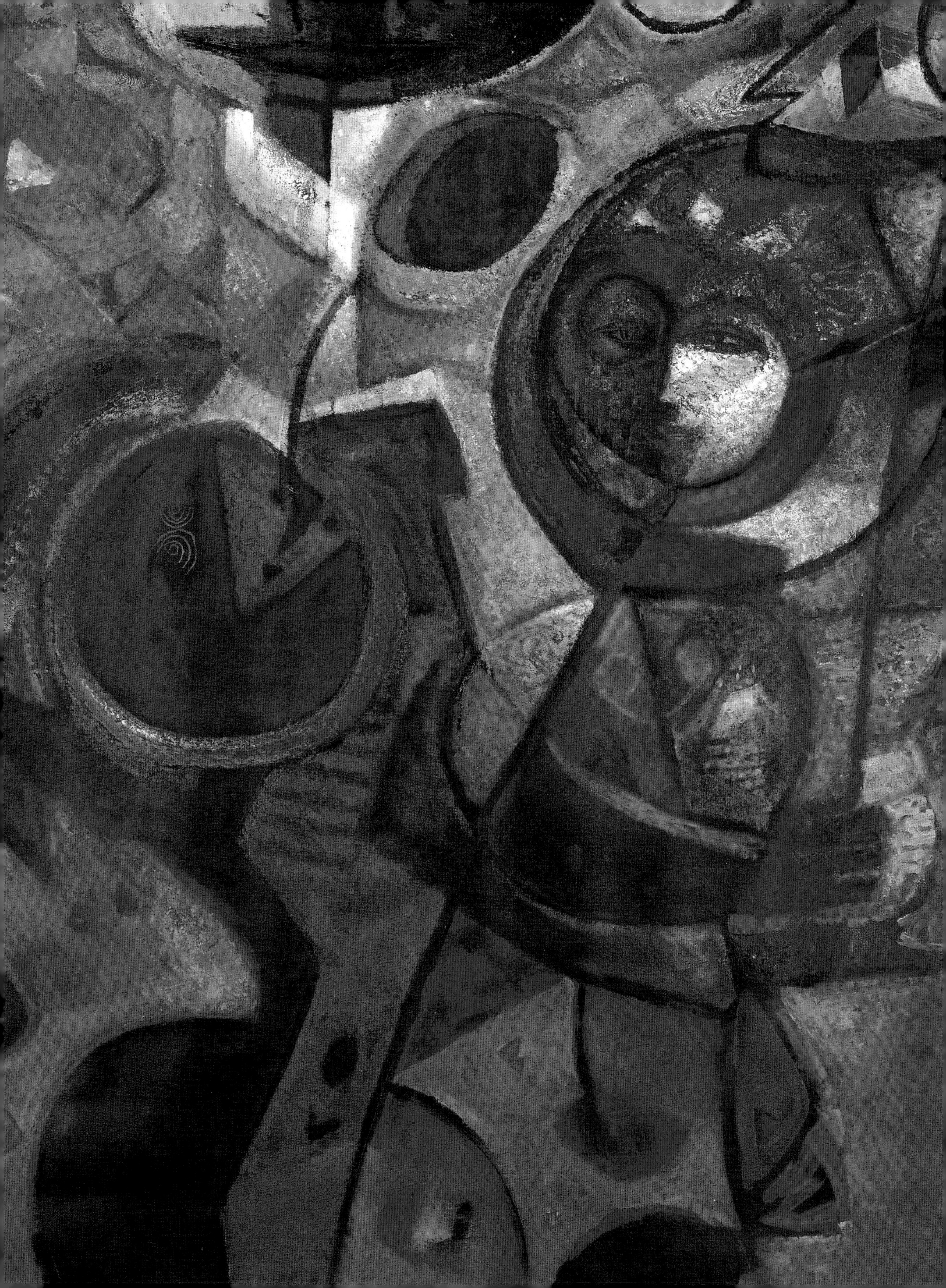

Contents

Acknowledgments 13

Preface 16
Gloria Gordon

Introduction 19
Samella Lewis and Mary Jane Hewitt

The Antilles: Fragments of Epic Memory 29
Derek Walcott

Caribbean Cultural Identity 37
Rex Nettleford

Trinidad Carnival: History and Meaning 43
Errol Hill

Carnival and Its Place in Caribbean Culture and Art 49
Peter Minshall

Caribbean Art and Culture from a Haitian Perspective 59
Gerald Alexis

Artists of Haiti: Reflections on a Narrative 65
Richard A. Long

Modern Art of the Spanish-Speaking Caribbean 71
Shifra M. Goldman

Catalogue of Works 95

Selected Exhibitions of Participating Artists 209

Glossary 221
Mary Jane Hewitt

Selected Bibliography 223

Index of Artists 227

Acknowledgments

Caribbean: the very word conjures up a host of visual, mental, and physical associations: lush vegetation, inviting beaches, enticing music, culturally rich peoples. Many have viewed the Caribbean from the outside, visiting the islands as tourists. Rarely are we given the opportunity to explore this diverse region through the eyes and experiences of its artists. *Caribbean Visions: Contemporary Painting and Sculpture* provides a long-awaited chance to investigate in one setting the wide range of artistic talent that this area has spawned in recent years. Works by fifty-six painters and sculptors from Barbados, the Cayman Islands, Cuba, the Dominican Republic, Guyana, Haiti, Jamaica, Puerto Rico, St. Thomas, St. Vincent, and Trinidad and Tobago are presented here, brought together under the auspices of Art Services International. In keeping with our mission to bring the fine arts of the world to American audiences, we are pleased to have assembled the dynamic works that comprise *Caribbean Visions.*

Vital to the successful completion of this endeavor have been the artists themselves, whose roots in the Caribbean have greatly affected their lives. They have all remained deeply committed to their homelands, even those who have left the islands to pursue their personal artistic quests. Their works exhibit an exciting array of images, ideas, and forms, each of which speaks of the unique experience of being from the Caribbean. This presentation would not have been possible without their generosity and that of the many collectors and institutions who have agreed to part with works for the duration of the traveling exhibition.

Working in close conjuction with us in organizing this presentation has been Dr. Samella Lewis, noted Caribbean scholar, Guest Curator of the exhibition, and a major contributor to the catalogue. Her perseverance and insight into recent developments in the Caribbean art world have honed this spectacular array of color and shape. We thank Dr. Lewis for her unfailing belief in this project, and we extend to her our warmest congratulations on its completion.

Others who have added to our expanding awareness of the Caribbean include the authors who have contributed essays to this catalogue. Our regards are sent to Dr. Gloria Gordon, Derek Walcott, Professor Rex Nettleford, Dr. Richard A. Long, Gerald Alexis, Peter Minshall, Dr. Errol Hill, and Dr. Shifra M. Goldman. Dr. Mary Jane Hewitt also made an important contribution to this catalogue. We appreciate the scholarship that they share with readers of this ground-breaking text, and we thank them for their efforts and interest in this exhibition.

Art Services International is extremely grateful to the Lila Wallace-Reader's Digest Fund for the major financial support it has provided to the organization of this hemisphere-wide project and for initially putting us in contact with Gloria Gordon, our Exhibition Consultant. At the Fund we acknowledge the endorsement of Christine M. DeVita, President, and George V. Grune, Chairman. We thank the Fund as well for its support in developing the educational aspects of the exhibition, in particular the enlightening video that accompanies this presentation. We com-

Myrna Báez
Retrato de un sueño (detail)
(see p. 179)

mend the Fund's focus on attracting a diverse public to the arts, making culture an active part of everyday life.

Additional support for *Caribbean Visions* was provided by a generous grant from Metropolitan Life Foundation. We offer our sincere thanks to the Foundation for recognizing the importance of this project, and for its contributions to the enrichment of our culture. In addition, we acknowledge the interest and encouragement we have received from the Barbados Investment and Development Corporation through E. Anton Norris, Chief Executive Officer.

Our sincere appreciation is directed to Edward Wegel, President of BWIA International Airways, for the generous participation of BWIA as Official Caribbean Carrier for *Caribbean Visions* and for his awareness of the contribution that Caribbean talent has made to the culture of our western hemisphere. We are indebted to Cheryl Lai Fang, Corporate Communications, for her tireless attention to the details of this international endeavor.

Art Services International is most pleased to recognize USAir for the support it has provided as Official United States carrier. We extend our special gratitude to David Low and S. Buzz Bisnath for their recognition of the certain contribution that the exhibition will make to American cultural awareness.

Also offering their able assistance to this project have been Manuel Biascochea, Director of the Puerto Rican Film Commission; Elizabeth Ruth Johnston of Johnston Art International; Pat Ramsey, Director of the Jamaican Artists and Craftsmen Guild; and Maud Duquella of Galeria Botello. Althea Silvera, Special Collections Librarian at Florida International University, provided curatorial assistance.

Lending their enthusiasm to this international endeavor are the ambassadors of the countries represented in this exhibition who have graciously agreed to serve as Honorary Patrons. It is an honor to acknowledge these distinguished persons: His Excellency Dr. Courtney N. Blackman, Ambassador of Barbados; His Excellency Dr. Odeen Ishmael, Ambassador of Guyana; His Excellency Dr. Richard Bernal, Ambassador of Jamaica; Wanda Rubianes, Esq., Director, Puerto Rican Federal Affairs Administration; and Her Excellency Corin McKnight, Ambassador of Trinidad and Tobago.

Numerous embassy representatives have generously contributed their assistance to this project. We wish to thank in particular Pamela Stroude, Second Secretary, and Roy Clarke, Commercial Counsellor, of the Embassy of Barbados; and June Persaud, Minister of Counsel, and Annette Harris, Executive Secretary to the Ambassador, of the Embassy of Guyana. At the Embassy of Jamaica we are grateful for the efforts made by Mrs. Richard Bernal, wife of Ambassador Bernal, and to Basil Bryan, Deputy Chief of Mission, and Maxine Anderson, Information Officer. Our sincere appreciation goes to Yvonne Cervoni, Executive Assistant to the Director, Puerto Rican Federal Affairs Administration; and to Desmond Parker, former Cultural Attache of the Embassy of Trinidad and Tobago.

This exhibition could not accomplish its purpose without the interest and endorsement of colleagues in museums throughout the United States. As always, it is a pleasure to recognize those who have joined us in exploring the Caribbean art of today: Suzanne Delahanty, Director, and Kate Rawlinson, Associate Curator, of the Center for the Fine Arts in Miami; John E. Bullard, Director, and Daniel Piersol, Chief Curator of Exhibitions, of the New Orleans Museum of Art; and Patrick McCaughey, Director, Gertrud Bourgoyne, Curatorial Administrator, and Kristin

Mortimer, Deputy Director, of the Wadsworth Atheneum in Hartford. It has been an extremely satisfying experience to work with each of them.

Our editor Nancy Eickel and designer Polly Franchine have been most successful in capsulizing the great diversity of styles and aesthetic approaches of these Caribbean artists. Working in conjunction with the printing firm of South China Printing Company, their efforts have culminated in this volume, which handsomely documents the roots and directions of contemporary Caribbean art.

Once again, it is with great pleasure that we acknowledge the staff of Art Services International. Deserving special recognition for her Herculean effort is Ana Maria Lim, Assistant Director, who has been instrumental in coordinating arrangements with the vast number of individuals connected with this project and its accompanying educational video. Douglas Shawn, Anne Breckenridge, Kirsten Simmons Verdi, Betty Kahler, Patti Bruch, Sally Thomas, Ralph Logan, and David Paper have all contributed their professional abilities to the completion of this important project, and we enthusiastically commend their efforts.

Lynn K. Rogerson
Director

Joseph W. Saunders
Chief Executive Officer

Preface

The realization of this exhibition is certainly a *cause célèbre.* Early presentations of works by Caribbean artists, such as the one held at the Trinidad and Tobago Tourist Board in New York City in 1970, which featured paintings by six Trinidadian artists, including Boscoe Holder and LeRoy Clarke, received much acclaim from the American artistic community and verified that Caribbean art was ready to be part of the mainstream.

Also in the early 1970s, the late Romare Bearden remarked that, although he took cruises in the Caribbean every year and consistently looked for information on Caribbean artists, there was simply nothing about them in print. This casual statement instigated a journey that has culminated in *Caribbean Visions: Contemporary Painting and Sculpture.* The challenge was to bring together the work of artists from throughout the region, allowing their voices to tell their own story and sing their own song. Each painter and sculptor had become aware of the aesthetic in his/her own environment and had directed attention to the endless variety of forms and colors, the richness of textures, the force, rhythm, and triumph of human interaction, and the poetry of nature and man. Assembling the artists and writers who would reflect the diversity of art and life in the region would offer to the world a profound and valuable statement about Caribbean realities and potential.

A number of people provided encouragement at the early stages of this endeavor. Outstanding among them was Dr. Samella Lewis, whose book *African American Art and Artists* served as a model for this publication on Caribbean artists. Others who expressed immediate interest in the project were the late M.P. Alladin, Director of Culture, Ministry of Education and Culture, Government of Trinidad and Tobago, and Roy Boyke, Director of Key Publications of Trinidad and Tobago, as well as the late Errol Barrow, Prime Minister of Barbados, and Errol Hill of Dartmouth College. Throughout the Caribbean, people recognized the need for such an overview of the region's art, and many supplied names of artists and writers who should be included. Geraldo Mosquera and Martha Llanos of Cuba, Ardry Bratton, a collector of Haitian art in New York City, Eneid Routte Gomez of Puerto Rico, and Rene Louis of Martinique were especially helpful. Both Derek Walcott and Rex Nettleford encouraged the continuation of work on this project in the early 1980s.

In the course of defining the concepts of what Caribbean art entails and in organizing this exhibition, a new generation of artists had emerged and honed their skills by studying the "old masters" of the Caribbean. A vibrant art scene in Trinidad and Tobago provided the impetus to view the work of newcomers Wendy Nanan and Christopher Cozier, while still enjoying Ken Morris and his panmen in copper repoussé, Boscoe Holder and his lyrical heads, LeRoy Clarke climbing to El Tuchuche, Luise Kimme carving her glorious creatures, and Peter Minshall and the *mas.* Correspondence with Selden Rodman in Haiti, Jim Rudin of the Poui Gallery in

Grenada, and Anne Walmsley in London unearthed valuable information on several of these artists, among them Ronald Moody, who had spent a large part of his career in England.

During the past two decades, numerous people have touched this project—Oswald Glean Chase, Archie Hudson Philips, Lowery Sims, Edward Habib, and many others—and they have all eagerly waited to see it come to fruition. The wait has ensured that an exhibition of the highest quality has been produced, one that will demonstrate to the world what Caribbean artists have to offer.

Gloria Gordon
Project Consultant

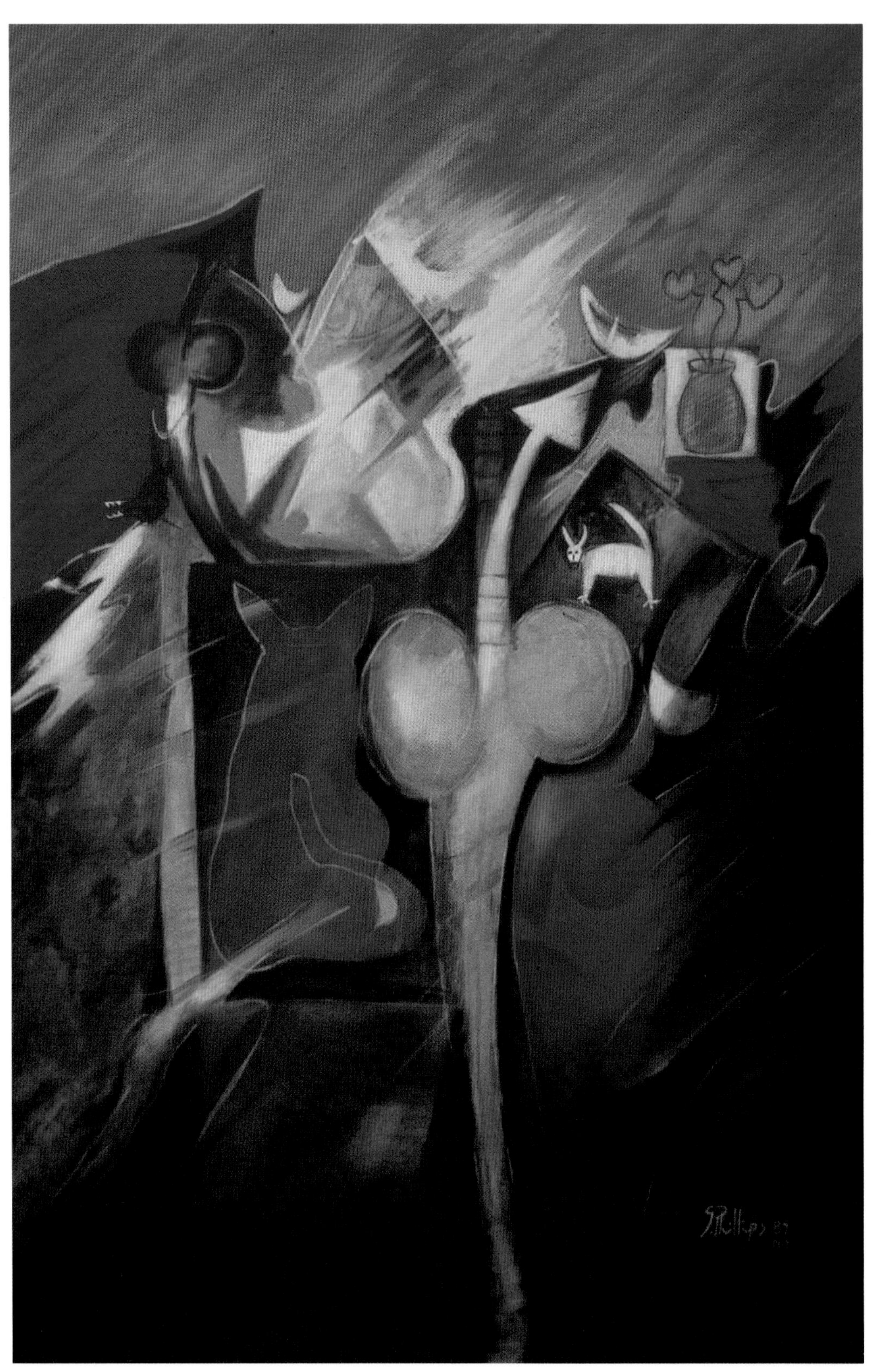

Introduction

Samella Lewis and Mary Jane Hewitt

The Caribbean comprises a region of sixteen independent countries, three French *departments,* five British colonies with varying degrees of autonomy, a commonwealth and a territory of the United States, and six semiautonomous members of the Kingdom of the Netherlands.[1] Or, if the notion of a Caribbean community as reflected by the participating nations in CARIFESTA (The Caribbean Festival of the Arts) were used as a guide, it would include all the Central and South American nations that border the Caribbean Sea and those that touch the Atlantic Ocean but have been identified as Caribbean through circumstances of cultural identity and colonial history, e.g., Bermuda, the Bahamas, Guyana, and Suriname.[2]

The term "West Indies" lost currency with the failure of efforts to federate the then-British colonies of Jamaica, Barbados, and Trinidad and Tobago in the mid-1950s and the pressures for independence exerted due to European colonialism. The only remaining entity that bears this paradoxical name is the University of the West Indies. The term now preferred is "Caribbean."

The linguistic patterns of this large and diverse region include Amerindian languages, English, Spanish, French, Dutch, and various creole languages that incorporate within them Amerindian and African words and syntax, as well as languages from India, Indonesia, China, and the Middle East. Equally diverse are religious orientations: various African cosmologies, such as *Vodoun, Santería, Shango,* and *Kumina,* Roman Catholic and Protestant Christianity, and several Hindu, Muslim, and Buddhist practices, all of which reveal themselves in Caribbean festival arts and in monocultural as well as syncretic manifestations. As Professor Rex Nettleford observes in his illuminating essay, these nations are engaged in a process of creolization, displaying an uncanny awareness of the complexity and interconnectedness of all phenomena because of their very separateness. National and individual identity is therefore rooted in cultural cross-fertilization.

•

The intent of *Caribbean Visions* is to present a comprehensive view of contemporary painting and sculpture in the region by featuring works created by artists who well reflect, and are inspired by, a Caribbean consciousness. Through a variety of media and styles, these artists expose us to the region's everyday activities that contribute to the composition and structure of their cultures. An effort has been made to avoid stereotypical generalizations and to explore the essence of the Caribbean people. Although they share geographic, historic, social, and economic conditions, the artists of this multicultural population express their creativity in unique ways. We have made a special effort to consider this art from the point of view of those who produce it rather than from within the context of our own perspective.

Genaro Phillips
Tropic II
(see p. 124)

Caribbean Visions is the first exhibition of its scope and size to travel outside the Caribbean. The participating artists are largely academically trained, native to the Caribbean, and either still live and work there or have resettled abroad, most often in the United States. Their works were known to the exhibition's curator and/or were recommended by specialists in contemporary Caribbean art. An attempt was made to be as comprehensive as possible in terms of geography, without sacrificing quality, and to reflect the rich cultural diversity of the region.

The uniqueness of contemporary Caribbean art lies within the artists' sense of space, their perceptions of light and color, and the geographic identification with the Caribbean, despite the location of their ancestral homeland or their current residence. As is universally true of the visual arts, environment must be given serious consideration in understanding how and what artists see, feel, and express. Flora, fauna, light, color, tropical air, and physical surroundings distinguish the Caribbean from other regions of the Western Hemisphere. Unfortunately, the physical environment has generally served as the principal focus that tourists and other visitors consider to be the main asset of the entire region.

Such close examination of works by Caribbean artists will reveal not only their individual qualities but also their unique ways of organizing form and content, their self-perceptions, and their aesthetic interpretations. Contemporary Caribbean visual arts reflect a large cultural spectrum. Caribbean artists have found unity in diversity. Their differences have sparked a sense of freedom that has evoked quality and depth to their artistic expression. It is our belief that the uniqueness of today's Caribbean artists lies in their liberation from the constrictions of historical convention. With that sense of freedom they are recreating themselves through "the arts of the imagination." Guyanese writer Wilson Harris expressed the belief that "Caribbean man is involved in a civilisation-making process," or at least that the possibility to do so continues.

> I believe the possibility exists for us to become involved in perspectives of renascence which can bring into play a figurative meaning beyond an apparently real world or prison of history. . . . A cleavage exists in my opinion between the historical convention in the Caribbean and Guianas and the arts of the imagination. I believe a philosophy of history may well lie buried in the arts of the imagination.[3]

Dr. Shifra Goldman concludes her comprehensive analysis of works by Spanish-speaking Caribbean artists with the astute observation that "artists have successfully crossed borders that politicians have not," which further reinforces our thesis and that of Wilson Harris. Perhaps the arts are the only means of liberating people and nations from historical convention, particularly when that convention is based on a variety of contradictory models: a plural society, a creole society, a national society, a syncretic/synthetic ideal, and a folk/maroon interpretation.[4]

Harris and Brathwaite look to ancestral legacies as "gateways" or "thresholds" to a new world, an "underworld imagination" that is not bound by these contradictory models.

> *Limbo* and *vodun* are variables of an underworld imagination. . . . The trickster of *limbo* holds out a caveat . . . of conscience and points to the necessity for a free imagination which is at risk on behalf of a truth that is no longer given in the collective medium of the tribe. The emergence of the individual works of art is consistent with—and the inevitable corollary of—an evolution of folk *limbo* into symbols of inner cunning and authority which reflect a long duress of the imagination.[5]

The *limbo* dance was born on the slave ships of the Middle Passage, it is said, because there was so little space in the cramped holds of the ships that the African captives contorted themselves into human spiders to move about. The trickster figures strongly in Caribbean folk culture and is often characterized as Anancy, the wily spider "who makes a way out of no way." Symbols of the *limbo* and trickster are key underpinnings of contemporary Caribbean art, which is at once affirmative/assertive and subversive.

Professor Brathwaite limits his observation regarding this creative affirmation/subversion process to the African and Amerindian, but the same holds true for those who came later and joined the creolization process.

> In the Caribbean, whether it be African or Amerindian, the recognition of an ancestral relationship with the folk or aboriginal culture involves the artist and participant in a journey into the past and hinterland which is at the same time a movement of possession into present and future. Through this movement of possession we become ourselves, truly our own creation. . . .[6]

•

In the case of Haiti, it has been a long journey from the revolutionary leaders' selection of French and English artists to interpret the Haitian people and their history, to the selection of popular or self-taught Haitian artists to represent their country's world of art, to the analysis and documentation of Haitian art by Haitian art historians. As described in the essays by Dr. Richard Long and Mr. Gerald Alexis, modern and contemporary Haitian art emerged earlier than 1944, when the Centre d'Art in Port-au-Prince opened with Dewitt Peters from the United States as director. This is not to negate the importance of the U.S. role in the development of training and exhibition opportunities for Haitian artists. Actually, interaction between Haitians and North Americans began in the late nineteenth century and continued through the period of the Harlem Renaissance, when social and literary representatives of the African American community visited the island in response to concerns about the U.S. occupation of Haiti and their interest in the Haitian Indigenist Movement. Contact broadened in the 1930s when African American visual artists began to interact with and influence leading Haitian artists. Haitian writers and painters served as Caribbean pioneers in furthering the concept of indigenization *(indigenisme),* an idea that spread throughout the Caribbean region as the twentieth century progressed.

The works of contemporary Haitian painters, such as the late Luce Turnier and Edouard Duval Carrié, offer a broad spectrum of subject matter and content that is revealed when each of their expressions is examined. While Turnier was concerned with semiabstract figurative forms that refer to working class people, Duval Carrié chose to explore life through a highly personal blend of surrealism and spiritualism. Both artists, although stylistically different, share connections with the intensely rich flavor of the indigenous Haitian cosmology. Whereas both Turnier and Duval Carrié frequently lived and worked in Paris, their aim seems to have been to use the styles and techniques learned in Europe to forge an individual style suitable to chronicling life in their native land. Singular differences of content and style are common throughout the Caribbean. Duval Carrié provides insight into age-old symbols, manifestations of ancient and contemporary beliefs. Turnier's version of ordinary people was expressed through figures that reflected her concept of social, personal, and aesthetic points of view.

•

A tireless champion of metal sculpture, Ken Morris (1924–1992) is justly regarded as the leading inspirational force behind this art form, now so popular in Trinidad and Tobago. Having worked as a professional artist since 1955, Morris is known for the expressionistic form and vibrant, vigorous style of his sculptures. His art grew out of ideas and images that stemmed from his own environment, usually experiences that offered views of traditional contemporary life on the twin islands.

Morris credited Carnival with changing attitudes on art and artists in Trinidad. It provided an outlet for creativity and participation that led to the discovery and recognition of countless numbers of imaginative individuals.

> I was beating metal to create art and some other people were beating pots to create music. People were looking for something to do. I identified with the steel band. A lot of things came out of that time. Trinidad was a breeding ground for creativity.[7]

Initially, satisfying the needs of Carnival rather than creating art was the principal purpose behind Ken Morris's art activity. The demands of Carnival to create works following a different theme each year inspired him to experiment with achieving his goal of producing more sophisticated and challenging works that would remain relevant throughout the year. He was concerned that beautiful works were discarded simply because Carnival was over. In this same vein, Professor Errol Hill and Mr. Peter Minshall, in their respective essays, offer their understanding of the history and meaning of Trinidad Carnival and the place of Carnival in Caribbean culture and art.

In Trinidad and Tobago, two artists with contrasting views of the African Caribbean heritage are Francisco Cabral and LeRoy Clarke. Cabral relates his views in sculpture and assemblages primarily from a political perspective, while at the heart of Clarke's expressions are allegories and religious beliefs. Both artists see and define "their Africa" with energy, even though from divergent viewpoints.

Francisco Cabral's sculptures usually consist of installations composed of independent objects that together form a narrative whole. Closely resembling architectural and environmental assemblages, they are poignant in their message and undeniable in their presence.

LeRoy Clarke grew up in a closely knit, primarily African tribal community, which made him profoundly aware of African Caribbean religious beliefs, practices, and folklore, particularly the ceremonies and deities that would later inform his work. This poet-painter-philosopher articulates a vision of a people who "need to see the light and touch it." "I became an *Obeah* man, a light-bringer," he observed. Clarke turned to the mystical past and transformed the powerful symbols of that mythology into a visual language that, for him, could translate preachings of spiritual ascendancy.[8]

Shengé Ka Pharoah, who was born in and spent much of his early life on these twin islands, currently lives in New York City. Consequently, he sees his African roots from a different perspective than that of Clarke or Cabral. Shengé's work shows marked influences of the mythic qualities of ancient cultures, as well as the creativity spawned by today's graffiti artists and the inspiration to be found in discarded materials salvaged from the urban environment. As a Rastafarian, Shengé has much in common with Ras Akyem Ramsay and Ras Ishi Butcher, two Rastafarian artists from Barbados. The common bond these artists share seems to be locked in their Rastafarian beliefs which, although originating in Jamaica, are now recognized as being part of an international culture and lifestyle.

Shastri Maharaj and Wendy Nanan are two of the most highly regarded artists of East Indian descent in Trinidad and Tobago. Their works, although contemporary, focus on ancient customs that are firmly established in East Indian Caribbean communities. By interweaving their cultural, social, religious, and aesthetic concerns, these artists render harmonious relationships between ritual and ordinary happenings. Ever mindful of their Caribbean environment, both Nanan and Maharaj freely interject images of their place and time into their compositions.

The enchanting visual narratives of Shastri Maharaj are reminiscent of the magic scrolls found in early Ethiopian paintings and the Buddhist caves of India. The intense red and green palette, enriched with black outlines, evokes a "dream world" in which the participants hope to have their wishes fulfilled. The spontaneity of the composition gives rise to a freedom only the imagination can render.

•

The island of Jamaica was visited by itinerant European artists as early as the seventeenth century, but not until the twentieth century did an indigenous school of Jamaican art arise. Pioneers in this movement included Edna Manley—born in England of a Jamaican mother and an English father, Edna married her cousin Norman Manley and moved to Jamaica with him in 1922—Albert Huie, and Ronald Moody. The Institute of Jamaica, founded in 1879, played a key role in furthering the island's arts. Spurred on by Mrs. Manley and Philip Sherlock, Secretary/Librarian at the Institute in the late 1930s, it consolidated the link between the nationalists and the local art scene.

Dr. David Boxer, Director of the National Gallery of Jamaica and himself a respected artist, summed up this process, having continued the course begun in the 1930s as "the intimate interrelationship between art and life, between art and the process of nation building," declaring it to be a "key characteristic of the Jamaican school."[9] Reviews of the 1992 and 1993 Annual National Exhibitions held at the National Gallery of Jamaica; an enlightening article by Veerle Poupeye-Rammelaere, Curator at the National Gallery of Jamaica, that appeared in a special Caribbean issue of *Revue Noire;* and works chosen for this exhibition document the broad range of expressions that enliven contemporary Jamaican art, including the avant-garde works of David Boxer as artist.

Social concerns continued to be recorded in aesthetic terms in the 1990s, and environmental awareness emerged as a major topical issue. In 1992, an archaeological find of valuable Taíno sculptures in a cave in St. Ann, Jamaica, and the acknowledgment of Columbus's first voyage to the Caribbean five hundred years earlier provided numerous themes for artists. Dr. Nadine Scott used the term "trans-avantgarde" to describe some of the work, "going, as they do, beyond the conventional ideas of avant-gardism."[10]

Veerle Poupeye-Rammelaere marked the 1960s as an era of rebellion against the nationalist stigma that had been attached to Jamaican art and the conceptual and stylistic limitations of the early movement on the part of several young Jamaican artists, most of whom had studied abroad.

> This resulted in a diversification of interests and the initially somewhat forced introduction of new concepts such as abstraction. During the same period, the Black Consciousness movement, Rastafarianism, Jamaica's turbulent political life and the harsh socio-economic realities facing a developing country, provided a new ideological impetus, which gave new meaning to the issue of cultural identity in Jamaica. Today, there is a self-confident and highly inventive Jamaican avant-garde, although only a few of these artists have chosen to deviate from the tradition of a humanist, message-oriented art in favor of "art for art's sake."[11]

Counted among the innovators was Margaret Chen, a Jamaican artist of Chinese ancestry who embraces abstract geometric forms and combines them with somber brown and gold colors characteristic of Asian screen painting. She creates monochromatic paintings, usually on multiple canvases or plywood that are distinguished from one another by size and tonality but nevertheless comprise the whole. Chen apparently prefers subtle changes in surface patterns and structure, which convey a quiet, timeless feel that appeals to the philosophical nature of experience.

Christopher Gonzalez, one of Jamaica's leading sculptors, is generally known for his carved wood sculptures. His work is always figurative and ranges from the organic and sensual to the expressionistic. Gonzalez allows subject matter to govern the surface treatment of his figures, all of which suggest growth and strong emotion. His works possess epic significance and are provocative in their contours and spatial organization.

Albert Chong is equally at home with sculpture and installations that reflect his Jamaican origins. Currently a resident of Boulder, Colorado, his work consists of symbols and images that serve as reminders of his Jamaican homeland. Thrones, bearing a close relationship to nature, are assembled from found objects. Although created from discarded materials, these intriguing works reflect Chong's sense of spirituality and respect for higher powers.

•

The work of Karl Broodhagen is considered by many to mark the beginning of contemporary art in Barbados. An artist-teacher who migrated from Guyana to Barbados as a teenager, Broodhagen served as a mentor for the transitional group of artists who were instrumental in recreating a neglected history of Barbados through their art. In the Barbados of Broodhagen's early years, virtually all interest in the visual arts was based upon a Eurocentric perspective. His example encouraged ordinary people of all races to envision themselves with strength and dignity. In his sculpture *Benin Head* (p. 131), Broodhagen reaffirms the deity of motherhood and womanhood. In creating such images he turned away from models and allowed the sculpture's form to rise from the wealth of his knowledge and the essence of his understanding. Thanks to Broodhagen, the flame of multiculturalism still burns in Barbados.

Contemporary artists in Barbados endeavor to express their serious concerns through a variety of media. At a "festival" held in an abandoned sugar refinery in 1992, visual, performing, and literary artists presented works that they had been invited to create in support of the continued production of sugar. Individuality was not sacrificed, as artists imbued the subject with serious meaning and approached it from their own perspectives. Through their participation artists reached beyond the borders of Barbados and connected with a larger world where important ideas, unseen, are made visible. In Barbados, artists who employ various styles and media strengthen their expressions by banding together and supporting each other's differences.

One member of this old/new breed of serious practicing artist is Annalee Davis, a socially concerned Barbadian who produces paintings, prints, and performance pieces that register protest against oppression and neglect. Her works are dramatic compositions containing expressive figurative forms that are seemingly projected with an x-ray vision to suggest a fourth dimension. Davis frequently uses geometric forms to abstract her figures and to add strength and forcefulness to her mission of creating meaningful works of social and aesthetic value.

•

Dudley Charles, a remarkable painter from Guyana who currently lives in Maryland, focuses on color and movement as the two essential elements in his compositions. Clearly the flora and fauna of the Guyanese rainforest have strongly influenced his art and his aesthetic vision. His ability to project his understanding of light and color stems from an intense love of nature and a close relationship to its spiritual qualities. The artist's appreciation of nature and his vivid sense of color are not only associated with his landscapes but are also present in his figurative style in which color and movement constitute the basic elements of his expressive, yet beautifully balanced paintings.

•

Numerous themes and subjects resonate throughout the work of these Caribbean artists: nationalism/indigenism, romantic love, mysticism, religious practices, satire, antibureaucracy, antitechnology, the figurative celebration of deities and legendary figures, respect for nature in all its forms, the excitement brought by Carnival throughout the Caribbean, the folk roots of culture, and visual narrative language. When these paintings and sculptures are contemplated together, it becomes obvious that a uniqueness of expression typifies the region, and yet the individuality of the artist is still quite prominent.

Professor Nettleford sees the entire Caribbean, indeed all of the Americas, as a product of the process of cross-fertilization, "actualised in simultaneous acts of negating and affirming, demolishing and constructing, rejecting and shaping," which is most evident in the creative arts. Carnival celebrations make life bountiful and endurable, and thus achieve the fundamental aim of this process, according to Professor Errol Hill, while Mr. Minshall sees Carnival as culture, as art.

For Nobel laureate Derek Walcott, the *Ramayana* festival of Hindu origin, which he observed being celebrated in the village of Felicity, Trinidad, proved to be a culture-specific occurrence replete with its own particular set of aesthetics. Experiencing this event as an outsider, even though he is from the region, served as the inspiration for Mr. Walcott's contemplation of what it truly means to be Caribbean and an artist. As he concluded, survival is the visible poetry of the Antilles, and celebrations such as *Ramayana* and the multicultural Carnival are key rituals in that survival.

The continuation of the Haitian art movement throughout that country's recent turbulent history is nothing short of miraculous. Gerald Alexis notes that Haitian modernism, in its development, was and still is, open to external influences, although it does rely strongly on its vernacular components and, like the rest of the Caribbean, is the result of a continual process of cross-fertilization. Dr. Richard Long confirms that contemporary Haitian artists share a visual patrimony and solidarity with other Caribbean artists and similarly considers Wifredo Lam to be a "tutelary spirit of the art of the Caribbean."

Dr. Shifra Goldman reinforces Lam's "tutelary spirit" by pointing out that the Cuban artist's legacy was "the first vision ever of 'modern art from the standpoint of Africa within Latin America.'" For her, Lam symbolizes the unities and the cultural interrelationships among Cuba, the Dominican Republic, and Puerto Rico, and his artistic influence resonates throughout the Caribbean.

Also important in the region's contemporary visual arts are the Biennial exhibitions held in Puerto Rico, Cuba, and the Dominican Republic, which have brought together scores of painters and sculptors. In this way, as Dr. Goldman observes, artists have frequently crossed borders that politicians have not. Such respect for cultural diversity can in turn form a solid foundation for new perspectives on art and the definition of "universality."

The concept of Caribbean artists being involved in a "civilisation-making process" and throwing off the fetters of history can be traced to Wilson Harris, while the belief in falling in love with the world in spite of painful history and past antagonisms can be attributed to Derek Walcott. Caribbean creative artists, in the wholeness of their fragmentation, are uniquely positioned to do both. We pay special tribute to the pioneers—Wifredo Lam of Cuba, Edna Manley of Jamaica, Pétion Savain of Haiti, and Karl Broodhagen of Barbados—who have led the way. The challenge that lies ahead is clear.

1. Mark Kurlansky, *A Continent of Islands: Searching for the Caribbean Destiny* (Reading, Massachusetts: Addison-Wesley, 1992).

2. Gordon K. Lewis, *The Growth of the Modern West Indies* (New York and London: Monthly Review Press, 1969).

3. Wilson Harris, "History, Fable and Myth in the Caribbean and Guianas," *Caribbean Quarterly* 16, no. 2 (June 1970), p. 6.

4. See Edward Brathwaite, *Contradictory Omens: Cultural Diversity and Integration in the Caribbean* (Mona, Jamaica: Savacou Publications, 1974), pp. 57–58.

5. Ibid., p. 17.

6. Edward Brathwaite, "Timehri," in *Is Massa Day Dead? Black Moods in the Caribbean,* edited by Orde Coombs (Garden City, New York: Anchor/Doubleday, 1974), p. 42.

7. The artist in conversation with Samella Lewis.

8. Gloria Mark Gordon, "To See the Light and Touch It: The Vision of LeRoy Clarke," *The International Review of African American Art* 8, no. 1 (1988), pp. 34–38.

9. Foreword to *Jamaican Art: An Overview* (1990).

10. Nadine A.T. Scott, "1992 The Annual National Exhibition, National Gallery of Jamaica," *Jamaica Journal* 25, no. 1 (October 1993), pp. 45–53.

11. Veerle Poupeye-Rammelaere, "The Years Between the 20's and Dub Poetry," *Revue Noire* 1, no. 1, special Caribbean volume (September–November 1992), pp. 33–34.

Samella Lewis, Ph.D., Professor Emerita of Art History, Scripps College, of the Associated Colleges of Claremont, California, is an artist and art historian. She is also the founder and Editor-in-Chief of *The International Review of African American Art,* published by Hampton University, Hampton, Virginia.

Mary Jane Hewitt, Ph.D., is a cultural historian whose primary research interest is comparative African American culture. She serves as Associate Editor of *The International Review of African American Art.*

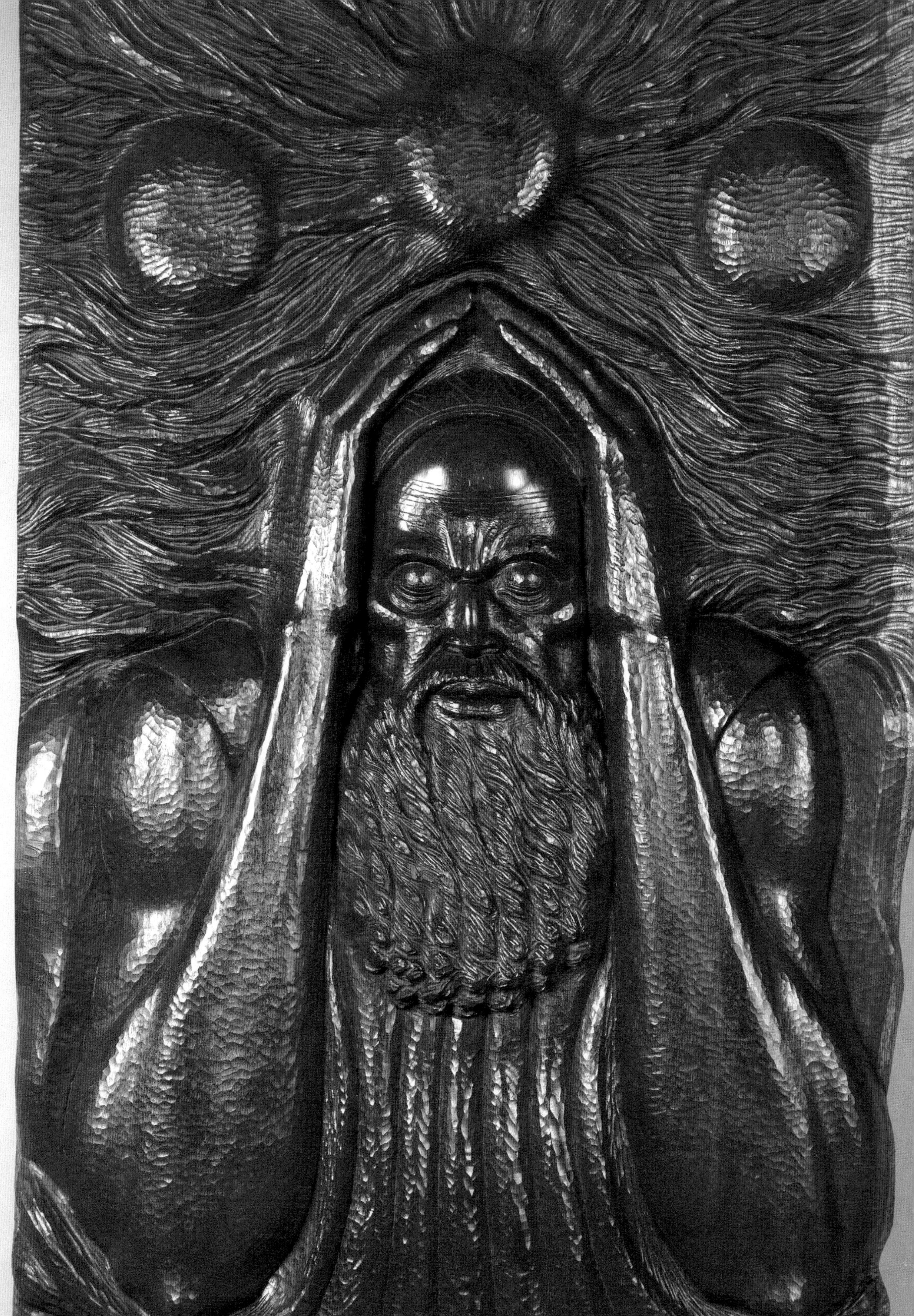

The Antilles: Fragments of Epic Memory

Derek Walcott

Felicity is a village in Trinidad on the edge of the Caroni plain, the wide central plain that still grows sugar and to which indentured cane cutters were brought after emancipation, so the small population of Felicity is East Indian, and on the afternoon that I visited it with friends from America, all the faces along its road were Indian, which, as I hope to show, was a moving, beautiful thing, because this Saturday afternoon *Ramleela*, the epic dramatization of the Hindu epic the *Ramayana,* was going to be performed, and the costumed actors from the village were assembling on a field strung with different-colored flags, like a new gas station, and beautiful Indian boys in red and black were aiming arrows haphazardly into the afternoon light. Low blue mountains on the horizon, bright grass, clouds that would gather color before the light went. Felicity! What a gentle Anglo-Saxon name for an epical memory.

Under an open shed on the edge of the field, there were two huge armatures of bamboo that looked like immense cages. They were parts of the body of a god, his calves or thighs, which, fitted and reared, would make a gigantic effigy. This effigy would be burned as a conclusion to the epic. The cane structures flashed a predictable parallel: Shelley's sonnet on the fallen statue of Ozymandias and his empire, that "colossal wreck" in its empty desert.

Drummers had lit a fire in the shed and they eased the skins of their tablas nearer the flames to tighten them. The saffron flames, the bright grass, and the hand-woven armatures of the fragmented god who would be burned were not in any desert where imperial power had finally toppled, but were part of a ritual, evergreen season that, like the cane-burning harvest, is annually repeated, the point of such sacrifice being its repetition, the point of the destruction being renewal through fire.

Deities were entering the field. What we generally call "Indian music" was blaring from the open platformed shed from which the epic would be narrated. Costumed actors were arriving. Princes and gods, I supposed. What an unfortunate confession! "Gods, I suppose" is the shrug that embodies our African and Asian diasporas. I had often thought of but never seen *Ramleela,* and had never seen this theater, an open field, with village children as warriors, princes, and gods. I had no idea what the epic story was, who its hero was, what enemies he fought, yet I had recently adapted the *Odyssey* for a theater in England, presuming that the audience knew the trials of Odysseus, hero of another Asia Minor epic, while nobody in Trinidad knew any more than I did about Rama, Kali, Shiva, Vishnu, apart from the Indians, a phrase I use pervertedly because that is the kind of remark you can still hear in Trinidad: "apart from the Indians."

Christopher Gonzalez
The Sage (detail)
(see p. 161)

It was as if, on the edge of the Central Plain, there was another plateau, a raft on which the *Ramayana* would be poorly performed in this ocean of cane, but that was my writer's view of things, and it is wrong. I was seeing the *Ramleela* at Felicity as theater when it was faith. . . .

The performance was like a dialect, a branch of its original language, an abridgement of it, but not a distortion or even a reduction of its epic scale. Here in Trinidad I had discovered that one of the greatest epics of the world was seasonally performed, not with that desperate resignation of preserving a culture, but with an openness of belief that was as steady as the wind bending the cane lances of the Caroni plain. We had to leave before the play began to go through the creeks of the Caroni Swamp, to catch the scarlet ibises coming home at dusk. In a performance as natural as those of the actors of the *Ramleela,* we watched the flocks come in as bright as the scarlet of the boy archers, as the red flags, and cover an islet until it turned into a flowering tree, an anchored immortelle. The sigh of History meant nothing here. These two visions, the *Ramleela* and the arrowing flocks of scarlet ibises, blended into a single gasp of gratitude. Visual surprise is natural in the Caribbean; it comes with the landscape, and faced with its beauty, the sigh of History dissolves.

We make too much of that long groan that underlines the past. I felt privileged to discover the ibises as well as the scarlet archers of Felicity.

•

The sigh of History rises over ruins not over landscapes, and in the Antilles there are few ruins to sigh over, apart from the ruins of sugar estates and abandoned forts. Looking around slowly, as a camera would, taking in the low blue hills over Port of Spain, the village road and houses, the warrior-archers, the god-actors and their handlers, and music already on the sound track, I wanted to make a film that would be a long-drawn sigh over Felicity. I was filtering the afternoon with evocations of a lost India, but why "evocations"? Why not "celebrations of a real presence"? Why should India be "lost" when none of these villagers ever really knew it, and why not "continuing," why not the perpetuation of joy in Felicity and in all the other nouns of the Central Plain: Couva, Chaguanas, Charley Village? Why was I not letting my pleasure open its windows wide? I was entitled, like any Trinidadian, to the ecstasies of their claim, because ecstasy was the pitch of the sinuous drumming in the loudspeakers. I was entitled to the feast of Husein, to the mirrors and crepe-paper temples of the Muslim epic, to the Chinese Dragon Dance, to the rites of that Sephardic Jewish synagogue that was once on Something Street. I am only one-eighth the writer I might have been had I contained all the fragmented languages of Trinidad.

Break a vase, and the love that reassembles the fragments is stronger than that love that took its symmetry for granted when it was whole. The glue that fits the pieces is the sealing of its original shape. It is such a love that reassembles our African and Asiatic fragments, the cracked heirlooms whose restoration shows its white scars. This gathering of broken pieces is the care and pain of the Antilles, and if the pieces are disparate, ill-fitting, they contain more pain than their original sculpture, those icons and sacred vessels taken for granted in their ancestral places. Antillean art is this restoration of our shattered histories, our shards of vocabulary, our archipelago becoming a synonym for pieces broken off from the original continent.

And this is the exact process of the making of poetry, or what should be called not its making but its remaking, the fragmented memory, the armature that frames the god, even the rite that surrenders it to a final pyre; the god assembled cane by cane, reed by weaving reed, line by plaited line, as the artisans of Felicity would erect his holy echo.

•

Poetry, which is perfection's sweat but which must seem as fresh as the raindrops on a statue's brow, combines the natural and the marmoreal. It conjugates both tenses simultaneously: the past and the present, if the past is the sculpture and the present the beads of dew or rain on the forehead of the past. There is the buried language and there is the individual vocabulary, and the process of poetry is one of excavation and self-discovery. Tonally the individual voice is a dialect; it shapes its own accent, its own vocabulary and melody in defiance of an imperial concept of language, the language of Ozymandias, libraries and dictionaries, law courts and critics, churches, universities, and political dogma, the diction of institutions. Poetry is an island that breaks away from the main. The dialects of my archipelago seem as fresh to me as those raindrops on the statue's forehead, not the sweat made from the classic exertion of frowning marble, but the contradictions of a refreshing element, rain and salt.

Deprived of their original language, the captured and indentured tribes create their own, accreting and secreting fragments of an old, epic vocabulary from Asia and from Africa, but to an ancestral and ecstatic rhythm in the blood that cannot be subdued by slavery or indenture, while nouns are renamed and the given names of places accepted like Felicity or Choiseul. The original language dissolves from the exhaustion of distance like fog trying to cross an ocean, but this process of renaming, of finding new metaphors, is the same process that the poet faces every morning of his working day, making his own tools like Crusoe, assembling nouns from necessity, from Felicity, even renaming himself. The stripped man is driven back to that self-astonishing elemental force, his mind. That is the basis of the Antillean experience, this shipwreck of fragments, these echoes, these shards of a huge tribal vocabulary, these partially remembered customs, and they are not decayed but strong. They survived the Middle Passage and the *Fatel Rozack,* the ship that carried the first indentured Indians from the port of Madras to the cane fields of Felicity, that carried the chained Cromwellian convict and the Sephardic Jew, the Chinese grocer and the Lebanese merchant selling cloth samples on his bicycle.

And here they are, all in a single Caribbean city, Port of Spain, the sum of history, Froude's "non-people." A downtown babel of shop signs and streets, mongrelized, polyglot, a ferment without a history, like heaven. Because that is what such a city is, in the New World, a writer's heaven.

•

A culture, we all know, is made by its cities.

Another first morning home, impatient for the sunrise—a broken sleep. Darkness at five, and the drapes not worth opening; then, in the sudden light, a cream-walled, brown-roofed police station bordered with short royal palms, in the colonial style, back of it frothing trees and taller palms, a pigeon fluttering into the cover of an eave, a rain-stained block of once-modern apartments, the morning side road into the station without traffic. All part of a surprising peace. This quiet happens with every visit to a city that has deepened itself in me. The flowers and the hills are easy, affection for them predictable; it is the architecture that, for the first morning, disorients. A return from American seductions used to make the traveler feel that something was missing, something was trying to complete itself, like the stained concrete apartments. Pan left along the window and the excrescences rear—a city trying to soar, trying to be brutal, like an American city in silhouette, stamped from the same mold as Columbus or Des Moines. An assertion of power, its decor bland, its air conditioning pitched to the point where its secretarial and executive staff sport competing cardigans; the colder the offices the more important, an imitation of another climate. A longing, even an envy of feeling cold.

In serious cities, in gray, militant winter with its short afternoons, the days seem to pass by in buttoned overcoats, every building appears as a barracks with lights on in its windows, and when snow comes, one has the illusion of living in a Russian novel, in the nineteenth century, because of the literature of winter. So visitors to the Caribbean must feel that they are inhabiting a succession of postcards. Both climates are shaped by what we have read of them. For tourists, the sunshine cannot be serious. Winter adds depth and darkness to life as well as to literature, and in the unending summer of the tropics not even poverty or poetry (in the Antilles poverty is poetry with a V, *une vie,* a condition of life as well as of imagination) seems capable of being profound, because the nature around it is so exultant, so resolutely ecstatic, like its music. A culture based on joy is bound to be shallow. Sadly, to sell itself, the Caribbean encourages the delights of mindlessness, or brilliant vacuity, as a place to flee not only winter but the seriousness that comes only out of culture with four seasons. So how can there be a people there, in the true sense of the word?

They know nothing about seasons in which leaves let go of the year, in which spires fade in blizzards and streets whiten, of the erasures of whole cities by fog, of reflection in fireplaces. Instead, they inhabit a geography whose rhythm, like their music, is limited to two stresses: hot and wet, sun and rain, light and shadow, day and night, the limitations of an incomplete meter, and are therefore a people incapable of the subtleties of contradiction, of imaginative complexity. So be it. We cannot change contempt.

Ours are not cities in the accepted sense, but no one wants them to be. They dictate their own proportions, their own definitions in particular places and in a prose equal to that of their detractors, so that now it is not just St. James, but the streets and yards that Naipaul commemorates, its lanes are short and brilliant as his sentences; not just the noise and jostle of Tunapuna, but the origins of C.L.R. James's *Beyond a Boundary;* not just Felicity village on the Caroni plain, but Selvon Country, and that is the way it goes up the islands now: the old Dominica of Jean Rhys still very much the way she wrote of it; the Martinique of the early Césaire; Perse's Guadeloupe, even without the pith helmets and the mules; and what delight and privilege there was in watching a literature—one literature in several imperial languages, French, English, Spanish—bud and open island after island in the early morning of a culture, not timid, not derivative, any more than the hard white petals of the frangipani are derivative and timid. This is not a belligerent boast, but a simple celebration of inevitability: that this flowering had to come.

On a heat-stoned afternoon in Port of Spain, some alley white with glare, with love vine spilling over a fence, palms and a hazed mountain appear around a corner to the evocation of Vaughn or Herbert's "that shady city of palm-trees," or to the memory of a Hammond organ from a wooden chapel in Castries, where the congregation same "Jerusalem the Golden." It is hard for me to see such emptiness as desolation. It is this patience that is the width of Antillean life, and the secret is not to ask the wrong thing of it, not to demand of it an ambition it has no interest in. The traveler reads this as lethargy, as torpor.

Here there are not enough books, one says, no theaters, no museums, simply not enough to do. Yet deprived of books, a man must fall back on thought, and out of thought, if he can learn to order it, will come the urge to record, and in extremity, if he has not means of recording, recitation, the ordering of memory that leads to meter, to commemoration. There can be virtues in deprivation, and certainly one virtue is salvation from a cascade of high mediocrity, since books are now not so much created as remade.

Cities create a culture, and all we have are these magnified market towns, so what are the proportions of the ideal Caribbean city? A surrounding, accessible countryside with leafy suburbs, and if the city is lucky, behind it, spacious plains. Behind it, fine mountains; before it, an indigo sea. Spires would pin its center and round them would be leafy, shadowy parks. Pigeons would cross its sky in alphabetic patterns, carrying with them memories of a belief in augury, and at the heart of the city there would be horses, yes, horses, those animals last seen at the end of the nineteenth century drawing broughams and carriages with top-hatted citizens, horses that live in the present tense without elegiac echoes from their hooves, emerging from paddocks at the Queen's Park Savannah at sunrise, when mist is unthreading from the cool mountains above the roofs, and at the center of the city seasonally there would be races, so that citizens could roar at the speed and grace of these nineteenth-century animals. Its docks would not be obscured by smoke or deafened by too much machinery, and above all, it would be so racially various that the cultures of the world—the Asiatic, the Mediterranean, the European, the African—would be represented in it, its humane variety more exciting than Joyce's Dublin. Its citizens would intermarry as they chose, from instinct, not tradition, until their children find it increasingly futile to trace their genealogy. It would not have too many avenues difficult or dangerous from pedestrians, its mercantile area would be a cacophony of accents, fragments of the old language that would be silenced immediately at 5 o'clock, its docks resolutely vacant on Sundays.

This is Port of Spain to me, a city ideal in its commercial and human proportions, where a citizen is a walker and not a pedestrian, and this is how Athens may have been before it became a cultural echo.

The finest silhouettes of Port of Spain are idealizations of the craftsman's handiwork, not of concrete and glass, but of baroque woodwork, each fantasy looking more like an involved drawing of itself that the actual building. Behind the city is the Caroni plain, with its villages, Indian prayer flags, and fruit vendors' stalls along the highway over which ibises come like floating flags. Photogenic poverty! Postcard sadness! I am not re-creating Eden; I mean, by "the Antilles," the reality of light, of work, of survival. I mean a house on the side of a country road, I mean the Caribbean Sea, whose smell is the smell of refreshing possibility as well as survival. Survival is the triumph of stubbornness, and spiritual stubbornness, a sublime stupidity, is what makes the occupation of poetry endure, when there are so many things that should make it futile. Those things added together can go under one collective noun: "the world."

•

This is the visible poetry of the Antilles, then. Survival.

If you wish to understand that consoling pity with which the islands were regarded, look at the tinted engravings of Antillean forests, with their proper palm trees, ferns, and waterfalls. They have a civilizing decency, like Botanical Gardens, as if the sky were a glass ceiling under which a colonized vegetation is arranged for quiet walks and carriage rides. Those views are incised with a pathos that guides the engraver's tool and the topographer's pencil, and it is this pathos that, tenderly ironic, gave villages names like Felicity. A century looked at a landscape furious with vegetation in the wrong light and with the wrong eye. It is such pictures that are saddening, rather than the tropics themselves. These delicate engravings of sugar mills and harbors, of native women in costume, are seen as a part of History, that History which looked over the shoulder of the engraver and, later, the photographer. History can alter the eye and the moving hand to conform a view of itself; it can rename places for the nostalgia in an echo; it can temper the glare of tropical light to elegiac monotony in prose, the tone of judgment in Conrad, in the travel journals of Froude.

•

These travelers carried with them the infection of their own malaise, and their prose reduced even the landscape to melancholia and self-contempt. Every endeavor is belittled as imitation, from architecture to music. There was this conviction in Froude that since History is based on achievement, and since the history of the Antilles was so genetically corrupt, so depressing in its cycles of massacres, slavery, and indenture, a culture was inconceivable, and nothing could ever be created in those ramshackle ports, those monotonously feudal sugar estates. Not only the light and salt of Antillean mountains defied this, but the demotic vigor and variety of their inhabitants. Stand close to a waterfall and you will stop hearing the roar. To be still in the nineteenth century, like horses, as Brodsky has written, may not be such a bad deal, and much of our life in the Antilles still seems to be in the rhythm of the last century, like the West Indian novel.

By writers even as refreshing as Graham Greene, the Caribbean is looked at with elegiac pathos, as prolonged sadness to which Lévi-Strauss supplied an epigraph: *Tristes Tropiques.* Their *tristesse* derives from an attitude to the Caribbean dusk, to rain, to uncontrollable vegetation, to the provincial ambition of Caribbean cities where brutal replicas of modern architecture dwarf the small houses and streets. The mood is understandable, the melancholy as contagious as the fever of a sunset, like the gold fronds of diseased coconut palms, but there is something alien and ultimately wrong in the way such a sadness, even a morbidity, is described by English, French, or some of our exiled writers. It relates to a misunderstanding of the light and the people on whom the light falls.

These writers describe the ambitions of our unfinished cities, their unrealized, homiletic conclusion, but the Caribbean city may conclude just at that point where it is satisfied with its own scale, just as Caribbean culture is not evolving but already shaped. Its proportions are not to be measured by the traveler or the exile, but by its own citizenry and architecture. To be told that you are not yet a city or a culture requires this response: I am not your city or your culture. There might be less *tristes tropiques* after that. . . .

It is not that History is obliterated by this sunrise. It is there in Antillean geography, in the vegetation itself. The sea sighs with the drowned from the Middle Passage, the butchery of its aborigines, Carib and Aruac and Taíno, bleeds in the scarlet of the immortelle, and even the actions of surf on sand cannot erase the African memory, or the lances of cane as a green prison where indentured Asians, the ancestors of Felicity, are still serving time.

That is what I have read around me from boyhood, from the beginnings of poetry, the grace of effort. In the hard mahogany of woodcutters' faces, resinous men, charcoal burners; in a man with a cutlass cradled across his forearm, who stands on the verge with the usual anonymous khaki dog; in the extra clothes he put on this morning, when it was cold when he rose in the thinning dark to go and make his garden in the heights—the heights, the garden, being miles away from his house, but that is where he has his land—not to mention the fishermen, the footmen on trucks, groaning up mornes, all fragments of Africa originally but shaped and hardened and rooted now in the island's life, illiterate in the way leaves are illiterate; they do not read, they are there to be read, and if they are properly read, they create their own literature.

But in our tourist brochures the Caribbean is a blue pool into which the republic dangles the extended foot of Florida as inflated rubber islands bob and drinks with umbrellas float toward her on a raft. This is how the islands, from the shame of necessity, sell themselves; this is the seasonal erosion of their identity, that high-pitched repetition of the same images of service that cannot distinguish one island from the other, with a future of polluted marinas, land deals negotiated by ministers, and all of this conducted to music of Happy Hour and the rictus of a smile. What is the earthly paradise for our visitors? Two weeks without rain and a mahogany tan, and at sunset local troubadours in straw hats and floral shirts beating "Yellow Bird" and "Banana Boat Song" to death.

•

There is a territory wider than this—wider than the limits made by the map of an island—which is the illimitable sea and what it remembers. All of the Antilles, every island, is an effort of memory; every mind, every racial biography culminating in amnesia and fog. Pieces of sunlight through the fog and sudden rainbows, *arcs-en-ciel.* That is the effort, the labor of the Antillean imagination, rebuilding its gods from bamboo frames, phrase by phrase.

Decimation from the Aruac downward is the blasted root of Antillean history, and the benign blight that is tourism can infect all of those island nations, not gradually but with imperceptible speed, until each rock is whitened by the guano of white-winged hotels, the arc and descent of progress.

Before it is all gone, before only a few valleys are left, pockets of an older life, before development turns every artist into an anthropologist or a folklorist, there are still cherishable places, little valleys that do not echo with ideas, a simplicity of rebeginnings, not yet corrupted by the dangers of change. Not nostalgic sites but occluded sanctities as common and simple as their sunlight. Places as threatened by this prose as a headland is by the bulldozer or a sea-almond grove by the surveyor's string, or from blight, the mountain laurel.

One last epiphany: a basic stone church in a thick valley outside Soufrière, the hills almost shoving the houses around into a brown river, a sunlight that looks oily on the leaves, a backward place, unimportant, and one now being corrupted into significance by this prose. The idea is not to hallow or invest the place with anything, not even memory. African children in Sunday frocks come down the ordinary concrete steps into the church, banana leaves hand and glisten, a truck is parked in a yard, and old women totter toward the entrance. Here is where a real fresco should be painted, one without importance, but one with real faith, mapless, Historyless.

How quickly it could all disappear! And how it is beginning to drive us further into where we hope are impenetrable places, green secrets at the end of bad roads, headlands where the next view is not of a hotel but of some long beach without a figure and the hanging question of some fisherman's smoke at its far end. The Caribbean is not an idyll, not to its natives. They draw their working strength from it organically, like trees, like the sea almond or the spice laurel of the heights. Its peasantry and its fishermen are not there to be loved or even photographed; they are trees who sweat, and whose bark is filmed with salt. But every day on some island, rootless trees in suits are signing favorable tax breaks with entrepreneurs, poisoning the sea almond and the spice laurel of the mountains to their roots. A morning could come in which governments might ask what happened not merely to the forests and the bays, but to a whole people.

A noted author, lecturer, and playwright, Derek Walcott was awarded the Nobel Prize in literature in 1992. His Nobel lecture, which appeared in *The New Republic* on 28 December 1992, is presented here in abridged form with the permission of The Nobel Foundation.

Caribbean Cultural Identity

Rex Nettleford

The entire Caribbean, like all of the Americas, is the creation of that awesome process of cross-fertilization resulting from encounters that occurred on foreign soil among the civilizations of Europe, Africa, and Asia, and the ancient Amerindian civilizations that developed and flourished on American soil long before Columbus set foot there. The development of this creation has helped to shape the history of the world for over half a millennium and has resulted in distinctive cultural spheres in the Western Hemisphere, each claiming its own inner logic and consistency.

The island nations of the Caribbean, which, along with the mainland territories of Guyana and Belize, are grouped into a subregion, are conscious of the dynamic of their own development. It rests firmly on an agonizing and challenging process, "actualised in simultaneous acts of negating and affirming, demolishing and constructing, rejecting and reshaping."[1] Nowhere is this process more evident than in the creative arts. This is not to neglect other indices of culture, such as linguistic communication, which underpins the oral and indigenous scribal literature of the region. Similarly, religion and kinship patterns reveal the texture and internal diversity that occur when disparate cultural elements are synthesized. In this region of the world, the result is an emerging creole lifestyle, a nascent ontology, and an epistemology that all speak to the Caribbean experience and to existential reality.

Today many Caribbean citizens struggle to gain currency and legitimacy worldwide (and sometimes even among their own people) for being native-born and native-bred, which is the original meaning of "creole."[2] Whites born in the American colonies were regarded as "creoles" by their metropolitan cousins. Jamaican-born slaves were similarly differentiated from their "salt-water Negro" counterparts freshly brought in from West Africa. The term "creole" was soon appropriated by, or attributed to, the mulatto (half-caste), who defiantly claimed certified rootedness in the colonies, an assertion not as easily justified by those of pure African or European descent.

To this day *genuine* Caribbean expressions are regarded as those that have been "creolized" into new indigenous forms that differ distinctively from the original elements from which they first sprang. Some of those original elements, especially those with European sources, in turn reinforce their regional claims through politics, economic control, or cultural penetration. Despite this, the Caribbean is becoming ever more conscious not only of its own unique expressions but also of the dynamism and nature of the processes that underlie these expressions.

•

Claude Fiddler
Jack-o-Lantern (detail)
(see p. 192)

At the end of the twentieth century, the Caribbean is therefore aware of two major forces that are at work in the world at large. One force is the threatening homogenization of humankind via the globalization of the economy and the penetration of the collective conscious through advanced communications technology. The other is the countervailing effort on the part of various groups to be more firmly rooted in the specificity of their realities based on ethnicity, religion, race or class, and gender. Such dialectical tension is scarcely new to the Caribbean.

In an effort to root the certitude of self and society in the region's realities, the Caribbean has been grappling with the urge to govern itself, to control its own destiny, and to define itself on its own terms rather than on those of the imperial powers who for five centuries have determined the psycho-cultural space inhabited by their colonial charges.

The "struggle," exhausting as it may have been, has not been altogether without rewards. Would-be "victims" long ago learned to transform liabilities into assets, calling into play the creative imagination and intellect to produce astounding works of art and literature. They address the ongoing quest for the irreducible kernel of Caribbean existence. The creative exercise attempts to define the region's sense of place and purpose in a world that, given half a chance, would continue to marginalize the creolized, cross-fertilized millions who inhabit the diverse countries washed by the Caribbean Sea.

Nevertheless, this is not possible, if only because the disparate elements that form the different communities in the region have devised strategies of resilience and cultural survival that surpass that very survival. Admittedly, the Caribbean still carries a plurality of designations which match the stubborn internal plurality of self-perceptions. Consequently, not only is there an Anglophone Caribbean, but the Francophone, Dutch-speaking, and Hispanic segments of the former tropical outposts of empire still endure. Some prefer to be known as Afro-Caribbean, Indo-Caribbean, Chinese Caribbean, and the like. And, following the old indulgences of plantation America, others segregate themselves into white, brown (with varying degrees of skin tones thrown in for good measure), and black.[3]

Yet, as I have said elsewhere, the region's

> pedigree of struggle for freedom and rehumanisation on the part of the majority of the population dates back almost to the beginning of the era of Caribbean history that followed on the fateful encounter of the Old Worlds of Europe and of Africa on the one hand with the ancient civilisations of the Americas on the other. The stage was therefore set from very early for the quest for self-definition in what came to be ahistorically labelled the "New World." . . .
>
> The opposition of one category of inhabitants to another itself compounded the issue of identity within the context of political and cultural power play. Cultural identity was therefore a part of the genesis and the subsequent nurturing of an entire hemisphere. In this sense the contemporary United States and Latin America are no different from the Caribbean. Only that as part of the hemisphere the Caribbean, of necessity, approached the issue from the specificity of its own experience; and it is that specificity that has fed the creative vision, artistic sensibility and aesthetic energy of the region.[4]

That specificity manifests itself in the dialectical approach to everyday living, just as it does in the polyrhythmic nature of the region's textured lifestyle. It appears in its fertile bed of musical creativity (traditional and contemporary/popular), in the range of expressions in the theater (drama, dance, and chorus), in the visual arts (painting, sculpture, and ceramics), as well as in the multilayered, multifaceted festival arts that range from the largely secular Jonkonnu and masquerade, through the Muslim-derived Hosay, to the all-Caribbean, pre-Lenten Carnival (or Mardi Gras), which has spread to the Caribbean diaspora in the North Atlantic.[5]

As an example, the religious expressions share commonalities that have been integrated into life from one end of the Caribbean to the other, covering Cuba's *santería,* Haiti's *vodun,* Jamaica's *pukkumina,* Trinidad's *shango,* Brazil's *candomble,* Guyana's *cumfa;* and zion revivalism has also spread throughout the region. All of these speak to an eloquent point of power in a landscape carved out of Africa-in-the-Americas.[6]

•

The Caribbean also remains a thriving laboratory of "creole languages," which in turn have given rise to emergent oral and scribal literatures. Louise Bennett and her heirs, in addition to Jamaican dub poets such as Mutabaruka, speak and write in the popular tongue of that island, while Paul Keens-Douglas of Trinidad and Grenada tells his stories in the vernacular of the eastern Caribbean.[7] These languages have inspired deceptively conventional writers, such as Aimé Césaire and Edouard Glissant of Martinique, Nicolás Guillén, a former poet laureate, and Alejo Carpentier of Cuba, and Derek Walcott, the Nobel laureate, Kamau Brathwaite, and Lorna Goodison of the Commonwealth Caribbean, to name a few.[8] Similarly, while the music of the Mighty Sparrow and Lord Kitchener of Trinidad calypso fame,[9] of Bob Marley, Jimmy Cliff, and Peter Tosh of the Jamaican reggae world,[10] and of the exponents of *zouk* in the "French Caribbean" speak to identities peculiarly Caribbean, their appeal is no less universal.

Despite persistent colonial attachments to a Eurocentric ideal among many, there are enough Caribbean artists and others of vision who are seized by the fact that universality, as Herman Melville once said, is a "culturally specific concept, used to maintain a hierarchy and a dominance over other cultures."[11] All voices worth their sound are, indeed, "culturally specific." As such, the Caribbean voice resonates within the region's borders and around the world with a certain authority of place and authenticity of purpose, even while it admits to the fragility of the creative process, the mutability of all things, and the certainty of continuous change that is reflected in the dynamism of a never-ending dialogue. Against the historical backdrop of a myth of relations, as Edouard Glissant so aptly describes the Caribbean reality,[12] is a deep understanding and acceptance of a need not only to negotiate differences but also to come to terms with the dilemma of difference that drives newly independent states in the Caribbean to raise as their national mottos such phrases as "Out of many, one people," "One people, one nation, one destiny," or "Together we strive, together we achieve."[13]

•

There is an uncanny awareness in the Caribbean of the complexity of things, of the interconnectedness of all phenomena due to their very separateness, and of the centrality of an intercontextuality to the achievements of all civilizations worth remembering—from those of the ancient Mediterranean through the Golden Age of Spain, when Iberians, Moors, and Jews lived and worked together, to that of the modern Americas of which the Caribbean is an integral part. Identity is therefore rooted in factual cross-fertilization and is at this time perched, albeit precariously, on the cutting edge of such questions as, How do we understand ourselves? What is really going on in the fields of art and literature? What drives us towards a civil society? Such questions serve as sources of energy for the exercise of the Caribbean collective and individual creative imagination. They also bestow upon the region the skills needed to cope with ambiguity and contradictions, without fear of psychic disintegration. Where else in the world could one with ease and confidence describe the self as part-African, part-European, part-Asian, part-Native American, and *totally* Caribbean?

Herein lies a celebration of heterogeneity, of unity in diversity, and of the method that underlies all that appears to be madness! Against the background of such differences, such contradictions, such contrariness, even such chaos, is a unifying space in which an identity that defies stasis while it promotes order and stability is now being forged. *Caribbean Visions: Contemporary Painting and Sculpture* is clearly meant to be a celebration of all this!

1. Rex Nettleford, *Caribbean Cultural Identity—The Case of Jamaica: An Essay in Cultural Dynamics* (Los Angeles: UCLA Press, 1979), p. 181.

2. See Edward Kamau Brathwaite, *The Development of Creole Society in Jamaica 1770–1820* (Oxford: Clarendon Press, 1971).

3. See M.G. Smith, *The Plural Society in the British West Indies* (Berkeley: University of California Press, 1965). See also Vera Rubin, ed., *Social and Cultural Pluralism in the Caribbean* (New York: New York Academy of Sciences, 1960) and David Dabadeen and B. Rinsley Samaroo, eds., *India in the Caribbean* (Hansib: University of Warwick, 1987).

4. Rex Nettleford, *Inward Stretch, Outward Reach: A Voice from the Caribbean* (Basingstoke: MacMillan Press, 1993), pp. 49–50.

5. John Nunley and Judith Bettelheim, *Caribbean Festival Arts* (Seattle: University of Washington Press, 1988).

6. George Eaton Simpson, *Religions, Cults of the Caribbean Trinidad, Jamaica and Haiti* (San Juan: Institute of Caribbean Studies, University of Puerto Rico, 1970).

7. See Louise Bennett, *Jamaica Labrish,* edited by Rex Nettleford (Kington: Sangster's, 1966). See also her *Selected Poems,* edited by Mervyn Morris (Kington: Sangster's, 1982).

8. J. Edward Chamberlin, *Come Back to Me My Language: Poetry and the West Indies* (Chicago: University of Illinois Press, 1993).

9. Gordon Rohlehr, *Calypso and Society in Pre-Independence Trinidad* (Port of Spain, 1990). See also his "Sparrow and the Language of Calypso," *Caribbean Quarterly* 14, nos. 1–2 (1968).

10. Stephen Davis, *Reggae Bloodlines: In Search of the Music and Culture of Jamaica* (Garden City, New York: Anchor Press, 1977). See also Carolyn Cooper, *Noises in the Blood: Orality, Gender and the "Vulgar" Body of Jamaican Popular Culture* (London: MacMillan Press, 1993).

11. Quoted from an unpublished and undated draft of a paper entitled "Toward an American Sensibility," by Henry Louis Gates, Jr.

12. Edouard Glissant, "Creolization in the Making of the Americas," *Race, Discourse and the Origin of the Americas, A New World View* (Washington, D.C.: Smithsonian Institution Press, 1992).

13. These are the national mottos of Jamaica, Guyana, and Trinidad and Tobago, respectively, which became independent in the 1960s.

Rex Nettleford is Director of the School of Continuing Studies, Professor of Continuing Studies, and Pro Vice Chancellor at the University of the West Indies. He is also the founder, artistic director, and principal choreographer of the National Dance Theatre Company of Jamaica.

Trinidad Carnival: History and Meaning

Errol Hill

Probably few, if any, human societies do not have a Carnival of some form or fashion. Although the word itself derives from the Latin term *carne levare,* which means "farewell to flesh," and obviously refers to the feasting prior to Christian Lent, the roots of the festival extend much deeper into pagan belief and tradition. The true origins of Carnival are found not in Christian observance but in those seasonal rituals by which human beings have sought, from time immemorial, to win the favor of those forces that govern the fertility of the earth and the womb. Thus, the fundamental aim of Carnival celebrations is to prolong life and, by appeasing the gods, to make life endurable and even bountiful. As part of these rituals the spirits of ancestors or tribal heroes were invoked to intercede on behalf of living members of the family and community, to help ensure survival, that most basic of human urges.

As is well known, the Roman Catholic Church long ago exercised a penchant for adopting pagan rites that were too ingrained in people's consciousness and traditions to be eradicated by fiat. If the Church could not stamp out what it considered to be a heathen practice, it would incorporate that practice into its ecclesiastical calendar and assign it Christian significance. It was a simple matter of "if you can't beat 'em, join 'em." Thus, what might have been the pagan worship of nature deities or revered ancestors became a Christian rite of purification of the spirit through the denial of the flesh, namely, the forty-day Lenten period. And since the pagan celebration involved feasting and revelries, these festivities were permitted as a last concession before the abstinence of Lent began. Some such transformation constituted the origin of Carnival as practiced in the Catholic countries of Europe at the time when the New World became known to them.

With the conquest of the Americas and the imposition of Christianity on the indigenous populations, as well as on those peoples who would subsequently be transported as slaves from Africa or as indentured servants from Asia, the European Carnival was itself transplanted to the peoples of Latin America and the Caribbean. In North America it found a toehold as the Mardi Gras of New Orleans, where French influence was strong in the Louisiana territory, but elsewhere in Anglo-Saxon American the English Church stood emphatically opposed to this custom and did not encourage its practice. Instead, it fostered celebrations around the twelve days of Christmas, with the mummings and disguisings of the Shooters Day parade in Philadelphia being a notable example. In North Carolina and in the Anglophone Caribbean countries such as Jamaica and the Bahamas, the *Jonkonnu* masquerades associated with Christmas became established.

I have suggested that all peoples stage festivals similar to Carnival, even though the modes of observance differ from place to place. It is understandable, therefore, that the Christian Carnival, once brought to a new country and to people of different religious, racial, and ethnic backgrounds, would undergo significant change both in its manner of expression and, more important, in its intrinsic meanings. Those peoples who constituted the basic population units

Shengé Ka Pharoah
Omra (detail)
(see p. 206)

in the Caribbean—of Amerindian, African, and much later, Asiatic origins—also celebrated their Carnivals. On my wall at home hangs a framed engraving, dated 1818, of a "Festival of the New Yam in West Africa." In it, crowds of people assemble to make music, to dance, sing, and masquerade as they celebrate the first reaping of the yams, a staple food crop. This is only one of the many types of masquerades I witnessed during a two-year sojourn in western Nigeria in 1965–1967.

•

The Amerindians were quickly eliminated from the Caribbean island chain to make way for the slave populations that were imported to work the large sugar plantations. Indeed, the process of "creolization" began during slavery, when the transplanted European Carnival assumed new modes of celebration as the white ruling class introduced masquerades that dealt with their new lives on the tropical plantations. Europeans initiated the *canboulay* procession (*cannes brulees,* meaning burnt canes) in imitation of the bands of slaves who would be awakened from their beds to put out cane fires. When the African slaves, finally freed in 1838, began to participate in the Christian Carnival, aspects of their own inherited customs were manifested even as they were constrained to observe those alien customs of the dominant ruling class who withdrew from participating in the street parades. A somewhat similar situation later occurred with the indentured Asians who were able to transfer their festivals almost intact to their new home, not having endured the deprivations of slavery. The result of this racial and cultural mix in a new environment was the establishment of a syncretic carnival. In outward form it was still a Christian liturgical festival, but inherently it perpetuated traditions and modified them to suit the new surroundings and controls under which these rituals were practiced.

Today, many of the ancient beliefs associated with the pre-Christian Carnival have faded and rituals of old have lost much of their pristine significance. Times change and customs become outmoded; new meanings supersede old. A festival remains vigorous and vital only as long as it can satisfy the changing needs of a people and give impetus to their aspirations. Local differences in the observation of Carnival exist among groups or countries. Nevertheless, it is still possible to determine common meanings that inhere in Carnival today, both in its home countries of the Caribbean and in its further remove to migrant communities and metropolitan cities, such as Brooklyn, Toronto, and London.

•

What are some of the basic meanings of Carnival, more commonly called the "masquerade" (and often shortened to "mas"), as it has been observed by the people of Trinidad and Tobago for almost two centuries? Let us be sure that in considering the Carnival we are dealing not only with the masquerades that parade the streets but also with the calypso, traditionally the Carnival music of Trinidad, and the steel band, which beginning in the 1940s became the primary form of making music during Carnival.

It has been argued that all commemorations are a return to the source, to the very origins. G.S. Metraux sees the re-enactment of mythical or historical events, using symbol and allegory, as a common feature of all festivals. What, one might ask, was at the root of the sometime belligerent element of the Trinidad Carnival, with its stick fighters, the whip-wielding Pierrots, the molasses-daubed *Jab Molassi,* the nightly processions with their defiant cries, the verbal assaults of the Midnight Robbers, the piquant jibes of the calypsonians? What are these if not a re-enactment of the experience, real or imaginary, of slavery? Certainly the canboulay procession of the nineteenth century was seen as such by the authorities who did everything lawfully possible to suppress it once the masquerade had been appropriated by former slaves.

The Wild Indian masquerades began as portrayals of Orinoco Indians who came to South Trinidad in their canoes to trade their wares. The military bands in Carnival were originally attempts to parody the annual muster of troops that were assembled at Christmastide to thwart rebellion by the slaves who were allowed a holiday from their year-long drudgery. And the parade of *jouvay* characters—the *Soucouyant, Diablesse,* Phantom, *Loup Garou, Papa Bois,* and other creatures from the country's folklore with which the Carnival of old began in the predawn hours—was surely one way of recalling the ancient beliefs in these mythical beings. The term *jouvay (jour ouvert,* meaning daybreak), which is still used to signify the predawn masquerading, derives from the cry of one of these characters, the Soucouyant. According to the folktale, this blood-sucking creature sheds her skin at night and flies through the air to attack her victims, knowing that she must resume her natural form before daybreak. The Soucouyant is unable to don her skin because her enemy, having found it, has sprinkled salt upon it. As day approaches she is left crying, *"Jouvert, jou paka ouvay"* (Is it daybreak or not daybreak?) These exotic characters have disappeared from the Carnival and in their place are the old mask bands of today, many of which still daub their skin with mud or burnt coal.

•

It is usually agreed that Carnival represents a reversal of established order. Such occasions allow the underdog to assert some self-importance. Automobiles are banned from streets and revellers have the right of way. As the calypsonian Lord Kitchener described it in a song in 1963, "The road made to walk on carnival day." Anyone who has seen two masqueraders greet each other in the middle of a street, feet astride, arms stretched wide, each claiming his piece of territory as he turns slowly to display the intricacies of his costume, can vouch for Kitchener's assertion. You may be a garbage collector on the days before and after Carnival, but on Carnival day you can be a king and the road belongs to you.

This subversion of the established social order has led to the view that Carnival is "a national safety valve" that helps to maintain the collective sanity of a people living under stressful conditions. Causes of stress can be the high rate of unemployment, tensions created by living in a polyglot society, an outrageously inadequate infrastructure where little works as simply or smoothly as it should, and a heavily devalued currency when not so long ago, during the oil boom, "money was no object," to quote a former prime minister. The argument is that this safety valve annually releases the built up stress that might otherwise erupt in some kind of violent revolt against the system.

While there is doubtless some truth in the proposition, it is a curious fact that chaos does not result from the apparent subversion of established rule during the Carnival celebrations. True, from time to time in the past, street battles have occurred between rival masqueraders or steel bandsman in fierce competition with each other, and there have always been unseemly elements in the Carnival which the prim and proper among us would prefer not to confront. When Trinidad experienced a seven-month state of emergency in 1970–1971, following an army mutiny that had a popular following, the government decided it was better to permit the Carnival be held than to risk further alienation by denying people their most cherished festival. This action clearly demonstrated the official view that the mas players impose a sense of order on themselves in planning and producing their magnificent costumes, in saving the considerable sums of money needed to pay for them, in parading the streets and presenting the costumed bands in the spectacular sections on competition stages, in the arduous practicing of the steel bands, and in composing and singing the calypsos. All these activities demand skill, intelligence, forethought, discipline, and order of a kind that is hardly encountered in other areas of daily life.

Moreover, as is known from the historical record, Carnival bands such as the Dragons, Wild Indians, and Borokits were accustomed to holding pre-Carnival ceremonies in their band headquarters. They crowned a king and queen, and elected princes and potentates, thus replacing their permanent relegation to the lowly working class with a two-day hierarchy of their own in which they were temporarily elevated to the aristocracy. One might well ask, How is it possible for a cosmopolitan country such as Trinidad and Tobago to produce a mammoth festival year after year, voluntarily, with a minimum of government interference? It takes imagination, organization, talent, and virtue, and yet the country is unable to run its daily affairs with the same skill and dedication.

Competition plays a significant role in the Carnival celebrations. Each year a king and a queen of all the masquerade bands are crowned. The best costumed individual, the finest masquerade band, and the most pleasing steel band performance are acknowledged, and a calypso monarch is selected. There are several ways, both positive and negative, to interpret this competitive element. Certainly individual and group prestige is at stake, as there is pecuniary interest in winning a first prize. While the monetary return is a major consideration for the big band organizers, it would be naive to think that the few hundred or thousand dollars in prize money can adequately compensate a mas maker for the considerable effort, energy, and creativity that are involved in organizing a Carnival band, in designing and meticulously building a prize-winning costume, in composing and singing a calypso, or arranging the music and rehearsing for a steel band performance. Some big band organizers have literally given their lives in the service of mas. Harry Basilon, George Bailey, and Wilfred Strasser are but a few of the masquerade martyrs.

More positive than negative factors are at work here. Group loyalty and group solidarity play a large part in this eagerness to excel, the striving for perfection being one of the most laudable aspirations humans can have, and the willingness to accept, however grudgingly, the judgment of one's peers. These are all integral elements of the competitive spirit and provide tremendously powerful motivations upon which a perceptive and sensitive administration can draw to help build a country and give its people a feeling of participation in its development and its destiny.

The Trinidad scholar Clement London considers Carnival to be a revitalizing force in the community. Under its demanding pressure, cultural materials at first rejected by society as dissonant or abhorrent, primarily because they emanated from an underprivileged class, eventually come to be embraced by the entire populace as unique products of the country's latent skill and creativity. The history of the calypso in the past century and of the steel band since the 1940s are glaring examples of the power of Carnival to conserve and revitalize the culture of the people of Trinidad and Tobago. I can still recall with what concern, but also with determination, Carlyle Kerr, the late Lennox Pierre, and I, all members of the Trinidad and Tobago Youth Council, took Ellie Manetts of Invaders Steel Band into the studio of Radio Trinidad to give the first ever demonstration on the airwaves of steel pan music. That was in 1947. We have come a long way since then.

One aspect of the revitalization movement is national awareness of cultural heritage. As ex-colonials, the people of the Caribbean have been so long exposed to the dominant European and North American culture that some are unable or unwilling to recognize what is indigenous to the region. Several years ago I was invited to attend a planning meeting to consider the establishment of a School of Music in Trinidad. The proposal, to which only two of all those asked to attend the meeting demurred (myself being one), was to have certain rooms in the projected building earmarked for the teaching of various conventional instruments—piano, violin, cello, flute—with the supposed aim of eventually being able to staff a symphony orchestra. All very laudable, to be sure, but when I asked what facilities were planned for teaching steel band music, the reply was, "Oh yes, that, too!"

•

People extricating themselves from the colonial yoke would seem to undergo three phases of emancipation. The first is *political* freedom, when the reins and symbols of power are transferred from the hands of the colonial authority to those of locally elected leaders. Next comes *economic* freedom, which is more difficult to secure in those small countries that, with limited natural resources, are often dependent on foreign markets and foreign capital for their development. At the very least these countries should be able to plan their own economies through regional and bilateral links. One would like to believe that this second freedom can be more easily achieved if the third freedom, that of *cultural* freedom, were fully exploited by a people realistically willing to assert their cultural independence and treasure their own heritage. It is in this sense that Carnival can foster socio-economic change.

Recognition of Carnival as a national festival means more than acknowledging its reappearance for a few days each year. It requires seeing Carnival as a symbol and expression of the broad-based desire to lay claim to a national identity, an identity that would be fearlessly willing to discard economic and cultural patterns of behavior that have proved unworkable or unproductive and to establish instead a more equitable system of sharing the spiritual life and material wealth which the nation is capable of producing. If this entails sacrifice, that is a price the nation should be willing to pay. A positive national identity can serve as a catalyst for transferring into the daily workplace the group loyalty, work ethic, camaraderie, and sacrifice that are associated with Carnival preparations and presentations.

Finally, as a creative artist and practitioner in a theater that embraces not only acting, movement, dance, song, gesture, and music, but also language and rhythm, conflict and contrast, symbol and metaphor, satire and burlesque, costumes and, yes, masking, I find Carnival to be a great resource for preserving and revitalizing these essential ingredients of a national theater. Several Caribbean dramatists, both at home and abroad, have realized this fact and have written plays incorporating elements of the Carnival since my own folk musical *Man Better Man* was first produced in 1961. Much more can be done in this regard.

Carnival is theater—stunning, infectious, massive, participatory, and communal—but by its very nature it is effervescent. It sparkles for all too brief a period, then subsides until it is brewed over again a year later. The job of artists is to take this rich and ever-renewing storehouse of artistic ingredients and transform them into more permanent art forms that will survive throughout the year and for generations to come, to produce exalting dramas, dance and musical compositions, symphonies and operas, paintings and sculptures, and indigenous crafts. This must be done with the same invention, resourcefulness, skill, and meaning that already exist in the annual Carnival, which passes from our consciousness on Ash Wednesday morning. Only when works as I have described have been actually produced can it be said that Caribbean artists have fulfilled their mission, that they have contributed towards that recognition of a cultural heritage and identity, without which nationhood is little more than an empty boast, full of sound and fury, yet signifying nothing.

Dr. Errol Hill, a playwright, director, actor, teacher, and native of Trinidad, is the John D. Willard Professor of Drama and Oratory, Emeritus, at Dartmouth College, Hanover, New Hampshire.

Carnival and Its Place in Caribbean Culture and Art

Peter Minshall

The original suggested title for this essay was "Carnival and Its Impact on Caribbean Culture and Art." This proposed line of inquiry seems to reflect the unexamined assumption that Carnival is peripheral to Caribbean culture and art, having an impact upon them but not included among them. The following writing proposes a different line of inquiry. Its premise is that Carnival, and the forms of creative expression that are encompassed within the festival, *is* culture, *is* art. The relevant questions are: What is the place of Carnival in Caribbean culture and art? Why do such stereotyped notions persist that fail to consider the arts of Carnival as valid contemporary forms alongside the more conventional (imported) arts? And what do Carnival and its forms have to offer the Caribbean artist as potential media for artistic expression and communication?

Carnival: Ancestor to the Arts

Carnival, in its general and universal sense, can be considered the precursor to all the performing arts. This festival of life—which celebrates the life force, the renewal of life in the spring, the life-giving force of the sun and its god-power—is a cultural-religious expression common to many ancient civilizations, from the Holi festival in the East to the Dionysian celebrations of the Greeks to the many rituals of song and dance from the African continent and the Americas. Such a celebration of the life force naturally expressed itself in dance, in music, and in masked costume, as a means to express the human energy of the celebrants and to invoke the presence and power of the deity. Without demanding precise historical evidence, it seems likely that these ancient expressions of movement, music, mask, and ritual had something to do with the origin and evolution of what we know today as dance, classical music, theater, and opera.

Of course, our latter-day forms are much more disciplined, sophisticated, and refined than the original festivals and rituals from which they were spawned, which allows them to achieve a greater level of complexity. But there are elements of the raw Carnival aesthetic which the refined arts tend to lack, and which to this day retain a vital and valuable power.

Carnival in Trinidad

LeRoy Clarke
Pantheon
(see p. 196)

Carnival as it has appeared in Trinidad in this century is a direct descendant of those ancient celebrations, manifested in a small, multicultural society. It is moot to debate the precise origins of Trinidad Carnival, since the nature of the festival is universal in its ancient roots. The custom of Carnival probably was introduced to Trinidad by the French immigrants, in the domesticated form that resulted from having been processed through the Roman Catholic adoption of the original pagan festival. It also seems reasonable to assume that, although the style and aesthetic of this mannered form of "carnival" would have been very European, the African creoles would immediately have recognized the essential business of masking, dressing up, and parading to music, for these elements would have been part of the various life-celebrating festivals and rituals of their own origins. Suffice it to say that the Trinidad Carnival, as it manifested itself over the next century and a half, is observed on a date that is determined by the Catholic calendar, possesses a vigor and an energy that is to a major extent creole-African in nature, and displays a set of forms and styles that has been informed by the immigrant cultures of Europe, Africa, China, India, and the Middle East, as well as the neighboring cultures of the New World.[1]

To evaluate the place of Carnival in Caribbean culture and art, it is helpful to realize that Carnival incorporates a broad range of forms and activities. Carnival in Trinidad includes: lyrical songs (calypso and soca), instrumental music (steel bands and brass orchestras), and costumed masquerade along with the dance and movement by which it is presented (mas). Carnival also includes the season of heightened social activity and interaction via fetes, work in mas camps, heated discussion over the merits of particular calypsos, pan orchestras, mas bands and their kings or queens, and in general a heightened level of human energy and rhythm and interaction. Carnival is not an art form; it is bigger than that—it is a Festival of the Arts.

Mas: An Analysis of the Form

The most visual of these forms is what we call *mas'*: the tradition of costumed masquerade in the Trinidad Carnival. In the Carnival context, at that level of familiarity that breeds contempt, mas is dressing up in a costume that conforms to a theme chosen by the band leader, and jumping up in the streets, to music, for the two days of Carnival. From an objective, analytical standpoint, however, mas has many different characteristics or possibilities that qualify it as a unique brand of performance art and make it of potential interest to the contemporary artist or observer of art.

Mas is a popular form, which means ordinary members of the community experience the artwork not merely by observing it, but by participating in it. Because it requires sacrifice on the part of these participants (long ago, by spending time to make the costume; nowadays, by spending money to purchase it), the experience has a characteristic of being valued, being keenly desired, which imbues the performance with a special vitality.

Mas offers the participant an opportunity for transformation, to transcend the conditions of daily existence; and the opportunity to be part of a transient but highly charged community of people, to be part of something larger than oneself. It provides a license or excuse to express oneself in a manner that is free and unrestrained as compared to ordinary daily existence during the balance of the year.

Mas is a vehicle for the expression of human energy. A mas often magnifies and articulates that human energy. This can create a type of kinetic that is especially exciting because it is human-driven (rather than mechanized) and hence is rhythmically responsive and vital, and because it happens at a larger-than-life scale. In particular, the discipline of a single live human performer carrying and motivating a huge kinetic structure, which could be referred to as "dancing mobile sculpture," is one that is unique to the Trinidad Carnival.

Mas is relevant to the community in which it occurs, because a mas band must appeal to, and be approved by, its players in order to be realized. This relevance may be achieved by tapping

Callaloo Dancing Tic Tac Toe Down the River, from the mas band *Callaloo,* by Peter Minshall, Trinidad Carnival 1984.

One of the most pure examples of "dancing mobile sculpture," this mas reaches fourteen feet into the air and is over forty feet wide. Photo by Norton Studios.

into a prevailing current of dissatisfaction, or defiance, or pride, or celebration; or, it may take the form of escapism, mirroring a reluctance or an inability to engage in day-to-day reality.

Mas is a performance art. It is not merely visual; a mas costume displayed on a mannequin is not mas. The mere costume relates to the actual work of mas in much the same way that a musical note on a page relates to a performed symphony. Mas involves visual art and three-dimensional sculpture as well as music, dance, mime, and sometimes even speech. It is more than shape, or form, or structure, or "costume"—it is a costume performed. In local terms, one "plays" a mas—and the music and the movement are essential to that "playing."

Though it is performance, mas does not easily fit into the mold of any one of the more conventional performing arts. It is theatrical, but it is necessarily broader of stroke, more symbolic, simpler than conventional narrative theater. It involves dance, but this dance is often more spontaneous than choreographed; or, it is dance that is aimed at articulating the mas that is worn, more than the body that is wearing it. It is most akin to what has become known as simply "performance" or "performance art,"[2] yet the mas had these characteristics, naively and unselfconsciously, long before the term "performance art" was coined.

Mas is capable of treating a wide range of subjects, from the purely abstract and kinetic to the thematically weighted and profound, from the surreal to the literal, from the light and frothy to the highly dramatic. The language of mas is broad, simple, symbolic, bold, and strong. Hence, it is difficult for a mas to convey a detailed plot or complex emotions or philosophy; but mas can communicate mood, emotion, thematic content, and even tell or illustrate a story. Though the primary theme or message of the mas may be broad and bold, the work of art may have many layers and resonances of meaning by virtue of its extremely public quality, its social dynamics, and the individual human energies brought to it by each of its many participants.

A mas band of many hundreds or thousands of participants can be conceived as a "visual symphony" passing in linear fashion before the eye. It may begin with an overture, and follow as movements of highs and lows; the staccato contrasted with the lyrical; the forte with the pianissimo, building to a visual/kinetic denouement and closing with an emphatic climax. As such, the visual, sculptural, and kinetic possibilities of a mas band are not only many and varied, but dynamic. Not only can the artist create line, form, and volume, but he can have it move and flow. He can set it to music and watch it dance. And among his media are the live human energy and spirit of the mas players.

Because of these many and varied characteristics—especially the large scale, the human energy, the musical rhythm that drives it, the necessary broadness and directness of dramatic content—mas can have an impact on the observer that is visceral, immediate, and very powerful.
Of course, not every work in this medium lives up to its potential. Just as the medium of two-dimensional representation can produce its teary-eyed clowns on black velvet or its pornographic graffiti, so too there are works in the mas that are not worthy of mention. But the characteristics described above do make it a form that is capable of a wide range and depth of artistic expression, and thus confirm it as a valid medium in which an artist may choose to work.

This has not always been immediately apparent.

Mas: Cultural Bias and Self-Contempt

To the First World artist, mas is likely to appear exotic. While he might applaud it as "wonderful" and "fantastic," he is not likely to look at a work in the mas according to the same terms by which he evaluates a work at the Brooklyn Academy of Music Next Wave Festival or the Institute of Contemporary Art in London. And to the native Trinidadian, although he may love his mas, he will not have the cultural self-confidence to think it worthy of a place alongside paintings in the Louvre or performances on Broadway, not until the First World itself recognizes it as such. Yet, if one considers the extent to which a work in the mas engages members of the community, by comparison to a work in the medium of painting or sculpture, this alleged "exoticism" begins to fall away.

Certainly mas can be distinguished from "folk art." It has no linear or pure tribal origin—it is a new form created through a process of synthesis within a young creole culture of many transplanted cultural inputs. Neither is it a seasonal recreation of traditionally established forms and images. To the contrary: the community demands that mas remain constantly contemporary. Anything that smacks of repetition is decried. Even in the very commercial mas bands of current times, what little costume there is will from year to year follow the latest trends in the cut, print, and pattern of the Spandex. In theme and content as well, topicality is the norm for those mas bands that are not purely escapist fantasy. (Indeed, the very preponderance of escapist fantasy themes probably reflects a current in society, which only serves to reinforce the position of mas as a socially responsive and contemporary form.)

Of particular challenge to the contemporary artist is the transitory nature of the form. A work in the mas requires months of design, development, and construction, and yet is performed only once, after which it ceases to exist. This may seem incomprehensible, even a bit frightening, to an artist entrenched in the world of excruciating scholarship, chemically sophisticated restoration, and atmospherically controlled preservation. But there is something instructive, and liberating, about a work that sparks to brilliant life but once, to extinguish itself in the ashes of a festival that, phoenixlike, will re-emerge in the next season in a new and different form.

This very transitory nature of the form mitigates against it being taken seriously by the conventional art world. It is difficult to catalogue a mas, to give its dimensions, to specify the media in which it was executed. Mas tends to fall between the cracks of conventional artistic disciplines. There is no museum or university department to which it can comfortably be assigned.

Yet, it is precisely those characteristics that make it difficult to define as a medium or form of artistic expression that should make the medium of mas appeal to the contemporary artist. The field of art "performance" has been described as a natural searching in response to the growing irrelevance of conventional object-oriented art to the dynamic modern world.[3] Mas can offer the same opportunity to transcend the object in favor of the experience, yet in a manner that is not elite and inaccessible, but by its nature popular and participatory.

Carnival and the "Fine Arts"

In the Caribbean in particular, the relation between the so-called fine arts and Carnival has always been rather ambivalent, if not troubled. Objectively speaking, the mas is a relatively new, synthesized, and uniquely Trinidadian form of expression, while two-dimensional painting and three-dimensional sculpture are conventional, First World–sanctioned forms that have been inherited directly from colonial sources. Yet, because the First World terms dominate cultural notions of what is "art," any young, talented island person who yearns to practice art will turn to painting and sculpture, not to the common, island-grown mas.

Still, anyone with the soul of an artist and the rhythm of a Trinidadian cannot but recognize the remarkable human energy of the Carnival, and the vitality of the creative impulse that surges within it. Some of our fine artists have paid tribute to this by depicting Carnival scenes in their paintings. Chris Cozier's series of large canvases that were exhibited at the 1987 Trinidad Art Society exhibition caught the mud and sweat and color of mas in the street. Jackie Hinkson's recent forays into oil painting include the huge, murallike *Masquerade,* peopled with an entire family of intense Carnival figures. The carnival paintings of Mr. Canute Calliste of Carriacou capture with breathtaking honesty and simplicity the character of real old-time mas and, in fact, are executed with the same intuitive sensibility with which the mas itself would have been made.

The mas aesthetic can be seen in manifestations other than literal representations of Carnival scenes, however, and these are perhaps the more direct links between the hand of the painter or sculptor and the designers and craftsmen who make the mas. The prodigious work of LeRoy Clarke is rife with painterly depictions of masks and masklike faces. His intricate and sophisticated brushwork could be seen as family to the painstaking beadwork, braid, and embroidery of the most lovingly crafted headpieces and Robber-capes.

The papier-mâché sculpture of Wendy Nanan is notable both for its choice of a technique that is a staple of old-time mas-making, and for its obviously short life span. The fragility of the work is as much a part of its character as is its shape. Francisco Cabral's chair sculptures also reflect the mas aesthetic in their "assembled" sort of quality and the very literal, almost naive symbolism that they employ.

The most direct relation between the fine arts and the mas was through the work of artist Carlisle Chang. Chang was one of the first among the fine artists—and his credentials as a painter and muralist have been established beyond question—actually to design and make mas. His creations in the 1960s and 1970s, such as *China: The Forbidden City* and *Land of the Kabuki,* brought to the mas an exquisiteness and a decorative balance that were unparalleled.

A quite different but no less intense relationship between the fine arts and the Carnival is exemplified in the life and work of artist and musician Pat Bishop. It is difficult, if not irrelevant, to say whether Bishop's painting is informed with a Carnival sensibility, or whether her conducting of the steel band has a classical discipline and aesthetic. Rather, she conveys the message, matter of factly and by example, that there is no essential distinction to be made between creative work in the Carnival and creative work in the classical arts. The lesson of Bishop's life work to date is that each and every creative endeavor is an effort to produce a work of art, and each such work must be approached with humility, tireless dedication, rigorous discipline, a fierce integrity, and a sense of service to one's community.

While Bishop has demonstrated what can be done in the form of music within the Carnival, her creative objectivity and willingness to ignore or transcend the stereotypes has yet to be emulated in Carnival's visual/theatrical/performing art, i.e., the mas. Chang raised the level of artistry in the mas by applying a painter's sensibility to mas design, and other Trinidad artists have engaged the Carnival peripherally by reflecting its energy and aesthetic in the more static disciplines of painting and sculpture. But an understanding of the essential character of mas as a form of expression, especially in light on contemporary thinking about art and society, leads to the conclusion that the form has dynamic possibilities that have only begun to be thought about, let alone explored.

For the present and the future, it is these dynamic possibilities that define the essential place of Carnival in Caribbean culture and art. That place is not to serve as a mere reference for artists to execute works in conventional media. It is for Carnival in general and the mas in particular to be available as media of expression in themselves.

Mas and the Artist

Of course, this is a daunting prospect. The artist's studio is a far safer and more comfortable place than is the sweat and industry of the mas camp, or the dust and heat of the street. And, admittedly, the state of the contemporary carnival is not one to inspire the artist to believe that great and important works might be produced there.

By contrast to the "golden era" of the mas, with its fancy sailor, the midnight robber, the pierrot, the devil, the fancy clown, and the bat, through the glorious era of George Bailey, the contemporary mas has in large part degenerated into a glorified fete, a swimsuit parade of minimal costuming based on meaningless, infantile, and escapist themes. Commerce has much to do with this decline, as do shifting lines of race and class, and the adoption of Las Vegas–style glamour as the prevailing and desired taste. But the decline may also be attributed to the

"Artist's Squares," for the mas band *Tantana,* by Peter Minshall, Trinidad Carnival 1990.

The special section of Artist's Squares in *Tantana* featured individual works by many of Trinidad's prominent painters. Lisa Henry Choo Foon designed the square on the left; Carlisle Chang, on the right, is shown performing the piece he designed.
Photo by Bruce Paddington.

neglect of the mas by those with creative talent and drive and ideas to express.

And yet, the mas still teases and intrigues the fine artist. A good few of them in Trinidad were coaxed out of their studios and into a mas camp a few years back to participate in a special section of "Artist's Squares" attached to the band *Tantana.* Each artist was invited to contribute a single work, seven-foot square in size, to be executed in appliqued cloth. Sixteen or so individualized tapestries, some of them worn and played by the artists who created them, paraded down the streets of Port of Spain and across the savannah stage as a section of "dancing paintings." It was a "performance" that, had it taken place in New York, might have raised the eyebrows of more than a few "conceptual" artists and critics.

This was undoubtedly an exciting experience for the artists involved, the craftspeople who were privileged to work with them, and those fortunate enough to witness the performance. But this barely scratches the surface of possibilities—the possibilities for the artists to develop the form, and for the form to develop the artists.

It is a form that is particularly appropriate for the Caribbean, and the world, today.

Mas is alive. It is capable of reflecting the essence of Caribbean people who move, sing, and dance through their daily lives, who play mas with their politics and their fashions, who have a very alive, excessive, larger-than-life human energy.

Mas, as a form, can be on the cutting edge of contemporary art. It can be public, participatory, multidisciplinary, multicultural, in-the-street and in-your-face. Historically and by its nature, mas is a synthesizing medium, joining and combining traditional or familiar forms and images, and transforming them into something new and contemporary.

Mas is huge in its potential range. With sufficient creative application, the opportunity exists for new work in the mas to push the envelope of its possibilities far beyond the current narrow confines of the bureaucratically sanctioned Parade of Bands and the King and Queen competitions.

And, mas may be something that Trinidad and the Caribbean can contribute to the rest of the world. Perhaps, because of its contemporary art characteristics, mas might be an exciting medium not only for Caribbean artists, but for artists everywhere. Perhaps, through the mas, Trinidad and the Caribbean can contribute a form of public/participatory/celebratory art that is especially valuable in this modern era of technology-driven and passively received culture.

1. Some commentators have maintained that various works that have appeared in the Carnival are African symbols and forms that have been remembered from the tribal past. (See John Nunley, "Caribbean Festival Arts: Each and Every Bit of Difference," *African Arts* 22, pt. 3 [May 1989].) These claims distort the facts to fit a preconceived anthropological thesis. Whatever African forms and symbols have appeared in the Carnival are much more likely to have been acquired in the same way that the Carnival has appropriated and processed the forms and symbols of Imperial Rome, Ancient Greece, tribal New Guinea, Elizabethan England, or the American West—via the encyclopedia, pulp fiction, or Hollywood. It is not necessary to manufacture anthropological links in order to document and celebrate the African contribution to the Carnival, which is the energy that drives it, the rhythm according to which it moves, and a fantastic instinct for appropriation, synthesis, and invention. (Daniel J. Crowley, "The Midnight Robber," *Caribbean Quarterly,* University College of the West Indies, vol. 4, nos. 3–4 [March–June 1956], p. 274). It is this contribution of the African creoles, aided and abetted by the East Indians, Chinese, Syrians and Lebanese, French creoles, Spanish, Portuguese, Scottish, English, German, and Dutch, that have conspired to create an annual festival of song, dance, and masquerade of new, unique, Trinidadian dimensions.

2. Many of the things that have been said about "performance" as an avant-garde discipline apply in equal terms to mas:

> Performance has been a way of appealing directly to a large public, as well as shocking audiences into reassessing their own notions of art and its relation to culture. . . .
>
> [B]y its very nature, performance defies precise or easy definition beyond the simple declaration that it is live art by artists. . . . For performance draws freely on any number of references—literature, theatre, drama, music, architecture, poetry, film and fantasy, deploying them in any combination.

> No other artistic form of expression can be said to have such a boundless manifesto. . . . The manifestos accompanying much of this work establish a framework and a utopian vision for an all-inclusive art that no painting, sculpture, or architectural monument can hope to achieve in itself.

RoseLee Goldberg, *Performance: Live Art 1909 to the Present* (London: Thames and Hudson, 1979), p. 6.

3. Ibid., p. 98.

Peter Minshall has produced seventeen major works in the Trinidad Carnival and has applied the same disciplines to various festival, stadium, and street-theater events around the world, including the ceremonies of the 1992 Olympic Games in Barcelona. The emphasis of his current work is The Callaloo Company, a small performance group that is exploring the possibilities of intimate theatrical performace based on the movement, rhythms, and images of the mas.

Caribbean Art and Culture from a Haitian Perspective

Gerald Alexis

In recent years, several opportunities have arisen to determine whether or not one can justly talk about Caribbean art and culture. These inter-island festivals and art exhibitions have proven that indeed, despite significant differences, a Caribbean vision exists that induces patterns of cultural expression shared by all creators in the region. This resemblance can easily be understood, for the Caribbean family has emerged from common races and cultures, blended in various proportions, from the time of the conquest of these islands in the late fifteenth century. Subsequently, these combinations of elements, including different socio-economic and political developments, can account for distinctions between each of these countries.

Like the greater Antilles, the island of "Ayti,"[1] which Columbus later named Hispaniola, was dominated during the prehistoric period by the Taíno culture. French appropriation of the western part of Hispaniola (then named Saint-Domingue) in the seventeenth century, its prosperous development, which created a greater need for African slaves, and thirteen years of bloody battle for independence were all factors that set a path for the evolution of Haiti which differs from that of its immediate neighbors Cuba, the Dominican Republic, Jamaica, and Puerto Rico.

Unlike on the other islands, where artworks from the colonial period have been preserved, the slave revolt on Saint-Domingue destroyed plantation homes and towns and with them the artistic treasures that, according to publications of the late 1700s,[2] had been brought to the colony from France. Although no evidence remains to support this assertion, it is believed that during the colonial period, freed slaves and mulattoes were trained as artists and worked primarily under the commission of less wealthy planters. One might be led to think that, with such a lack of artistic references, the new nation would have had to establish its own traditions in the arts.

On the contrary, the need to celebrate Haiti's independence and its heroes led the country's new leaders to call on French and English painters to record their grand feat. Portraits and historical scenes, created in fashionable European styles, thus became common forms of art throughout the nineteenth century. In Haiti and in other Caribbean countries, such official European art came to define the discriminatory taste of the elites and the upper middle class. Local artists, then few in number, had to comply with the standards set by their potential patrons. Victims of a total cultural alienation, little of their national or regional inclinations could be transferred to their canvases. In the mid-1800s, the concordat signed by the Haitian government with the Vatican strongly reinforced this alienation. Priests and nuns, sent to educate young Haitians, encouraged the obsequious copying of European images in their art classes. Amateur paintings of landscapes with snow-covered mountains and still lifes with apples and pears thus proliferated under the tropical sun.

Andre Juste
Early Hanging (detail)
(see p. 142)

This bent toward the European mode, from fashion to table manners, precluded the educated classes from seeing and appreciating what remained of the island's indigenous culture and of the cultures brought over by African slaves. Yet, in Haiti and elsewhere in the Caribbean, some forms of artistic expressions surely existed among the poorer classes, which were comprised largely of blacks. They had kept some of their heritage vivid, as is evident primarily in their music, their storytelling, and their clandestine religious rituals. The social structures that defined most Caribbean countries at the time assigned little importance to these strata, and whatever they created in the form of art went unnoticed.

•

An awakening to some form of national identity occurred in the areas of literature and poetry during the American occupation of Haiti from 1915 to 1934. In 1928, Dr. Jean Price Mars (1876–1968), a Haitian intellectual, published a series of essays under the title *Ainsi parla l'Oncle* (The uncle spoke in such terms). This document is today considered to have marked the origin of a cultural trend that is now referred to as the "Indigenist Movement." Price Mars criticized Haitian society and hoped for "its emancipation from these binding preconceptions that restrict its creators to the pale imitation of that which is extraneous to their own values."[3] He strongly emphasized the African origin of the Haitian people and exalted the traditions brought over by the slave trade. He pointed out, in conclusion, that this legacy still remained vivid among Haitian peasant families.

In its daily activities the Haitian peasantry had inspired William Edouard Scott (1884–1964), an African American painter who sojourned in Haiti and had a one-man exhibition in a fashionable private club of Port-au-Prince in 1930. Scott then received a distinction from the Haitian government for having revealed to Haitian artists the rich variety and potential of indigenous themes.[4] Rural genre scenes thus became the major subject in the works of painters who joined the Indigenist Movement. An immense gap, however, existed between these artists, who came from the elite and the upper middle classes, and the figural types they portrayed. Their works were therefore affected by an unfavorable superficial impression. Much had to be done to convince potential buyers of the interest and validity of such works. Their content suggested some kind of social involvement, and their formal elements showed an obvious lack of precision. Indeed, unlike Scott himself, his Haitian followers had received little artistic training. They thus were unable to master the intense light of the sun and to render properly the anatomy and movement of the figures depicted. Partly to overcome these technical difficulties, native artists in the 1930s turned to the natural beauty of the environment, generally painting from photographs. These appealing paintings conformed with the Indigenist idea that painters and poets should celebrate the beauty of the land. Furthermore, they eschewed all social content that might have been considered too radical.

These Haitian artists paid little attention to the fact that painters on many of the other islands, following a tradition established by foreign itinerant artists, fervently practiced landscape painting. They also ignored that in Cuba, at the time of the island's independence around the turn of the century, the intense play of light and shadows, the lush vegetation, and the picturesque sites were key elements in the works of Cuban painters who sought to define their national identity. Although these countries of the same region then had limited contact with one another, it appears that in the first half of the twentieth century, artists sought to create a mode of visual expression that would accent something which was truly theirs and by extension truly Caribbean: the environment. Equating such images with "Caribbean art" meshed perfectly with the idea of "paradise" that was being conveyed through advertising campaigns to promote the region's developing tourist industry. Yet there was, and still is, much more to being Caribbean.

Hector Hyppolite, *Grand Maitre,* oil on hardboard. 37x 25 in., Collection Musée d'art Haitien.

In Haiti, several factors came together in the late 1940s to bring about noticeable change in the visual arts. As mentioned earlier, the writings of Jean Price Mars revitalized the African component of Haitian culture and introduced intellectuals, writers, and painters to the popular religion of voodoo. Deeply rooted in the Black Continent, despite the combination of elements borrowed from the Catholic faith over the years, voodoo came to be regarded as an interesting field of investigation and led to the definition of a new facet of the Haitian spirit—this *real maravilloso* of which the Cuban writer Alejo Carpentier spoke. Also, Haitian painters, through travels in Europe and through books and other publications, had been introduced to modernism and sought to use this visual language in their own art. While they looked to Picasso, Braque, and Chagall for inspiration to rebel against the academic tradition, which was considered unsuitable to the Haitian soul and its lack of "raison raisonnante,"[5] these native artists found the essential qualities they were seeking in the works of their compatriots, who were labeled "primitives." These popular artists, whose works were featured at the opening of the Centre d'Art in 1944,[6] had proven that voodoo, born of the African tradition and beliefs, had perpetuated powerful means of artistic expressions other than music and dance. The oeuvre of "Hector Hyppolite (1894–1948), to name just one, had turned people's attention to Voodoo temples to find an art form which probably dates back from the years prior to independence."[7] In addition to the spiritual power in their free play of the unconscious, the work of these so-called primitives conveyed to the trained Haitian artists the aesthetic strength of their flat forms, their circular composition, and their particular use of colors. Included among these determining factors was the 1945 presentation of Cuban avant-garde art at the Centre d'Art in Port-au-Prince, an exhibition that previously had been shown at the Museum of Modern Art in New York.

This event represented Haiti's first major artistic exchange with a neighboring Caribbean country, and its repercussions were significant. It was "an appropriate example for Haitian artists since they could identify geographically with the Cubans and respond with no difficulty to the tropical boldness of their works."[8] Shortly thereafter the Cuban painter Wifredo Lam (1902–1982) made two sojourns in Haiti and held workshops at the Centre d'Art. Lam was, as Aimé Césaire put it, "the first in the Antilles to salute freedom."[9] He painted the tragedy of his country, thoroughly expressing the Negro spirit and the sculptural beauty of the blacks. Since that time, free from all aesthetic doubts, servility to any form of realism, and all documentary concerns, contemporary Haitian artists have adeptly confronted all of the various components of their individual personalities.

•

Experts have noted the subsistence of Amerindian elements in Haitian culture, with food and the traditions of basketry and pottery being among the most salient features. Archaeological finds in the 1940s and 1950s revealed the extraordinary complexity of pre-Columbian civilizations on the island. The design and anthropomorphic aspects of certain decorative motifs found on fragments of vessels caught the attention of artists. They in turn strongly urged their contemporaries in the international mainstream of art to "start over,"[10] to redefine their inner selves and their notions of truth and beauty, for "art is not a goal in itself, but rather a medium, a tool allowing the introspection into one's cultural roots and personality in relation with lost civilizations."[11]

Modernism, in its development in Haiti, was and still is open to external sources while it relies heavily on vernacular components. Haitian contemporary art is truly the result of this continual process of crossbreeding which one encounters throughout the Caribbean. The foreign art market, however, tends to perpetrate the old idea that Haiti is "the only country in the world whose artistic output [is] represented by works of naive painters, primitive not only in their approach, but also in their complete lack of academic training."[12] This false perception is attributable to the fact that, unlike Cuba, for instance, which entered the international art scene with an exhibition representing its own avant-garde, Haiti did so with an exhibition of works by its so-called primitive painters, which was overwhelmingly received by critics and collectors alike. The modern art of Haiti was then criticized for its "lack of distinction,"[13] for as one critic observed, "The more they become like us, the less they will be able to paint like themselves."[14] Obviously the critic overlooked that the inner self of the Haitian artist is not necessarily that of a person who lives close to nature, in a pre-industrial, pre-modern world. On the contrary, artistic vision can be that of a man exposed to modern concepts with both the opportunity and the right to comprehend Western conventions and adapt them to a Third World context.

Such is indeed the case of the contemporary painters and sculptors in Haiti whose art can be justly defined as a true reflection of the Haitian soul, which has been permeated with lost and distant civilizations and shaped by circumstances in the modern world. It is also the image of their inner selves, dominated by the Caribbean spirit upon which elements of French, English, Spanish, and American cultures have impressed very special qualities.

1. The Indian name supposedly meant "Land of Mountains."

2. Michel Philippe Lerebours, *Haiti et ses Peintres de 1804 à 1980,* 2 vols. (Port-au-Prince: L'imprimeur II, 1984), I: 44–46.

3. Pradel Pompilus, *Manuel Illustré de la Littérature Haïtienne* (Port-au-Prince: Editions Henri Deschamps, 1961), pp. 614–615.

4. Samella Lewis, *Art: African American* (Los Angeles: Hancraft Studios, 1990), p. 54.

5. This expression, referring to the Cartesian way of thinking, was used in the Western sense of the word by the Haitian painter Max Pinchinat in the foreword to *Max Pinchinat,* exhibition brochure (Port-au-Prince: Le Centre d'Art, 1949).

6. The Centre d'Art was inaugurated in Port-au-Prince in May of 1944 and was directed by Dewitt Peters (1902–1966), an American painter from California.

7. Excerpts were taken from notes by Pierre Monosiet, former director of the Musée d'Art Haitien, and were compiled and published in "Ainsi parlait Pierre Monosiet," *Le Nouvelliste* (Port-au-Prince), 10 December 1984.

8. José Gomez-Sicré, in the foreword to Eleanor Ingalls Christensen's *The Art of Haiti* (New York: S.A. Barnes and Company, 1971), p. 10.

9. Aimé Césaire, quoted by Maiten Bouisset in "Wifredo Lam," *Beaux Arts Magazine,* no. 71 (September 1989), p. 107.

10. Max Pinchinat, "Réflexions sur la Peinture," *Le Nouvelliste* (Port-au-Prince), 14 October 1949, p. 3.

11. Jean Claude Garoute, "From the HaitianTraditional Art to l'Ecole du Soleil," lecture presented at the Center for Contemporary Art, North Miami, Florida, March 1992.

12. *Naive Art of Haiti,* press release issued by The Carol Reese Museum of East Tennessee State University at Johnson City, 1967.

13. Mrs. Parker, Director of the Seligmann Gallery of New York, as quoted by Dewitt Peters in his *General Report on the Centre d'Art from September 1, 1947 to February 29, 1948,* found in the archives of Pierre Monosiet.

14. Mark Stevens, "Black Magic," *Newsweek,* 18 September 1978, p. 69.

As Director and Chief Curator of Georges S. Nader's Art Museum in Port-au-Prince, Haiti, art historian Gerald Alexis promotes contemporary Haitian and Caribbean art through exhibitions and lectures. He also serves as editor of *Cultura* magazine.

Artists of Haiti: Reflections on a Narrative

Richard A. Long

It was approximately fifty years ago that the existence of Haitian visual art struck the consciousness of the art public in the United States and elsewhere. At the same moment Katherine Dunham, through her concert-theatrical dance group, was presenting Haitian themes and movement to a large and enthusiastic audience. While the Haitian elements in Dunham's work were not always clearly perceived as such by her audiences, the work of Haiti's painters and sculptors was firmly attached to the persona of the Black Republic.

Haiti's entrance into the international art scene is a frequently recounted tale, first presented at length by Seldon Rodman in his 1948 book *Renaissance in Haiti: Popular Painters in the Black Republic.* Although some elements of Rodman's account were contested in Haiti from time to time, his involvement with the nation and its art was lifelong, and his subsequent writings include the guidebook *Haiti: The Black Republic* (1954) and *Miracle of Haitian Art* (1973).

Many Haitians felt that Rodman's books emphasized the popular or "primitive" artists fostered at the Centre d'Art in Port-au-Prince, and thus presented a narrow and even demeaning impression of art in Haiti. The eminent Haitian writer Philippe Thoby-Marcelin offered an initial response to Rodman in his book *Panorama de l'Art Haitien* (1956); a condensed English translation by Eva Thoby-Marcelin was published by the Pan-American Union in 1959. Michel-Philippe Lerebours made a definitive riposte in his two-volume *Treatise on Haitian Art.* Despite these two important works, what the art world outside Haiti understands of Haitian art derives largely from Rodman's account.

The role played by the United States at the outset of this "international" story is significant. Ironically, the support of the Haitian government, slight but crucial, would hardly have been extended to the Centre d'Art without American participation. Initially, the underlying foundation for the creation of the Centre d'Art was an English teaching program in Haiti, headed by Mercer Cook, an African American scholar. Cook had been a professor at Atlanta University and at Howard University in Washington, D.C. After a long international career that included a post as Ambassador to Senegal, Cook returned to Howard University.

Among the teachers on the staff of the English teaching program were Naomi Garrett and Dewitt Peters, a sometime painter. Garrett later wrote a doctoral dissertation at Columbia University, which was ultimately published as *The Renaissance of Haitian Poetry* (1963). Peters remained in Haiti as a mentor to the Haitian art movement. Along with a group of Haitian artists and intellectuals, he established the Centre d'Art, which served as the locus of the movement.

Edouard Duval Carrié
Danse de la Morte (detail)
(see p. 140)

The Centre d'Art opened in May 1944 in Port-au-Prince, and its founders planned to encourage and instruct young, aspiring painters who, presumedly, would come from the educated bourgeoisie. Quite unexpectedly, working class people with artistic hopes appeared on the scene, eager to participate. This surge in interest changed the major thrust of the Centre d'Art and led it to develop two wings: a "standard" art school and a less formal "primitive" program. Ultimately, emphasis shifted to the "primitive" movement, which caused discontent, accusations, and even secession by many of the schooled artists. Nevertheless, a tremendous fount of creativity was discovered among people who had had no previous access to artistic training.

The beginning of this heady tale is told in Rodman's *Renaissance.* A thirty-year history of Haitian art is provided in two books: Eleanor Ingalls Christensen's *The Art of Haiti* (1975), which provides a brief but balanced account, and the catalogue of The Brooklyn Museum's extensive exhibition *Haitian Art* (1978) by Ute Stebich.

In the two decades since these books appeared, much has happened in Haiti, both in and beyond the world of art. In 1972 the Musée d'Art Haitien du College St. Pierre opened under the directorship of Pierre Monosiet, who had been an assistant to Dewitt Peters at the Centre d'Art. The museum maintains a permanent collection and presents a series of temporary exhibitions of artists of all schools. Among these artists was a cadre that had long been associated with the Centre d'Art, as well as some artists who were products of the School of Visual Arts established within the framework of the University. Others were Haitian artists who had trained abroad.

•

From the foregoing, it is obvious that tension has existed between the widely known "primitive" artists of Haiti, who are predominantly of lower class origin and relatively unschooled, and the trained, academic artists, who are almost exclusively bourgeois in their social origins and are products of Haiti's francophone culture. This friction has been felt primarily by artists of the latter group. Furthermore, certain members of the Haitian elite are uncomfortable with the representation and interpretations of their land and culture by these popular painters.

The Brooklyn Museum exhibition of 1978 may have contributed to this opposition by defining Haitian art exclusively in terms of the popular painters and featuring certain themes. The museum's installation included "trained" painters who were not in the catalogue and were undoubtedly added due to pressure brought by the Haitian community of New York. It is the catalogue, however, which conveys the thrust of the exhibition and remains its document. The catalogue presented a frenzied, if not neurotic, obsession with *Voudun* (called voodoo in the catalogue) as the key to the art of the painters represented.

The 150 artworks represented in the catalogue were divided into three categories: history (19 works), voodoo and art (59 works), and everyday and festive life (72 works). The willingness to present Haitian art as "primitive" is exemplified by the inappropriate inclusion of several paintings in the "voodoo" category and by the ambiguous labeling of other works. Two examples of this forcing further illustrate the point.

The exhibition curator notes of *La presence de dieu* (The Presence of God), a painting by the pious Catholic servitor Castera Bazile, "The context of the *Presence of God* seems clearly Christian. Yet the remoteness of God and his noninvolvement are typical of the way the voodooist perceives God as the supreme force in the voodoo pantheon."[1] The commentary degenerates from this point. Of a 1975 painting by Ernest Prophete, a civil engineer born in 1950, the curator says: *"But . . . I Dreamt* is a vision of the artist's own death. He is led by two angels toward a light representing God, leaving the cemetery and the earth behind. . . . Even though the iconographical details of angels and God are of Christian origin, the choice of colors may stem from voodoo concepts."[2] Given the narrow view of Haitian art and artists it presented, the opulent Brooklyn exhibition could, without ingratitude, be perceived as a distinctly mixed blessing.

•

A more accurate history of Haitian art must include events preceding the founding of the Centre d'Art and the wide popularity of the primitive painters. During the 1920s, Haiti was one topic of interest and concern among the artists and intellectual leaders of the Harlem Renaissance, now regarded as a significant epoch of African American and of American cultural history. Reasons for this interest emanate from a whole tapestry of Haitian-African American interrelationships in the nineteenth century, culminating in the appointment of Frederick Douglass as United States Minister to Haiti in 1889. Four years later, in 1893, the Haitian government requested that Douglass be its Honorary Delegate to the World Columbian Exposition in Chicago. In that capacity Douglass made a statement which reflected the opinion of informed African Americans of the time.

> I consider Haiti as the original liberator of the 19th century. It was her example, both unique and courageous, which for the first time shocked the Christian world with an understanding of the manliness of blacks. . . . Until the moment that Haiti struck its blow for liberty, the conscious of the Christian world remained dormant in the presence of human slavery.[3]

In 1915 the United States occupied Haiti on various pretexts, an action widely and profoundly protested by African Americans through the NAACP and in other ways. James Weldon Johnson, a noted man of letters, traveled to Haiti in 1920 on behalf of the NAACP and upon his return published several articles criticizing the occupation. In the wake of Johnson's visit, many other African Americans journeyed to Haiti, including the writer Langston Hughes. The painter William Edouard Scott spent a year in Haiti in 1930–1931, and his activity there particularly inspired Pétion Savain, the principal figure on the Haitian art scene in the 1930s. Aaron Douglas, another distinguished African American painter, visited Haiti in 1938.

Two artists, Normil Charles and Archibald Lochard, opened a private art school in Port-au-Prince in 1915, the year of the occupation. Charles, a sculptor then about forty-five years old, had studied in France at government expense; Lochard, a painter, was the son of a painter who had been attached to the court of the self-proclaimed emperor Soulouque. Among students at the school were Charles's son Hubermann and André Lafontant, both of whom were to have an impact on their countrymen.

Thirty years later some pupils of Pétion Savain, such as Geo Remponeau, were active in Port-au-Prince at the founding of the Centre d'Art in 1944. Most of these academically trained artists who were to enjoy international attention emerged during the epoch of the Centre d'Art, including Luce Turnier and Antonio Joseph—both are mentioned in Rodman's *Renaissance in Haiti*—and the slightly older Lucien Price and Maurice Borno, each of whom died young.

Significantly, several academic artists seceded from the Centre d'Art in 1950 and formed a group known as the Foyer des Arts Plastiques. A group of artists associated with the Foyer created the Galerie Brochette in 1956. Numbered among this latter group were Nehemy Jean, Luckner Lazare, Dieudonné Cédor, Roland Dorcély, and Jacques Gabriel.

All of these artists and their activities and achievements belong to the narrative of Haitian art. While it would be impossible to list the names of Haiti's many artists, including six Haitian artists in this exhibition devoted to the Caribbean does underscore several points. The present artists of Haiti share a visual patrimony and solidarity with other artists of the Caribbean, and they are all aware of Cuban artist Wifredo Lam as a tutelary spirit of the Caribbean art world. Like other artists of the Caribbean, these Haitian artists are cosmopolitan and "internationalized." Luce Turnier, for example, lived in France, Italy, and the United States, and returned to Haiti for long periods. Bernard Séjourné lived in New York and returned to great commercial success in Haiti, his success inspiring imitators among technically proficient but less privileged artists.

Haitian art is today dominated by the work of trained artists, who trace their lineage back to the beginning of the century rather than to the opening of the Centre d'Art in 1944. What then of the popular painters who for so long wore the mantle of Haitian art? Theirs is an honored and honorable achievement, the product of a particular moment in time and of distinct social and cultural factors which, under the impact of globalization and modernization, are no longer in place. There will doubtless always be "outsider" artists of genius in Haiti, as elsewhere, but the popular movement, after fifty years, has become a new academicism, with all that state entails. Its practitioners are "trained" artists who occupy a shifting position in Haiti's present art scene.

1. Ute Stebich, *Haitian Art* (New York: The Brooklyn Museum and Harry N. Abrams, Inc., 1978), p. 88.

2. Ibid., p. 92.

3. Quoted from Richard A. Long and Eugenia Collier, *Afro-American Writing* (1985), pp. 89–90.

Dr. Richard A. Long is the Atticus Haygood Professor at the Institute of the Liberal Arts at Emory University in Atlanta, Georgia.

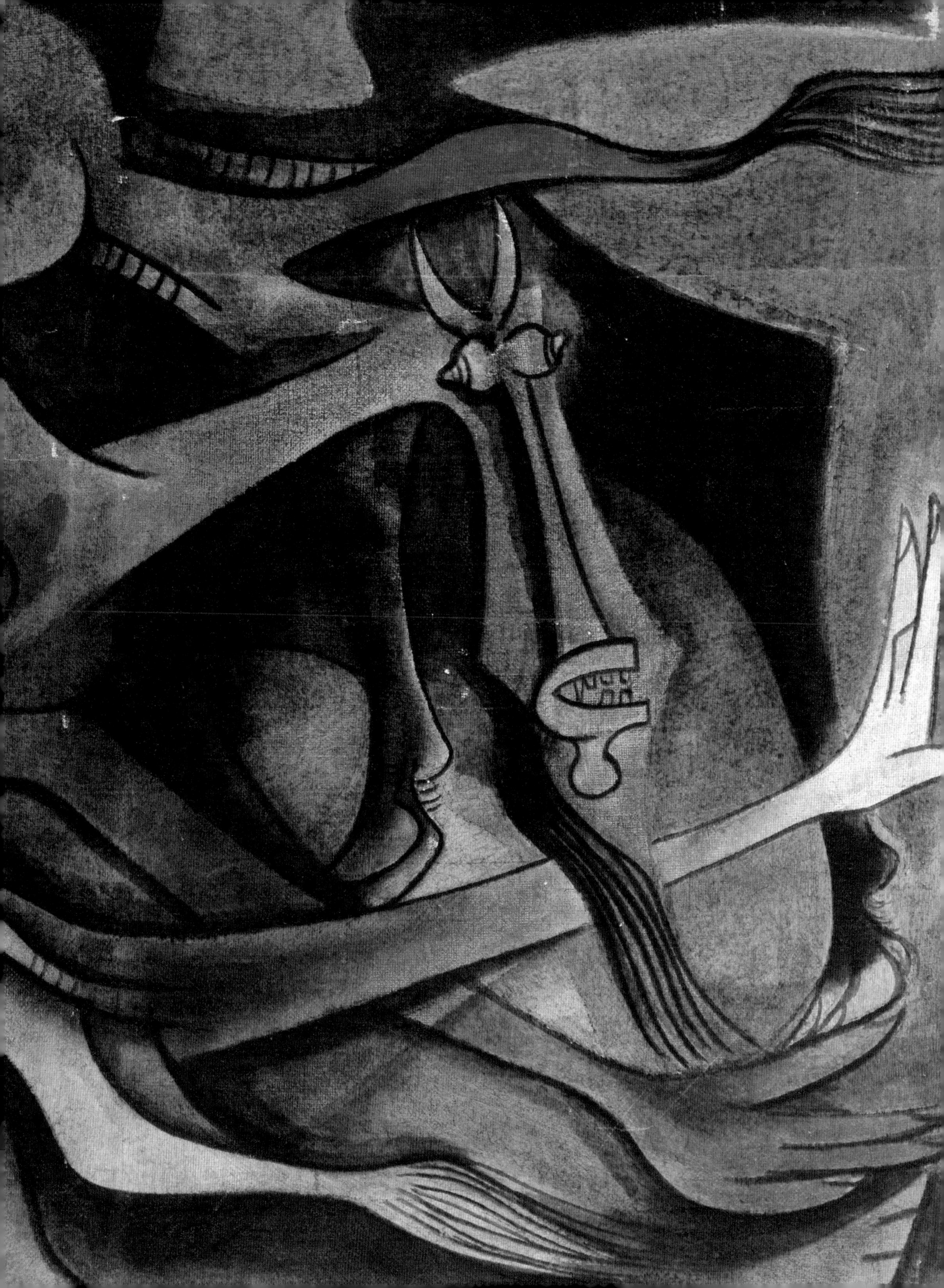

Modern Art of the Spanish-Speaking Caribbean

Shifra M. Goldman

It is absolutely fitting that at the heart of an enterprise called *Caribbean Visions* there should be a splendid work by the Cuban painter Wifredo Lam (1902–1982), a 1948 painting titled *Exodo* (Exodus).[1] In the same sense that his most well-known work, *The Jungle* (1943, Museum of Modern Art, New York), marked the beginning of a new, a mature, phase of his artistic production when he returned to Cuba after an absence of eighteen years in Europe and encountered the living traditions of his youth, *Exodus* marks the other boundary of that fertile period. Painted five years after *The Jungle,*[2] its fluidity, urgent sense of movement, monochromatic treatment, and relative simplification of forms announced that Lam had achieved and internalized a new aesthetic synthesis.

Comparatively, the static quality of *The Jungle* is evident in the way figures and vegetation alike are "planted," so to speak, in and on the earth, while its almost square space is densely filled with a complex of metamorphic beings and the stems, trunks, and translucent leaves of tropical foliage. Its rich dark spectrum of colors, which features blue-greens, red-oranges, and pale yellow-browns, illuminates a ground of umbers, blacks, and violets, all of which are contained within linear structures and a geometric grid.

Thematically, the painting represents a memory of Lam's past—the mistreatment and degradation of Africans—and the artist's desire to subvert that process. "The whole colonial drama of my youth seemed to be reborn in me," he said. The situation of blacks in Cuba had scarcely improved during his years of absence. The same poverty, the same discrimination, the same destruction of his people's dignity still existed. In response, Lam saw himself in a subversive role:

> By thoroughly expressing the negro spirit, the beauty of the plastic arts of the blacks . . . I could act as a Trojan horse that would spew forth hallucinating figures with the power to surprise, to disturb the dreams of the exploiters. I knew I was running the risk of not being understood either by the man in the streets or by the others. But a true picture has the power to set the imagination to work, even if it takes time.[3]

Lam himself never intended *The Jungle* to picture reality but to communicate a psychic state. "Look at my monsters and the gestures they make. . . . My idea was to represent the spirit of the negroes in the situation in which they were then. I have used poetry to show the reality of acceptance and protest."[4] By accentuating the monstrosity of his figures, Lam's work can be seen as a discourse between colonization and decolonization. Within the context of a primitivizing Western modernism (that "terrorized" aspects of "other" cultures without entering into their original meanings), Lam was fascinated by the transformative power of African art and the significance of image making as a means of articulating processes of change and liberation.[5] At the time, such a view could only be held by an African versed in the powers of African sculp-

Wifredo Lam
Exodo (detail)
(see p. 119)

Wifredo Lam, *The Jungle,* 1943, gouache on paper mounted on canvas. 7' 10 1/4" x 7' 6 1/2" (239.4 x 229.4 cm.), The Museum of Modern Art, New York. Inter-American Fund.

ture, by an African American such as Lam who was familiar with the syncretic religions of the Caribbean, by a writer such as Alejo Carpentier or by scholars such as Fernando Ortiz and Lydia Cabrera of Cuba, who were among the first to conduct in-depth studies of *Santería, Palo Monte,* and Afro-Cuban spiritual life. In the process of discovering this new pictorial and thematic terrain—of "graduating" from the African sculpture he so admired in Paris—Lam anchored his figures within the frame of the painting with cubic methodology, much as Picasso and Braque's exploration of early analytical cubism temporarily precluded them from the use of color and motion.

By contrast, *Exodus* flows. Though still defined by Lam's characteristic expressive lines within which volumetric beings emerge and terminate, there is no sense of fixed gravity, no vegetation, and no stability. *Exodus,* with its shades and tints of brown, draws the eye to enter a shallow horizontal space in which interlaced organic forms surge to and fro like waves, as if seeking an exit or an entrance. At the same time, darker areas form hollow cavities of negative space to suggest unknown crevices and depths in which dwell the shadows of living creatures with hooves and other appendages. One might say that *The Jungle* represented a "finding," an arrival, while *Exodus* (as its name implies) was a departure. The rooted forms of *The Jungle,* though surging with spiritual energy and with what André Breton called "convulsive beauty," convey neither the restlessness nor the anxiety of *Exodus.* Lam had reached a new point on his artist's compass, and he seemed ready to veer in a different direction.

And indeed, *The Jungle* and *Exodus* represent two distinct phases of history and Lam's location within it. The paintings mark the boundaries of World War II (1939–1945 in Europe; 1941–1945 in the Americas) as enacted in the life and intercontinental movements of the artist. They also indirectly signal the fact that while Lam found refuge and a new sense of identity in Cuba during the time that war raged in Europe, and that, while being in Cuba and the Caribbean (particularly with visits to Martinique and Haiti) deepened his childhood memories of the rituals of Santería[6] and brought them together with the profound lessons of cubism and surrealism which he absorbed and developed in Europe, neither Cuba nor the Caribbean could claim an art market sufficient enough to sustain him. Thus, during the war years, he traveled to the United States, particularly to New York, for the regular gallery exhibitions that provided him with not only a source of income but also continued contact with New York artists who admired his work and with the exile community of European artists and intellectuals.

In 1946, with the war over, Lam began a circuit of travel that led him to wander between Paris, New York, and Havana. Not until 1952 did he finally settle in Paris. It was during these peregrinations that he painted *Exodus,* which can be considered a symbol of his second exit from Cuba as well as of his internationalization as a painter and a world citizen. *Exodus* incorporates this process of displacement and uncertainty which was to continue for yet another four years.

Cuba

I have dwelt so extensively on Wifredo Lam because he represents, as has been pointed out by Cuban critic Gerardo Mosquera, the first artist to offer an overall vision of the African element in the history of gallery art. From 1941 on, when Lam renewed his contact with Cuba, his works became the vehicle for his own definitive kind of expression, the first vision ever of "modern art from the standpoint of Africa within Latin America." It created a "non-Western space within the Western tradition, decentralizing it, transforming, and de-europeanizing it." It was work at a crossroads, a location that later artists expanded into a multibranched and multileveled roadway.[7]

Consistent with the politics that prompted the artist (who was then studying in Spain) to serve the Republican cause during the Spanish Civil War (1936–1939), Lam also supported the 1959 Cuban Revolution. Not only did he repeatedly visit Cuba after establishing himself in Paris, but in 1980, having suffered a disabling stroke, he returned to Cuba in a wheelchair in order to fulfill his promise to participate in a demonstration against imperialism before the Office of U.S. Interests in Havana.[8] He died in Paris on 11 September 1982, and his ashes were then sent back to Cuba.

By 1983, the Cuban government passed legislation establishing the Wifredo Lam Center, charged with organizing the Havana Biennials that to date have taken place for ten years: in 1984, 1986, 1989, 1991, and 1994. These events, which put Cuba on the international artistic map, have brought together artists, critics, historians, and theoreticians not only from Latin

America but also, starting in 1986, from the entire Third World. Wifredo Lam was thus honored on a level equivalent to that of the Cuban writer and patriot José Martí.

Interestingly enough, the creation of the Center coincided with the emergence of a new generation of Cuban artists in the early 1980s, some of whom actively integrated an interest in Amerindian art and culture with the African spirit and elements of Santería. Known as "Volumen Uno" (Volume One), they marked the emergence of a new avant-garde within Cuban art. Born in the 1950s,[9] they were children of the 1959 Cuban Revolution who felt both the freedom and necessity to celebrate its culture and to critique its failings. According to Luis Camnitzer, the generation of artists that immediately followed Volumen Uno was not markedly distinguishable from it; however the third generation took a stronger critical approach,[10] especially as—for various reasons, including the stiffening of the U.S. blockade and the termination of the Soviet Union—the situation in Cuba deteriorated. The *Caribbean Visions* exhibition includes one artist from each of these three generations: José Bedia, María Magdalena Campos-Pons, and Tomás Esson, all recent arrivals to the United States. Luis Cruz Azaceta and Lía Galletti both emigrated to the United States at earlier dates, and neither received an art education in Cuba.

José Bedia

José Bedia (born 1959) has a profound interest in Amerindian and Afro-Cuban traditions. These interests are not, however, primitivistic appropriations such as those embraced by European modernists. Rather they mark the extrapolation of historical and living histories and rituals that were integrated into the work of artists who lived in their midst. As Bedia has commented, "I'm of the idea that things must be universal, but have as a focus or a starting point the local or regional point of view. It's important to retain the folklore or the national art and then make it universal, but starting from a local point of view."[11]

In carrying out his personal mandate, Bedia—while fully cognizant of international artistic modes—evolved a visual and iconic language uniquely his own. Working on paper or canvas, nailing his unframed pieces directly on the wall, or painting on the walls themselves (sometimes with his hands), Bedia eliminates as much as possible the paraphernalia mediating between his activity and the ultimate viewer. Line and flat forms based on a geometry of shaped spaces (circles, semicircles, rectangles, and squares, as well as numbered comic booklike sequences) that relate to his meaning rather than to purely formal considerations, contain figures of humans, animals, and syntheses between the two; vegetation; landscapes and houses; skyscrapers; and industrial objects such as ships, automobiles, trucks, and airplanes; bodies of water and mountains, etc., as well as spiritual and ritual beings and artifacts. To these he adds found or created three-dimensional objects that are adhered to the surface or stand free in space. Both paint and objects are often extended on the floor, creating an installation in which the corners of rooms—actually and pictorially—play an important role.

Finally, Bedia adds directly within the piece texts in Spanish or in African languages, depending on his intent. Thus it is evident that communication is a principal desire; that the artist has no interest in being esoteric or hermetic; that he wishes the commentaries as well as his visual language to be understood. Abstract cosmograms, connected throughout the Caribbean with religious practices, are an essential element in establishing the presence of ritual activities and, at the same time, providing an awareness of the complex philosophies and intellectual achievements of so-called primitive peoples.

While it is true that animistic and symbolic religious practices are associated with tribal and pre-industrial human groupings universally, it is not true that they can be universally understood, even by each other. Bedia has further rejected the universalist theorem based on European histories that compares and equates all spiritual configurations with the Egyptian-Mesopotamian-Greek models. He insists on the African and Amerindian mode as valid spiritual and human statements about earthly ecology and cosmic powers. To that he adds elements of history: for example, the transference of African belief systems to the Americas during the colonial period, or modern views of the Dakota Sioux, with whom he spent considerable time. Practices and artifacts (past and present) of Latin American Indian peoples are also invoked. Among these is the Mexican belief that certain individuals have animal counterparts called *nahuales* that protect their human counterparts with special knowledge. Harm done to either affects both.

As a practitioner and priest in the Palo Monte religious system, Bedia incorporates his spiritual insights into his work—no longer with the anger and passion of Wifredo Lam as an act of resistance and affirmation of the "negro spirit," but as a philosophical system as valid as any other in the contemporary world. Robert Farris Thompson, in discussing Bedia's work, notes his "affinity of vision" with that of Africa which, unlike that of Picasso, "restores the real metaphors of belief" and gives a place to "the most profound incursion of the influence of *nkondi* kongo in modern art." However, says Cuban art critic and theoretician Gerardo Mosquera, it is more appropriate to consider that Bedia is making "postmodern kongo culture." In other words, Bedia is producing "African cultural action within today's art," rather than "on top of" today's art.[12]

Bedia's painting *S. Silvestre* (St. Sylvester, 1993; p. 111) is the "portrait" of a spirit, given its syncretic name as a Catholic saint—a widespread phenomenon within many conquered cultures where Catholicism and the symbolic carriers of its belief system were enforced on unwilling peoples. To underline this point, Bedia has inscribed the names of this spirit in Spanish as well as in African languages of the Yoruba (Nigeria) and the Bantu (Congo). "Osain" of the former and "Gurunfinba" of the latter appear above the figure, as do other African terms and sacred linear diagrams. Silvestre is an asymmetrical spirit, says the artist. He has only one eye, one arm, one leg, and one testicle. As a spirit of nature and of plants, as the "mystical herbalist," he holds a plant in his hand.

María Magdalena Campos-Pons

One of the salient characteristics of modern and contemporary Latin American art is the continuum between the past and the present. Among the features that Guy Debord attributes to the power structures of First World society (the "society of the spectacle") is an eternal present,[13] unreferenced by history and its lessons. To consider the art of Magdalena Campos (born 1959) is to consider the new dimensions given an old history by this Afro-Cuban artist. Though references to Santería exist in her work, unlike many other Cuban artists this interest originally evolved from artistic rather than religious pursuits. Nevertheless, the memory of her grandmother, who was strongly involved in Santería, caused her, in more recent years as an artist, to wonder about this power.[14] Of greater moment to Campos was the history of women within the African diaspora, the brutality of slavery, and the continuing presence of racism in society.

To use the term "feminist" is to risk confusing Latin American feminism with that of Europe and the United States, where its platforms and programs were developed primarily by white middle-class women, with little or no understanding of the circumstances affecting women of color, women of the Third World.[15] Suffice it to say that Latin American feminism does not set itself against men, considering an alliance of the sexes to be crucial to liberation from colonialism and neocolonialism. It does, however, seek both a position of equality for women and, in

María Magdalena Campos-Pons, *La verdad no mata* (p. 113)

the arts, an expression of women's history and concerns. In Campos' work—like that of the women artists of her generation—sexuality, from the erotic to the reproductive, is of major interest, as is the right to express pleasure and personal emotion as a means of establishing a feminine identity. In fact, claims Luis Camnitzer, Cuban feminism is based on the idea of the oppression of feminine sexuality.[16]

Within the realms of mythic belief, the erotic also plays a role—from the days of Wifredo Lam and his close friend Carlos Enríquez, up to the present. Thus Campos videotaped *Rite of Initiation* (1988) and *Sacred Bath* (1991) to record performances using her nude body in ritual acts that evoked Santería without employing its symbolic system. She transformed the mythic into a personal expression, emphasizing the oneness of the universe through the interpenetration of her body with the landscape, and through the metaphoric interchanges of her body with plants, honey, water, and space itself.

Text and titles form an important aspect of Campos' work: in true postmodern style, they clarify and add to visual content. In the work *La verdad no mata* (The Truth Doesn't Kill You, 1992), three profile silhouettes of a woman's body (the artist's own) dominate the space. The first in black is carved in relief from the wood; the second is gouged out of the board and exists only in the negative; while the third, made of the missing positive and painted in yellow, has escaped her wooden confinement to stand free in space. An ax is embedded in her back, while a heart blooms from her chest. Many readings are possible: the black and the white (or the negative) have mixed and produced the mulatto (in this case, *mulata*) whose ambiguity in society ranges from being ostracized by both black and white, to being glamorized as an exotic lover who combines a lighter skin with the erotic appeal of African sexuality. It also includes a national or social symbol that denies the existence of blackness or Africanness in its constitution or, admitting its existence, ends by confirming as superior those closest to whiteness. All these racist-derived denials of identity cluster in the symbol of the ax-in-the-back, which is negated by the marvelous florescence of the heart. Located between the breasts and the womb (symbols of generation), the heart carries out the motif of the work: the truth does not (cannot) kill. This piece celebrates survival and the human spirit. Not incidentally, it is given a female form.

Tomás Esson

The work of Tomás Esson (born 1963) has been described as "difficult, aggressive, raw and, often, nasty. Looking at his paintings is often like being slapped in the face."[17] Others have referred to its "scatology," "obscenity," and "vulgarity." And there is no question that in his paintings the viewer encounters what Coco Fusco described as "sexual activity, sexual anxiety and excretory functions" and the propensity to render nature as "phallic."[18] So potent are some of the paintings that fall into these categories, so offensive to puritanical thinking, that there is a tendency to overlook their propensity to illustrate truly horrendous mutilations: legs, arms, heads, and torsos are lopped off, leaving exposed raw flesh, layers of fat, and cavities from which liquid substances often spurt. In addition, the extreme exaggeration of human and animal bodies, including their synthesis, is so grotesque that the forms challenge what is truly a remarkable realism in the rendering of monstrosities.

The problem, however, lies deeper. In contemporary society (though not in Cuba), both film and television produce much more shocking images of violence and sexuality that many people flock to see without a sense of impropriety, disgust, or accusations of perversion. What causes outrage over Esson's works is that they are defined as "fine art" rather than as caricature or pornography, and that their baroque realism and excellent facture makes them impossible to dismiss. Therefore, censorship is invoked, and Esson's works have been removed from exhibitions in various countries. In Cuba, censorship was exercised when Esson combined his outrageous fornicating and excreting figures with images of popular heroes such as Ché Guevara and Fidel Castro. By 1992 he had also targeted the United States flag, replacing its stripes with liquid-ejecting turds (a process he previously applied to the Cuban flag), but in compensation, he painted the stars as male and female versions of his favorite "talisman," or good-luck symbol.

Unlike Francisco de Goya, whose more horrific and pungent socially critical images were either executed as prints or kept from public view (his late "black paintings") and not published until after the artist's death, Esson's paintings are his major production. Closer in time, if not wholly in spirit, are the critical and subversive activities of the Situationist, Fluxus, and auto-destructive artists of Europe during the 1950s and 1960s. Utilizing what in one case was called the "aesthetic of revulsion,"[19] these artists searched for a radical leftist critique of capitalist society through an assault on its culture. In the process, they employed many of the critical "crudities" found in Esson's work. The paradox is that Esson, coming from a socialist country whose ideals he apparently has not abandoned, critiques the ossification and distortions (what he and his generation called the "hypocrisies") of the type of society that Fluxus artists considered utopian.

Dos deseos (Two Wishes; p. 114), a 1991 painting by Esson, is milder in tone than many that have appeared since he first began to exhibit in Havana in 1983. *Two Wishes* (whose immense size alone marks it as a major statement) is a self-portrait: the artist is decapitated but fully alive, with two oval clouds issuing from his forehead. One, lined with blue-gray, portrays the decapitated head of Fidel Castro from whose neck cavity spews a river of blood. The other cloud is lined with gold within which floats Esson's "talisman": a sausagelike red object with black horns from which radiates a dazzling light similar to an aura. Kellie Jones, in an Esson catalogue, described it as a "horned turd," a designation the artist does not disdain. Nonetheless, Esson considers the talisman to be a personal charm which he made of clay in Cuba to give his friends. Surrounded by light, he says, it becomes "sacred."[20] It appears regularly in his paintings, sometimes as a penis (with the "turd" as testicles), at other times with the horns crowning the head of his bull-like creatures, and in still other instances in a female incarnation when the talisman sports only one cut horn, a "vagina," and an empty horn socket. The Catholic-derived iconography reads clearly: while Esson's talisman takes him to heaven, Castro has been demonized and will descend to hell. Small wonder that the artist was welcomed in Miami.

Luis Cruz Azaceta

Still within the expressionist and painterly vein, but with a totally different iconography, is the Cuban artist Luis Cruz Azaceta (born 1942), who in 1960 was sent to the United States by his parents to live with relatives in New York. Though he had practiced drawing since childhood, the cost of an art education for the son of a military airplane mechanic in pre-revolutionary Cuba was prohibitively expensive and was never considered by his family. Thus Azaceta's art

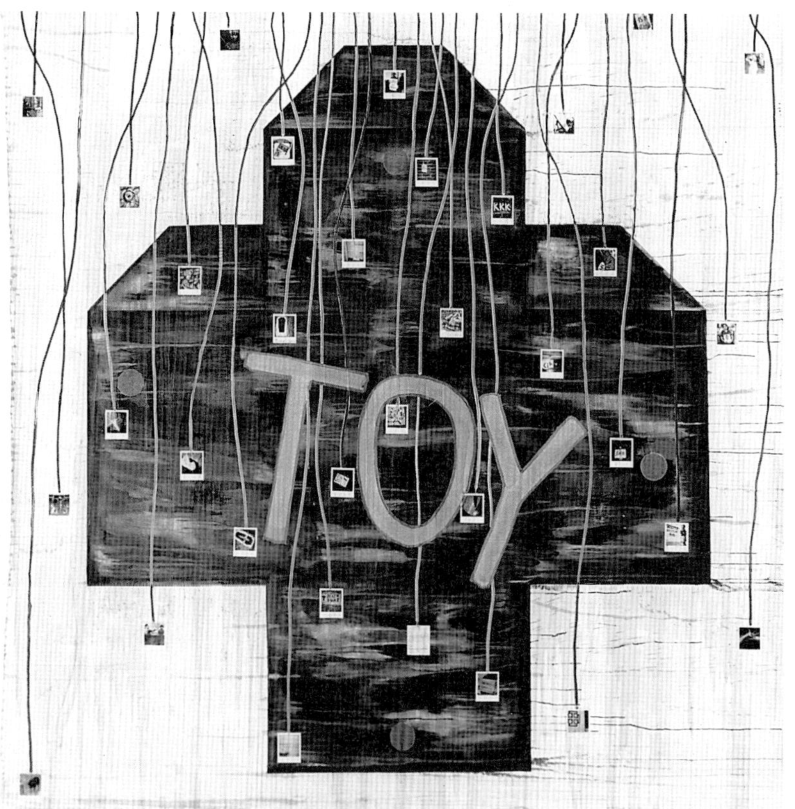

Luis Cruz Azaceta, *Toy* (p. 108)

education did not begin until he had established himself financially in the United States and was encouraged by teachers to study art. His four years at the School of Visual Arts trained him in the then-fashionable tenets of hard-edge geometric abstraction—particularly the repeated stripes practiced by leading artists at the time—an element once again employed in his paintings of the late 1980s. More immediate for Azaceta's future production, however, was his admiration for his teacher Leon Golub, a socially oriented expressionist painter who was originally from the Chicago School, and a visit to European museums in 1969, which totally changed his artistic direction.

For the next two decades, Azaceta worked on large-scale paintings, sculptures, and environments that focused on violence and alienation in New York City. Tormented by his still-painful estrangement from Cuba and an excruciating sensibility that caused him to find life in New York conflictive and psychologically destructive, Azaceta's work was full of personal anguish that inadvertently served as social criticism. With his own image at the center of his art, his work could be characterized as autobiography that had become visual sociology.

Azaceta considered New York violence among the worst anywhere; its climate of fear made him more aware of his vulnerability and mortality when walking on the streets or descending into the subways. Nevertheless, though based on daily experiences, he avoided the anecdotal to make the sense of violence seem as universal as possible in a world of growing despair and fragmentation. Working with frightening and metamorphic creatures, hybrids of humans with animals or machines, his desire was to generate compassion in the viewer.[21] "My work isn't political, per se. My concern is with humanity. I want to confront the viewer with life and what we are doing with each other. I paint to kill *la muerte* [death] and also to kill Cruelty, Injustice, Violence, and Hypocrisy."[22] Among the themes that surfaced during those years were murder, fires, the dog-eat-dog motif, exile, dictatorships in Latin America, abuse of children, suicides, racism, homelessness, and an entire series on the AIDS epidemic. As in his self-portraits, focus is placed on the "victim" rather than the perpetrator. In this sense, Azaceta's choice of subject stands at a polar opposite to that of Tomás Esson. One is in the defensive mode, the other in the offensive.

Without relinquishing his themes, Azaceta moved to a more somber palette, utilizing geometric abstract forms in a more simplified composition. If his early work was dense with figures and objects in heavily textured and brilliant colors, the later paintings use more grays, blacks, blues, whites, and browns, with reds and oranges as contrasts. On occasion, figures themselves have been banished, thus permitting content to be conveyed by form alone. Symbols continue to proliferate, while numbers, texts, and found objects adhered to the painted surface add new dimensions. One immense work of his "Broken Realities" series incorporated the entire box spring of a bed as a bitter reminder of homelessness.

In *Toy* of 1994, Azaceta places photographs on an enormous square canvas, ten by ten feet, upon which is rendered, on a ground of dripped pale orange and blue paint, a cruciform of two brown boxes that alternately suggest houses, jails, and coffins. Suspended vertically from the top are long painted cords or strings to each of which is attached a Polaroid photograph—some taken by the artist, others collaged on his Polaroid. Across the image is the single word "toy" written in green, while four red dots emphasize the crucifix form.

Not only do the cords form a counterpoint to the solid boxes, but they also create an almost musical diversion with their loose, free-flowing strands. Given the one-word text and the cords, the boxes also suggest a child's set of building blocks, until the written words on the photographs are taken into consideration: KGB, KKK, Racism, Mafia, CIA, and "other organized crime groups," as the artist explains. Reference is also made to victims, such as Native Americans, African Americans, Latin Americans, those eliminated by dictators, Jews killed during the Holocaust, etc. In this context, the word "toy" becomes ironic, even frightening. The cruciform has become a crucifixion.

Lía Galletti

While sharing many of the same problems as immigrants from elsewhere in the hemisphere, Cuban Americans have a particularly complex relationship with their adopted country owing to the intensity of U.S. involvement in Cuban affairs. Cubans came to the United States in two great waves: the approximately 215,000 who left the island between 1959 and 1962 (most of whom arrived in Miami) included ultraright landowners, business people, and members of the middle class; and the *marielitos* of 1980, who took their name from the boatlift that originated in Mariel, Cuba, with many trickling in between these dates. As of this writing, there are approximately a million Cubans dispersed among Florida, New York, New Jersey, Illinois, and California.[23] Both Azaceta and Lía Galletti (who was born in 1943 and left Cuba in 1960) belong to the first group, though their class position and their destination (New York) sets them apart from the above description.

As a woman, married very young and with children, Galletti's life took a far different course than that of Azaceta. Art training and entry into the art market—especially in the pre-feminist years of the 1960s when New York's avant-garde was dominated by white male artists—were not even considered or perhaps even possible. Azaceta himself had a difficult time until the Latin American "boom" of the 1980s opened the doors to many Latin Americans living in New York. By that time Galletti was in Miami, but without artistic training either in Cuba or the United States, her chances for recognition were very slim, if not inexistent. Nevertheless, her location in Florida, after the arrival of the marielitos, indirectly influenced some of her artistic choices. Among the artists who arrived in 1980 were a number (some of Afro-Cuban descent) trained at the San Alejandro Academy, who brought with them the vanguard ideas and interest in Santería that inspired the Volumen Uno generation. One such artist was Juan Boza, who had practiced Santería in Cuba and, in the United States, decided to erect altars with Santería references. Others, such as Carlos Alfonzo, were clearly influenced by Wifredo Lam, an interest that passed to the second generation of the early migrants to Miami. Furthermore, Afro-Cuban artists in New York had the opportunity of personally seeing *The Jungle* by Lam at the Museum of Modern Art.

Galletti married for the third time in the 1990s and moved to Washington, D.C., where her husband represents her through the "Human Corporation," named after a series of 1993 works under the same title, of which *Kiss in the Sky* (p. 116) and *Smell the Roses* (p. 117) are a part. Both paintings are loosely brushed and dependent on almost pure saturations of the three primary colors to which white, black, and brown have been added.

In 1993, when Esson and others of his generation from Cuba were among the most recent arrivals in Miami, Galletti exhibited in Kingston, Jamaica, a series titled "Oricha" (or Orisha, the name given Santería deities), and in 1994 she presented another such series in Lansdowne, Canada. With dim memories of Cuba, Galletti had revived her recollections of Santería, perhaps with a desire to reclaim some of her Cuban identity in her art. The attempt at a spiritual presence in *Kiss in the Sky* and *Smell the Roses* seems more Catholic than Afro-Cuban, perhaps because Santería was disdained by the middle and upper classes in Cuba before the revolution when her beliefs were being formed. Only artists whose formative years were spent in the Caribbean, or African Americans from the United States who adhered to Santería as an expression of their African heritage, could convincingly convey such beliefs if they chose to do so and/or were practitioners of Cuban or Puerto Rican Santería, the related Voudoun of Haiti, or the Gagá of the Dominican Republic.

Puerto Rico

Puerto Rico's artistic history, tied to its political history, is very different from that of Cuba. Though he did not directly participate in the Cuban avant-garde of the 1920s, Wifredo Lam is considered one among a number of artists who constituted the movement, not far behind the major countries of Latin America.[24] While Cuba and Puerto Rico both won their independence from Spain in 1898, through the intervention of the United States, Puerto Rico never achieved national sovereignty. It remains to this day a colony of the United States under the euphemism of being a Commonwealth. Puerto Ricans have partial U.S. citizenship rights: their highest elected official is a governor; they must serve in the U.S. armed forces; they have no representation in the Congress, etc. They can, however, move freely between Puerto Rico and the United States, and many Puerto Ricans are bilingual. A great many artists have studied in U.S. art schools, which has had immense consequences artistically and culturally. Identity and national consciousness are therefore an important part of Puerto Rican psychology.

With the exception of two notable painters, Francisco Oller (1813–1917) and Ramón Frade (1875–1954), Puerto Rican artists and intellectuals of the nineteenth and early twentieth century had to grapple with the effects of colonialism, extreme poverty, strict rules of censorship, and the lack of training centers and museums that would develop and exhibit their work. Not until 1950 were conditions favorable for such an undertaking.[25] At that time the Centro de Arte Puertorriqueño (CAP) was established, and its presence definitively changed the direction of Puerto Rican art, both aesthetically and thematically.[26] Among the important achievements of this era was the development of exceptionally fine printmaking, with linoleum prints, woodcuts and serigraphs being produced under the leadership of Lorenzo Homar. This practice was continued by his two disciples Antonio Martorell and Myrna Báez.

Myrna Báez

In addition to creating very fine serigraphs, Myrna Báez (born 1931) is known for the subtlety, delicacy, and dreamlike quality she imparts to her paintings by applying glazes of transparent color. Her personal iconography has been inspired by the human figure—most particularly female nudes—who appear in "estranged solitary interiors and environments. The psychological tensions that envelop them are augmented through the dissection of space into different planes of perception."[27] Báez's world is one of women into which men occasionally wander.

Connected but not confined to this feminine world are Báez's domestic interiors and their sources of light. Her primary instrument—the mirror—serves many functions, as does the window, which admits light and imagery but also doubles as a surface for reflection (in both senses of the word). Windows (such as the plate glass showcases of stores) also appear as foils in the outdoor urban environment. The third source of light is doorways, or curtained areas against which figures can be silhouetted or within which they can be framed; and the fourth is lamps. Located among these many transparencies and luminosities are female figures, standing, seated, or reclining on couches and beds. The combination of mirrors/windows/doorways, light and shadow, and sedentary women immediately suggests the work of Diego Velázquez and, to some extent, Goya. And indeed, in the 1950s, when Báez was in Madrid, surrounded by its great museums, she decided to give up her pursuit of medicine to become an artist. Not only did she study at the Royal Academy of San Fernando, as well as with the contemporary Spanish painter Juan Genovés, but after 1963 she was regularly invited to exhibit her work in Spain. In the 1960s she also studied lithography in New York, where she again enjoyed the city's many fine museums. It is not uncommon, therefore, to find numerous compositional references to Old Master paintings, particularly of the seventeenth to the nineteenth centuries, when the exploration of chiaroscuro reached a peak.

Báez's second principal theme is landscape—not only in its sweeping panoramas of plains, mountains, and ocean, but also in the distinctive details of tropical plants. "The land," says Jean Franco, "is the third member of the trinity [the indigenous and the African peoples are the other two] to which artists turned in their search for roots."[28] Though landscapes were primary themes in the early development of Latin American nationalisms that were in a process of self-discovery and valuation, they play a particularly striking role in island nations such as those of the Caribbean. Tropical foliage, the sea, clouds, mists, the effects of brilliant light, the color of shadows, the shapes of mountains, beaches, fish and fishermen, and sea birds all play a part in the daily life of Caribbean peoples. In Puerto Rico, the plantain is a staple food, much like corn in Mexico or bread in the United States. Consequently, the palmlike banana tree and the palm tree in its many varieties (although picturesquely used for tourist posters) have actually provided food, shelter, and clothing for many tropical peoples, and have inspired countless painters. The huge Caribbean ceiba (silk-cotton) tree, so named by the Taíno, that appears in Puerto Rican art serves as the site for Santería rituals, replacing the baobab of Africa. Some of Báez's most spectacular works depict bamboo clusters, maguey cacti with their flowering stalks erect, pine trees, mangroves, and the flame-colored *crotón.* One critic, who referred to them as "totemic plants," considered such paintings more original than generalized landscapes.[29] For Báez, mountainous scenes are infused with the female principle to such a degree that the mountain is breast-shaped.

Báez's two paintings, *Retrato de un sueño* (Portrait of a Dream, 1988–1990; p. 178), and *Entre cortinas* (Between Curtains, 1993; p. 179), encompass aspects of the female nude and its transparencies, as well as the landscape for which the seated nude provides both a foil and a frame. In *Portrait,* Báez maintains her ambiguities: the viewer is uncertain whether two women, one reclining, one sitting, are the same woman dreaming of herself or are representations of waking and sleeping persons. The net effect of transparencies and silhouettes is to generalize the figures: thus the seated figure in *Curtains* can be male or female. The theme is not the figure but the richly forested parkland and clouds whose greens and blues form counterpoints with the range of warm colors in the foreground and are contained within the verticals of the curtains, an old Dutch Baroque device for establishing spatial differentiation in depictions of interiors.

Arnaldo Roche Rabell

After studying architecture and design in Puerto Rico, Arnaldo Roche Rabell (born 1955) determined to be a painter and printmaker and happily chose for his training ground the rather idiosyncratic School of the Art Institute of Chicago. Since the late 1960s Chicago has been known for the Hairy Who, a group of artists who built a style based on comic books and expressionism that has been called "Absurd Humanism."[30] The School of the Art Institute subscribed to this "Chicago Imagist" aesthetic, which was in place when Roche arrived there in 1979. The artist continued to keep a part-time home in Chicago until he decided in 1993 to live exclusively in Puerto Rico. The collision, if it can be called that, of the extremely intense, sensitive Puerto Rican who is deeply committed to Catholicism, with the existential and ironic humor of Chicago Imagism, made a volatile mix that resulted in Roche's almost immediate recognition as a new talent.

A somewhat schizophrenic feeling about identity was a prime factor in Roche's work from the beginning. Not greatly interested in reading, his art serves as a primary release for his emotions and ideas that derive from strong dreams and personal experience. Judging from his paintings and statements, I believe that Roche is basically a realist in intent: his explosive expressionism is not a "style" but a way of being, of existing, in a manner not unlike the intense spiritual *realism* of Vincent van Gogh, who has been incorrectly linked with the esoteric and primitivized mysticism of Gauguin and the Symbolists.

An examination of Roche's working methods and themes reveals that one of his earliest techniques was absolutely physical, that of covering a canvas with black paint and rolling on it. Later he covered models with canvas or paper and rubbed pigment directly upon the surface contours of the body so that the figure's three-dimensional qualities were rendered in a spread-eagled way on a two-dimensional surface. The markings and objects that fill the space around his figures are not distinguished from the individuals in any spatial way; they generally coexist on the same plane, in the same reality. Physicality is likewise brought to the fore when he works the surface after the rubbing (or *frottage*) is complete. Roche prepares his canvases with thick layers of paint in the order of yellow, orange, red, and finally black. Then he "carves," gouges, and scratches that surface until the image is revealed at different layers of color. He uses his hands, along with a knife, spoon, hammer, and only occasionally, a brush. Thus the physical content remains constant in both technique and subject. As the artist explains:

> The image is not something from my imagination. It is from something real that was there. Of course I depart from the rubbing, but finally everything is about being physical and being real. . . . My intention is to touch people in an emotional and in a physical way. I put them under canvas or paper, and I trace them with my hands, just as I find them.[31]

The other aspect of Roche's "realism" is his use of the slide projector to relay a photographic image to the canvas. This technique, widely used by Chicago street muralists in the 1970s and 1980s, derived from the example of Mexican muralist David Alfaro Siqueiros. Whether Roche adopted this method from the muralists or from Pop artists is of little importance. The point is that photographs give an impression of reality beyond any other source of image making. Roche's manual techniques and his absolute frontal close-ups of his own facial features speak to realism that was, from the first, absolutely suffused with a strong Christian faith and overlaid with Puerto Rican mythology and social tensions. This is emphasized by his methods: crowning himself or covering his face with tropical foliage, including sugar cane leaves; evoking the African American presence in various self-portraits; and compulsively filling every inch of space with objects or markings defined by ridges and layers of textured paint, thus creating, according to one astute observer, a "vehement symbiosis of facture and representation," as well as a ritual and ceremonial approach that converts art into an "exercise in exorcism."[32]

In Roche's painting *Nadie es profeta en su propia tierra* (No One is a Prophet in his Own Land, 1993) the self-portrait appears, or rather disappears, behind a baroque veil of foliage and birds. Curly and wiry thorns cover the entire face, giving it the appearance of a cadaver or skull. The skin of the face behind is dark, while the thorns are white, suggesting death and partial burial, that is until the viewer notices the open blue eyes and the tiny portrait head (of the artist?) on the forehead, which is being pecked by a yellow bird. All the dark areas of the eyebrows, nose, and mouth (a double metaphor of clustered birds flowering outward) are composed of black and yellow dovelike birds. Roche's self-portraits, as with many of his figure paintings, are almost invariably reversed, like the negative of a photograph. Doubtless this arises from the technique of working from dark to light that is required by the rubbing technique, but it is also an aesthetic choice. Perhaps on a socio-psychological level it relates to the *mestizaje* between Europeans and Africans that comprises the Puerto Rican population, one of the most interracially mixed of the three islands. It is one more level on which the artist confronts his identity.

Diógenes Ballester

Like Roche Rabell, Diógenes Ballester (born 1956) has shuttled back and forth between Puerto Rico and the United States, obtaining art degrees in both countries. Trained in the traditions of realism and surrealism, and interested in abstract expressionism and conceptual art, Ballester slowly transformed his style to organic abstraction in which representational, figurative, and landscape elements play a role in dynamic and powerful works on a monumental scale. That an active social consciousness is at work is made evident by the artist himself:

> I use symbolic imagery and organic abstractions to depict the themes of struggle, vulnerability, and volition. Intense colors, layers of paint, thick impasto, scratched and blended surfaces create depth, movement, and dramatic contrasts which translate the experience of living within the urban landscape of human existence and interchange.[33]

Caught between two cultures, one of which treats him as the "other," Ballester transforms these struggles into paintings such as *The Anxiety of Life in the Midst of Conflict; Struggle Against Racism; Confrontation; The Struggle Against Alienation; Vulnerability: Tied and Liberated Being; Portrait of Existence; Powerless;* and finally, *Looking for Structure; Compressed Energy;* and *Spiritual Celebration.* In the titles alone emerges a dialectical ebb and flow among doubt, insecurity, alienation, and the exaltation of the spirit. "I live and work in intertwined worlds," says the artist. "I live and work under the never-ending influences of history, mythology and oral traditions; I live and work in a continuous culmination of today's diversity."

Both Roche Rabell and Ballester work on a large scale, with one crucial difference: Roche completes a complex idea within the space he designates, whereas Ballester, like a frustrated muralist, conceives his work in terms of monumental images that push at the borders of his support. Many of his paintings are fragments of much larger ideas that seem to await completion. His working technique is additive: paintings grow from one sheet of paper or linen to two, four, eight, or sixteen, each covering an entire wall in his cramped studio. In the process of growth, he regularly changes and overpaints what is no longer compatible.

Ballester's painting medium is as physical and visceral as that of Roche. He employs the ancient and difficult technique of encaustic, a method of hot wax painting that derives from ancient Greece but was replaced by tempera and oil paint during the medieval and Renaissance periods. "Paint cooks in Diógenes' house morning, noon and night," describes fellow artist Antonio Martorell, "in pots brimming with cadmium yellow, Sienna red, cobalt blue, Prussian and ultramarine blue, Spanish whites and Ivory, blacks, all of them richly mixed pigments spiced with melted virgin wax and applied, still scalding, to the hungry linen."[34] Adds the artist, "When I

Diógenes Ballester, *Magic of the Patchouli II* (p. 181)

stand over my encaustic mix heating in the melting pot, I can see and smell the blending of the crystal damar varnish with the stand oils. I watch and breathe in the fragrant bees' wax as it coheres with the dry pigment or oil colors. When I apply the mix on the linen surface I am drawn in by its matted mystic magnificence."

Sensuality is the final aspect to consider in the work of Ballester. It is implicit in his choice of painting techniques and explicit in the work itself. Luminous shadows, convoluted fleshy forms that turn in on themselves like body parts, rotundities, sweeping gestural shapes and stroked surfaces, cavities and bony structures, breastlike forms, warm earth colors and patches like seas and skies, and areas bathed in light and shadow are all characteristic aspects of his style. Both *Reminder of the Spirit* (1987–1993; p. 180) and *Magic of the Patchouli II* (1993) are resonant with these qualities. If *Spirit* is organic and visceral, then *Patchouli* anoints it with sensual fragrance.

María de Mater O'Neill

Like Myrna Báez, the two broad thematic concerns that intersect in the work of María de Mater O'Neill (born 1960) are portraiture and landscape. Contained within these currents are a plethora of subthemes that situate the particular painting within the artist's time and space. The point of intersection is at the node of autobiography, even though O'Neill's subjective self-portraits and landscapes never describe an objective reality. Rather, like the Italian Futurist painters of earlier in this century, O'Neill centers the world within her own persona and permits it to explode outward. She proceeds first and foremost with the self-portrait, which has been her ongoing preoccupation for almost a decade.

In the 1970s the woman artist in Latin America, as elsewhere, began to emerge from her chrysalis, not in the name of femininity, but of feminism, now remodeled to provide a metaphoric mirror for the self-portrait of the *indigena,* the *mestiza,* the black and mulatta, the creole woman. The Latin American woman strives to create an identity that is not only personal but also national, one that is not concerned with duplicating European standards of "beauty" but with creating new standards based on her own realities. Such an identity has long been part of a social problem that requires a political posture.

Through the self-portrait, O'Neill explores her personal and social identity in a seemingly frenzied expressionist style that is rooted to her decade of study in New York but that resolves itself with the colors and problematics of Puerto Rico. (She permanently returned to the island in 1988.) In all her recent paintings the point of contact with Puerto Rico is the island's geography itself. This she made amply clear with the 1993 series of paintings called "Mapa," which renders the map of her island as a small irregular rectangle anchored between the Atlantic Ocean and the Caribbean Sea. Land, water, and sky seen from an aerial perspective constitute this vision, which metamorphosizes in color and shape from painting to painting.

Aside from this stratospheric experiment, O'Neill's paintings are land-based, but they are hardly more visually stable since they emanate from within the artist. In a complex mix of narrative and symbolism, space is experienced in dreams or states of mind. Color and scale are arbitrary.

María de Mater O'Neill, *Autorretrato VIII* (p. 183)

Figures and objects are generally flat and described by lines that operate within color changes that are as variable as those of Kandinsky or Matisse. In other words, the narratives of line and color do not always coincide, since line expresses the shape of objects and color the shape of emotions. Textures do not correspond to real surfaces, but to the violence or suavity of painted surfaces, the admixture of mediums, and the variables of ground. Mixing oils, acrylics, and gouache with oil and encaustic crayons on cotton and linen canvas leads to a great variety of applied and base textures. In addition, texture relies on the loose and expressive method of application, which on occasion verges on the indecipherable. Symbols are frequently buried in the fragmented paint surface.

In *Autorretrato VIII* (Self-Portrait No. 8, or Nude in Front of the Mirror, 1988), modeled on a similar self-portrait by Myrna Báez—whom O'Neill served as a printmaking assistant and whom she considers her mentor and inspiration—the atmosphere and environment are totally at odds with Báez's calm and orderly interiors shown in full perspective. Not only is this world flat and frenzied, but it is also filled with symbols: moons, knives, faces, animals, a palm tree, people devouring each other, and a fatal profile whose eye-stare can be located by means of dashes. Some of these might be associated with Santería, but if so, they are highly personalized in a postmodern world, as is O'Neill's command of computers.

Nelson Santiago and **Juan Carlos Toca**

Although twenty years apart in age, Puerto Rican artists Nelson Santiago (born 1946) and Juan Carlos Toca (born 1966) are both fairly new to the art world. While Santiago was a late arrival, the younger Toca recently entered the realm of sculpture via his activity in architecture.

If the diasporic condition of Puerto Ricans has fostered feelings of alienation and identity, for Santiago these problems were further aggravated by being an "army brat" in a military family that was constantly on the move within the United States and Puerto Rico (with even a stint in Japan). His move to Miami in 1988 was punctuated by his discovery of the recently arrived Cuban artists Carlos Alfonzo and later José Bedia. The impact of the now-deceased Alfonzo and of Arnaldo Roche Rabell, both of whose works he saw in Washington, D.C.,[35] were fundamental to his own painting and can be detected in *Crouched Man* (p. 187) and *Fantasy of Symbols* (p. 186), both of 1993.

Earlier fascinated by the fragmented brushstrokes of the Impressionists, by the pointillism of the Post-Impressionists, and the intensity of Van Gogh, Santiago responded strongly to the cultural symbols of Alfonzo's semiabstractions because he recognized in them the visual language of Santería[36] in whose rituals he had been initiated in Puerto Rico. The work of Bedia went more deeply into the belief systems, but on an intellectual and philosophical basis and in a highly reduced style; Santiago was more impressed with the emotional quality and heavily textured surfaces of Roche. *Crouched Man* responds to the same anxieties and personal pressures found in works by Roche, the same complex surfaces and busy spaces, the framing technique that compresses the human body into anguished postures, and the use of saw-toothed forms, of eyes, knives, spirals, and other symbols. Color and light derive from Alfonzo. Santiago has evolved a personal language that reflects a certain decorativism at the expense of expression. The sincerity of the work, however, augers well for the future.

Juan Carlos Toca is more of a novice, thrust almost accidentally into sculpture through commissions from patrons who employed him as a draftsman and designer in commercial architectural enterprises. Based in Miami since childhood, he apparently harbors an obsessive need to prove he has absorbed the Puritan work ethic, presumably in an effort to counteract the stereotypes of Latin Americans and Latinos[37] in a city saturated (and controlled) by Cuban exiles and emigres, a situation that is still periodically protested as an expression of Anglo American xenophobia.

Working with sheets of stainless steel, copper, and other materials that he forms by hand, Toca's pieces are organic abstractions of creatures and plants. *Birds of Paradise* (1993; p. 189) is a copper fountain whose hollowed and segmented spiraling contours are based on the swan and are reminiscent of the mobius strip sculptures of Max Bill.

The Dominican Republic

Still another history confronts us in the case of the Dominican Republic.[38] Located on Hispaniola, the first island discovered by Christopher Columbus, it served as the initial viceregal seat. On its soil was carried out the first genocidal destruction of the Taíno/Arawak Indians, followed by those of Cuba and Puerto Rico. The history of the Dominican Republic is intimately tied to that of Haiti, which occupies one-third of the island and was established when the French took over the former Hispaniola, where they governed until the Haitian slaves ousted them in 1803 and set up the first black republic and the second independent nation in the Americas. The Dominican area was returned to Spanish control in 1814, and once again freed in 1821. Between 1822 and 1844 the area was invaded and occupied by the troops of the Haitian president, who settled the Haitians on Dominican land, where many remain to this day. When the Dominicans finally freed themselves in 1844, a residual fear of Haiti remained, which was (and is) ruthlessly exploited by Dominican politicians in the form of a "racist" policy that denies Dominicans are of African as well as European descent.

The regime of Rafael Leonides Trujillo Molina subjugated the Dominican people and enriched Trujillo and his cronies for thirty years (1930–1960). Desiring to appear as an art patron, Trujillo subsidized the National School of Fine Arts and the National Biennials (both begun in 1942). He also permitted into Santo Domingo Jewish refugees and those who were fleeing the Spanish Civil War, some of whom became influential art professors at the National School. So abusive was Trujillo's administration, however, that the United States covertly approved his assassination in 1961. The next year the first free elections were won by Juan Bosch, who ran against a U.S.-supported candidate. Bosch was in office only long enough to create (in 1963) the most democratic constitution in Dominican history, yet it was never passed into law.[39] There ensued, nevertheless, a period of euphoria that was shared by the country's artists.

During the last decade of the Trujillo regime, growing unrest and popular nonconformity were met by strict controls on the freedom of expression, despite state support of the arts. Artists were thus forced to present ideas in subtly disguised forms. A period of abstraction and symbolism followed this "somber decade."[40] The generation of the 1950s had already developed a marked nationalism and a shrewd use of social commentary, employing an expressionist style to portray folkloric rites, eroticism, the magical, the geography of the land, images of mulattoes, the autochthonous (Taíno) origins of the culture, and so on. An international language had already been set forth, one that blended the African elements of the nation with European idioms or, as has been said, "Picasso seen through Lam or Lam through Picasso."[41]

By the 1960s, the quest for "Dominicanness" had become compulsive, a necessary response to what was seen as a strong cultural penetration from outside the country, and a growing technocratic elite within. By 1968, amid reductions in arts funding and the rise of commercial patronage, which many of the artists rejected, some art instruction was delegated to Santo Domingo University. In defiance, a group of artists triumphantly proclaimed themselves as being self-taught. On this utopian wave, artists' groups were established to resist government/commercial control and to seek international ties,[42] which caused many young artists to go abroad. In fact, each of the four Dominican artists discussed here—José Perdomo, José García Cordero, Genaro Phillips, and Inés Tolentino—spent lengthy periods of time studying and exhibiting in the metropolitan cities of Europe and the United States. Born during the 1940s and 1950s, they pertain to the generations of the 1960s to the 1980s, with Tolentino being the last to begin her professional career in 1979. As such, they were part of the tumultuous and passionate 1960s and the activist 1970s until the heavy hand of *trujillista* president Joaquín Balaguer, installed in 1966 by the United States after the 1965–1966 invasion and occupation, once more instituted an oligarchic government and cut off whatever support had been given the arts and culture by the previous dictatorship. (Balaguer was re-elected in 1994.)

José Perdomo

Having studied graphics and participated in exhibitions in New York during the 1970s and 1980s, following his years at the National School of Fine Arts (1961–1965), José Perdomo (born 1943) combines, in the best Latin American tradition, the experimental languages of the metropolis with an immersion in Dominican history and culture. Since his first exhibition in 1966, Perdomo has preferred abstract modes of various types, and he decided in 1984 to work in series. Among them are "Tropics" (1988), "Search for Origins" and "Homage to the Children of the Sun and the Myths" (1990), "Tropics and Myths of the Caribbean" and "Memorable Signs" (1991), and his latest series, "El mundo mágico de JOP" (The Magic World of JOP, ongoing since 1992; p. 122).[43]

It is obvious from these titles that Perdomo's interests lie generally in the tropical Caribbean, and particularly in the pictographs and magico-religious symbols of the pre-Hispanic Indians that were discovered in island caves. Perdomo does not pretend to an accurate archaeology or a literal transposition of the cave drawings: rather he uses them as a springboard for his personal fantasies and pictorial experimentation. In fact, in the early 1980s, the artist was involved with sequential, semiabstract geometric signs which totally covered his canvas with linear fish or human figures that were slightly reminiscent of M.C. Escher's visual games. His most recent works do not relinquish this calligraphic approach, now contained within a painterly universe of cubic and organic shapes, and densely covered with streaks, meandering lines, signs, abstracted human forms, dots and masses of color, and patterns of light and shadow articulated through color. The influence of abstract expressionism is evident, but with a much higher keyed and more saturated color range dominated by the primaries. There is also a deliberate invocation of recognizable objects and symbols. That this is a personal iconography is confirmed by the series title. The "magical world" is erected on Taíno, African, and European mythologies, but surely JOP refers to the artist himself; this is *his* magical world.

José García Cordero

Probably one of the most versatile and multidimensional artists of the younger generation, José García Cordero (born 1951) has resided in Paris since 1977 and has made extended visits to the Dominican Republic. Architect, philosopher, critic, and painter, he was an active participant in the "groups" movement of the late 1960s and 1970s. The radicalization of Dominican artists and intellectuals that occurred during the 1960s paralleled similar enterprises throughout Latin America (particularly in the wake of fallen dictators and the Cuban Revolution) and the world—from Tokyo to San Francisco, Chicago, and Paris. By 1962, after the demise of Trujillo, numerous writers, poets, musicians, painters, and sculptors joined the "Art and Liberation" movement, followed by the artists' "Cultural Front" group of 1965, the group "Project" of 1968, the "Atlantes" of 1972, and "Group 6" of 1974, of which García Cordero was a member.[44]

Many phrases can be applied to García Cordero's paintings: a level of surrealism in abstract and figurative modes of which he was, at one time, one of the few practitioners in Santo Domingo; an oneiric quality; and a sense of fantasy and humor that pervades much of his work and his writing. The humor is ironic, however, while the fantasy is a commentary on the world of reality. He has not surrendered his critical posture, and the strange, invented creatures that populate his world are satirical to the same degree as are those of Pieter Brueghel. Indeed, he shares with the Flemish artist a similar emphasis on metamorphosis, on morality, and on making the impossible believable, or at least understandable, though miraculous events happen daily, and twice on Sunday.

As a regular leitmotiv, dogs appear constantly in drawings and paintings and possibly serve as a surrogate for the artist himself. Meek, erotic, soulful, with large eyes and pointed noses, their skulls inhabit the base of a carnivorous leafless tree. They rest on top of a small elegant table in the artist's studio, and one climbs to the top of an enormous pillar (like those occupied by the early Christian ascetics, or Stylites) in order to embrace a female Hellenistic nude. Still another accompanies the artist to a city traffic island from which he views a large Picasso painting on the "mainland" building. In still another painting, the heads of other dogs fill a boat in which refugees escape the Caribbean islands. Sailing on a sea of blood, their tails—or the tails of those who have capsized—emerge from the water like sea snakes. A *double-entendre* always waits below the surface.

García Cordero's wit and sophistication are exemplified in the pages of a publication named *El frío cálido* (The Hot Chill), which doubled as a catalogue for the exhibition *García Cordero y sus amigos x-tramodernos,* held at the Santo Domingo Museum of Modern Art in 1993. For that presentation, almost all the essays were written by the artist and illustrated with his work and that of his "x-tramodern friends" (a synonym for postmodern?), revealing a group of unorthodox artists, photographers, and writers with a shared sense of irony and humor.

Genaro Phillips

It has been said that Dominican art combines indigenous polyforms, African expression and color, Spanish baroquism and realism, and French impressionist luminosity, and it emphasizes color and composition over drawing.[45] As a general statement, this is a great simplification, but like all valid simplifications, it contains important elements. The fusion of Indian, African, and European peoples and cultural sources began with escaped slaves collaborating with the threatened Indians.

In the art of the Dominican Republic, images of black and mulatto people appear in social realist and semiabstract versions as early as the 1930s, and they continue to the present. By the

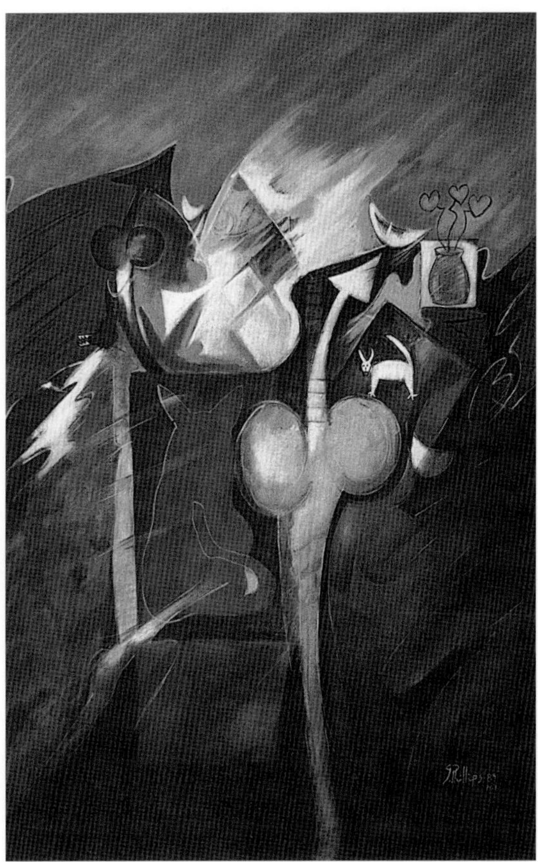

Genaro Phillips, *Tropic II* (p.18)

1940s, the strong influence of Wifredo Lam is evident, as it continues to attract young artists through its evocation of the African, the use of tropical landscapes and plants (particularly the coco palms and sugar cane that are ubiquitous in the region), and the geometric elements of cubism.

Genaro Phillips (born 1955), of Afro-Dominican descent, has drawn on all these sources and added to them his personal voice. Of a large and very poor family that depended on the work of his mother, he managed to obtain an art education that eventually permitted him to teach classes as well as to paint. Gradually moving from an academic style to a semiabstract one, Phillips proceeded on the plan of a number of young artists who, rather than abandon either figuration or abstraction, combined the two in a way that is recognized by many Dominican critics and art historians as the quintessential style of the island, a resolution of international modernist pressures and the desire to communicate to more than an elite audience.

Having lived in the countryside, Phillips observed the backbreaking labor and the miserable situation of the seasonal Haitian workers who cut the cane and still employ oxen to carry it to the sugar mill. This evoked the historical memory of African slaves during the colonial period and the popular saying that defined sugar cane as "something that has a very sweet flavor and a very bitter history." Such images were instrumental to his 1985 series of twenty-seven paintings entitled "Cuando la noche cae sobre los ingenios y los bueyes desaparecen" (When Night Falls over the Sugar Mills and the Oxen Disappear). The oxen became a metaphor for the exhausting labor of slaves who toiled under the threat of the whip. Night is the only time the oxen—and the slaves—can rest. These works reiterated, in a more poetic, even legendary form, his earlier abstracted works of sugar cane stalks and the wheels of the sugar mill.

In earlier paintings Genaro Phillips combined African-Taíno magical elements and artifacts, as well as a poetic social surrealism, with calligraphic marks, linear geometry, and saturated tropical color, yet his more recent works have evolved in a new direction. The influence of Wifredo Lam is pronounced; many of Lam's erotic symbols (breasts and testicles), elongated distortions, horns, profuse foliage, and African sculptural references reappear, but with a much more highly keyed palette than that of the Cuban master. The application is personal as well as tropical. In fact, *Tropic II* (1989) includes what appears to be a horned chair with the silhouette of an animal humorously inscribed on the chair back, while a plant equipped with testicles metamorphosizes into an arrow that points at the moon and terminates with a very domestic plant set in a pot. Greens, blues, red-purples, whites, and black dominate the foreground (a cool interior forest with a chair?) while flaming and textured reds, yellows, and oranges sweep across the upper space, radiations of a fierce sun. With this work, and the imposing diptych *My Sub-Conscious* (1989; p. 124), in which powerful organic forms, hearts, and arrows define but are not dominated by the calligraphic lines and markings, seem to suggest a new mature direction.

Inés Tolentino

It seems perfectly plausible that Inés Tolentino (born 1962), the daughter of a Dominican father and a French-born mother who is a prominent art critic, should, upon receiving her undergraduate degree in 1979, decide to pursue graduate studies in Paris toward a master's degree in art, and toward a doctoral degree in aesthetics with a focus on ethno-anthropology.

That Tolentino is a capable painter in traditional modes is evident from her past work. It is also apparent that portraiture, regardless of style, plays an important role in her work. Her paintings make clear three other points: much of her work is based on evocations of childhood memories that assume the fantastic by their context and presentation; she has formulated a symbolic language of popularly derived sacred and secular meanings; and photographs play a role in almost every painting.

Inés Tolentino has chosen the kind of imagery embraced both by a number of young Latin American women and by some who come from older generations. Her direction is personal, domestic, a recollection of a past that is not just her own but seems to derive from family albums, or books on history and customs of earlier periods. To this she adds an iconography of animals, signs, plants (sometimes vegetables), and various types of architecture. Memory plays a role, but the memory is whimsical, as is the style of deliberate naïveté. Simply drawn objects that simulate childhood efforts are composed with great sophistication. In *Las desventuras del perro mudo* (Misfortunes of the Mute Dog, 1992), three flat planes of black and sienna establish the space occupied by a Romanesque tower, a lively sequence of activities by the dog that cannot bark, and the portrait of a man with a ladder accompanied by multiple objects, including a terrified cat, crosses, the hearts and spades of playing cards, and glimpses of an apple tree partially painted and partially scratched into the paint surface. Various markings appear in all three sections.

The tower appears again in *Las desventuras de los amos* (Misfortunes of the Masters, 1992; p. 127), which features a wedding photograph connected by a ladder to the tower, motifs of dogs and cats, playing cards, a hat/shoe combination, and a field of crosses. Again, despite its playfulness, an astute use of color and organization is obvious. The very simplicity of the objects, the distinct sense of past events, and the humbleness of the settings and activities convey charm at the same time that they suggest a sense of meditation.

•

It has been my intention, based on the curatorial project that brought together the specific works, to construct the unities and variabilities to be found in just three nations of the Caribbean—the Spanish-speaking lands of Cuba, Puerto Rico, and the Dominican Republic. It is clear that each body of national work is subject to differences of generations, gender, and class, in addition to the subjectivities of the individual artists. To historical and social differences must also be added the very different relationships of each nation and artist to the metropolitan centers of economic and cultural power. Finally, as there has been opportunity to observe, the cultural *interrelationships* among the three countries are an important consideration, symbolized by the figure of Wifredo Lam and his direct or indirect influence throughout the region. It should also be noted that artists and intellectuals have been brought together at the Biennials of Puerto Rico (the oldest such exhibition, directed at all of Latin America and the Caribbean), of Cuba (the largest, embracing the Third World), and the Dominican Republic (uniting the Caribbean). Thus artists have successfully crossed borders that politicians have not.

1. Wifredo Oscar de la Concepción Lam y Castillo was born in Sague La Grande, Cuba, on 8 December 1902. His father Lam Yam was born in Canton, China; his mother Ana Serafina was of mixed African and Spanish heritage. His spiritual "godmother," a Santería priestess, brought him up under the guidance of this African-based religion, though he was never initiated as a priest. At the age of twenty-one, he sailed to Spain to study art. For a full chronology, see María R. Balderrama, ed., *Wifredo Lam and His Contemporaries* (New York: The Studio Museum in Harlem, 1992), pp. 90–97.

2. *The Jungle* was purchased in 1946 for New York's Museum of Modern Art by its new director, James Johnson Sweeney. It hung for some time near Picasso's *Guernica,* but in recent years it was moved to the lobby of the museum, close to the cloakroom—as critic John Yau pointed out—outside the linear historicity of MoMA's cubist or surrealist holdings on the second floor.

3. Max-Pol Fouchet, *Wifredo Lam* (New York: Rizzoli International, 1976), pp. 188–189.

4. Ibid., pp. 198–199.

5. Charles Merewether, "At the Crossroads of Modernism: A Liminal Terrain," in *Wifredo Lam: A Retrospective of Works on Paper* (New York: Americas Society, 1992), p. 15.

6. Santería refers to a variety of African religious complexes that were practiced by African slaves and their descendants and later adopted by wider segments of the Cuban population. The term "Ocha" refers to the worship of Yoruba-derived deities called *orishas,* and Palo Monte (or Mayombe) when referring to *brujería* or sorcery, which is primarily of Bantu origin. Ocha is considered to constitute the religious core of Santería. The resistance aspect of Santería was accentuated by its suppression, particularly in Cuba, during and after slavery. In response, practitioners disguised the deities and rituals behind a facade of Catholic icons and rites. See Steven Gregory, "Afro-Caribbean Religions in New York City: The Case of Santería," in Constance R. Sutton, et al., eds., *Caribbean Life in New York City* (New York: Center for Migration Studies of New York, 1994), pp. 287–302.

7. See Gerardo Mosquera, "Wifredo Lam," *Art Nexus,* no. 15 (January-March 1995), p. 74.

8. Antonio Nuñez Jiménez, *Wifredo Lam* (Havana: Editorial Letras Cubanas, 1982), p. 7. Lam's action parallels that of Frida Kahlo, who in 1954 (the year of her death), when confined to a wheelchair after a leg amputation, participated in a demonstration of ten thousand people in Mexico City to protest the U.S. overthrow of Jacobo Arbenz, the democratically elected president of Guatemala.

9. The most complete information about this generation and the two others that followed can be found in Luis Camnitzer's very useful book *New Art of Cuba* (Austin: University of Texas Press, 1994). Among the members of Volumen Uno, the main interests after a phase of photorealism were the exploration of Cuban kitsch, of Afro-Cubanism, Americanism (particularly the indigenous), and Cuban nationalism. Camnitzer, *New Art of Cuba,* p. 17.

10. Ibid., passim.

11. Quoted by Leah Ollman, "An Anthropological Artist," *Los Angeles Times,* 5 March 1995, Calendar Section, p. 51.

12. Gerardo Mosquera, in *Los hijos de Guillermo Tell: Artistas cubanos contemporáneos* (Consejo Nacional de la Cultura, Venezuela, and Banco de la República de Colombia, 1991), p. 18. In Cuba, as in other Caribbean cultures, and in Brazil, African-derived religious practices are not restricted to those of African descent but have been integrated by peoples of diverse heritages. Bedia, for example, is of Spanish ancestry, with no personal tradition to link him to Santería (see Camnitzer, *New Art of Cuba,* p. 41), but was introduced to the practices by other members of Volumen Uno.

13. Guy Debord, *Comments on the Society of the Spectacle,* translated by Malcolm Imrie (London: Verso, 1990).

14. Camnitzer, *New Art of Cuba,* p. 211.

15. There exist many documentary and anecdotal records of the clashes between First and Third World women over feminist policy and ideology, starting as early as the First World Conference for International

Women's Year held in 1975 in Mexico City. Cuban women, including artists, have interacted with well-wishing U.S. women visiting Cuba at various intervals during the 1980s.

16. Camnitzer, *New Art of Cuba,* p. 211.

17. Edward J. Sullivan, introduction to *Tomás Esson: Chá-Chá-Chá* (Monterrey: Galería Ramis Barquet, 1993), unpaginated.

18. Coco Fusco, "The Sacred Meets the Profane: The Work of Tomás Esson," *¡Que Calor! Paintings, Drawings, Installations Inspired in Havana, Miami and Hamburg* (Coral Gables, Florida: Fred Snitzer Gallery, 1991), unpaginated.

19. Stewart Home, *The Assault on Culture: Utopian Currents from Lettrism to Class War* (Stirling, Scotland: A.K. Press, 1991), p. 62.

20. Telephone conversation with the artist, 6 March 1995.

21. Interview with the artist, 1986.

22. Interviews with the artist cited in *Luis Cruz Azaceta* (Cologne: Kunst-Station Sankt Peter, and New York: Frumkin-Adams Gallery, n.d. [c. 1988]), pp. 11 and 34.

23. See "The Manifested Destinies of Chicano, Puerto Rican, and Cuban Artists in the United States," in Shifra M. Goldman, *Dimensions of the Americas: Art and Social Change in Latin America and the United States* (Chicago: University of Chicago Press, 1994), pp. 443–444.

24. See Shifra M. Goldman, "La década crítica de la vanguardia cubana/The Critical Decade of the Cuban Avant-Garde," *Art Nexus/Arte en Colombia,* no. 7/53 (January-March 1993), pp. 52–57, 201-204.

25. See Mari Carmen Ramírez, *Puerto Rican Painting: Between Past and Present* (Princeton, New Jersey: The Squibb Gallery, 1987), p. 14.

26. See "Under the Sign of the *pava:* Puerto Rican Art and Populism in International Context," in Goldman, *Dimensions of the Americas,* pp. 427–430.

27. Ramírez, *Puerto Rican Painting,* p. 91.

28. Jean Franco, *The Modern Culture of Latin America: Society and the Artist,* rev. ed. (Hammondsworth, England: Penguin Books, 1970), p. 140.

29. Marta Traba, "Myrna Báez: Notas sobre una pintura difícil," reprinted in *Myrna Báez: Diez años de gráfica y pintura* (New York: Museo del Barrio, 1982).

30. Barry Schwartz, who coined the term, described it as that which "gives the viewer upsetting fantasies, demonstrating that the imagination can think of nothing as upsetting as reality itself." This Pop sensibility, combined by certain artists with a witty, unorthodox political and social critique, was characteristic not only of the Hairy Who but also of a range of artists in the New York, the Midwest, and the Southwest. See Barry Schwartz in *The New Humanism: Art in a Time of Change* (New York: Praeger Publishing, 1974), pp. 133–135.

31. "Arnaldo Roche Rabell: An Interview." *Newsletter,* St. Louis Gallery of Contemporary Art (Summer 1988), unpaginated.

32. Enrique García Gutíerrez and Mari Carmen Ramírez, in *Eventos, milagros y visiones* (Río Piedras, Puerto Rico: Museo de la Universidad de Puerto Rico, 1986), pp. 3, 5–6.

33. Personal communication with the artist. Unless otherwise noted, all quotes from Ballester derive from the same source.

34. Antonio Martorell, "So Where is my Painting?" in *Diógenes Ballester: Celebración Espiritual* (San Juan: Museo de las Américas, 1993).

35. *Hispanic Art of the United States: Thirty Contemporary Painters and Sculptors* (Houston: Museum of Fine Arts, 1987). The exhibition traveled to Washington, D.C., where Santiago was living before moving to Miami.

36. Anthropologists agree that Santería is Cuban in origin, and the Puerto Rican variety seems to be a recent derivative. See Margaret E. Crahan and Franklin W. Knight, eds., *Africa and the Caribbean: The Legacies of a Link* (Baltimore: John Hopkins University Press, 1979), p. vii. Spiritualism is a contending belief in Puerto Rico, embraced by Nelson Santiago in his search for a spiritual identity and inherited from practices continued by his mother.

37. The term Latin Americans refers to those who live in the United States but were born and educated in Latin America and maintain relations with their country of origin. Latinos are those who were born in or immigrated to the United Stated and consider themselves primary residents of this country.

38. I would like to thank Elizabeth Ferrer, Director of Visual Arts at the Americas Society, and Dr. Silvio Torres-Saillant, Director of the Dominican Studies Institute Project, City University of New York, for the important materials that they provided me on contemporary art in the Dominican Republic.

39. See Norberto James, "First Person Singular," in Rachel Weiss, ed., *Being América: Essays on Art, Literature and Identity From Latin America* (Fredonia, New York: White Pine Press, 1991), pp. 51–60.

40. Jeannette Miller, *Historia de la pintura dominicana/History of Dominican Painting,* translated by Edison Antigua (Santo Domingo: Amigo del Hogar, 1993), p. 123.

41. Jeannette Miller, *Arte dominicano contemporáneo/Contemporary Dominican Art,* catalogue, The Signs Gallery, New York, 1981, unpaginated.

42. Miller, *Historia de la pintura dominicana,* p. 123.

43. Raquel Tibol, "El dominicano José Perdomo en México," *Proceso,* 8 November 1993, p. 55.

44. Miller, *Historia de la pintura dominicana*, p. 125 passim.

45. Carlos Dobal, quoted in *100 años de la pintura dominicana: Continuidad y ruptura* (Santo Domingo: Intergrafic, 1989), p. 30.

A specialist in modern Latin American art, Dr. Shifra M. Goldman is an art historian, author, and lecturer who now serves as Research Associate with the Latin American Center at the University of California, Los Angeles (UCLA).

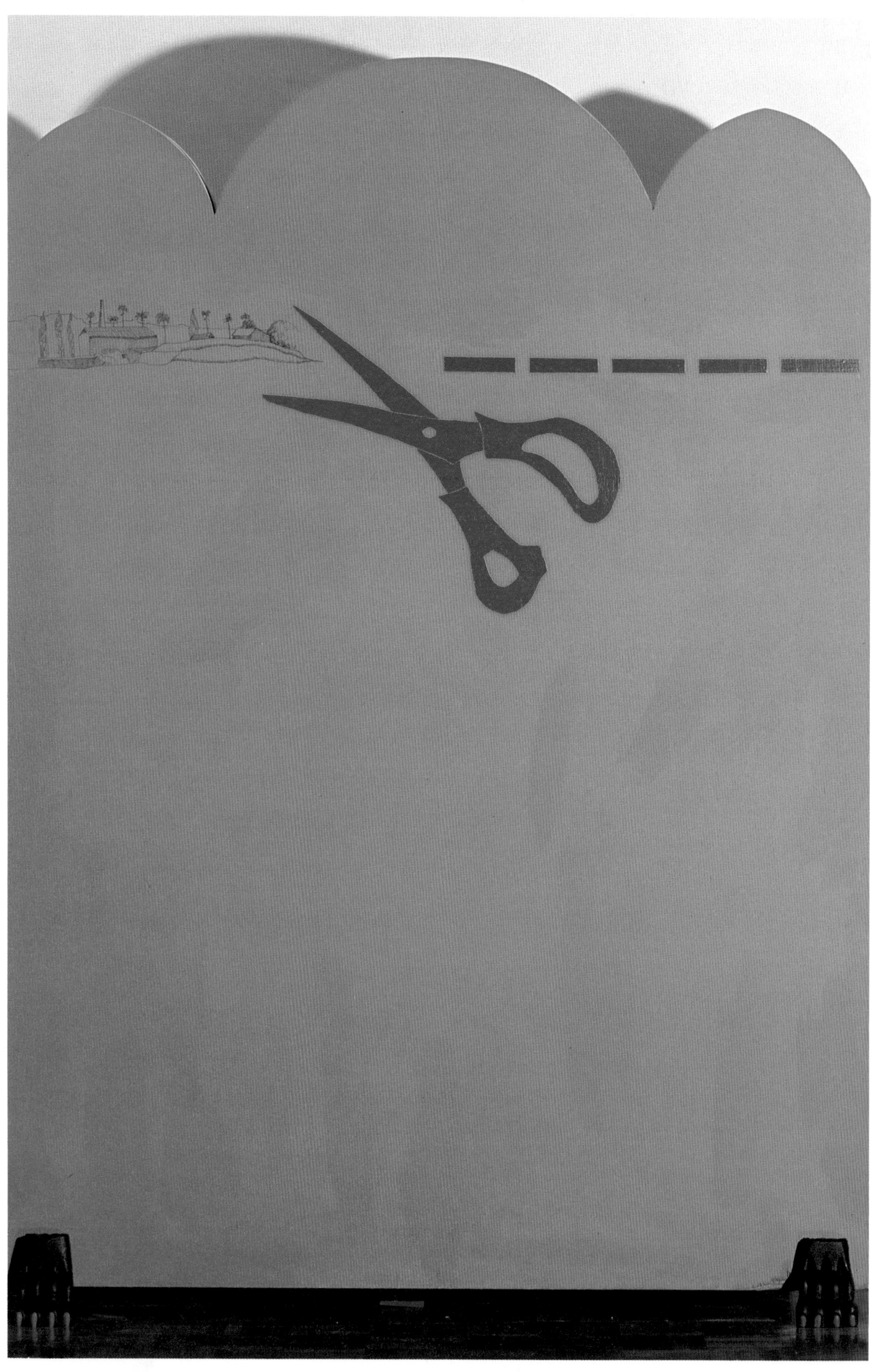

Catalogue of Works

Annalee Davis
The Things We Worship (back)
(see p. 99)

Ras Ishi Butcher

The interrogation and investigation of the Caribbean psyche is a challenge for us artists. We must trust ourselves and rely on our intuition and instincts, which have access to all primordial creativity . . . and bring into being in our artistic creations a freshness and flamboyancy that is not only amusing and exciting but is diapasonic and extraordinary. . . .

Being a vacuum, a spatial void, gives us limitless creative potential and rigor. Our creative potential is [in such a state of] metaphorical and transcendental flux that it knows no confinement to any academic and technical criteria or any stylistic and fashionable approach, but it allows us to make the obvious and simple miraculous. [We invest] the obvious with a certain amount of personal power, . . . or what some may say, a certain amount of "voodoo," an act of "black magic."

The black magic ritual is one of our peculiarities that we so much deny. . . . It is a gateway for me to cure my neuroses—my personal weakness, a gateway for mental stabilization—a means of vital importance, not only for economics or pleasure, but also to maintain my own sanity and sensitivity. Black magic comes from the depth of suffering, of being in tune with the most fundamental urges of existence. That faith abounds deep within that wholesomeness is absolute. It gives a sense of tranquility in a world where everything is under declension.

My act of black magic ritual reflects the untutored dimension of the void, of the dispossessed Caribbean man. It is without any "academic rigor," unbridled, unpretentious, without refinement. It has no social grace, totally uninhibited, raw and feral. The act of an artistic bastard.

Born: 1960, Bridgetown, Barbados

Education: Division of Fine Arts, Barbados Community College

Lives: St. John, Barbados

Cops and Robbers

1990

Oil on canvas

60 x 84 in.

Courtesy of the artist

(not shown)

Annalee Davis

My work has been influenced by conditions in my country and region, where mistaken identities, racial passions, and layers of betrayal simmer in isolated islands. The scars run deep and are compelling. I use my work to explore the wounds of these small island cultures, probing the hurts that simultaneously unite and divide a people. One of the central icons running through the work is the agricultural land, once bountiful, now lost to the highest bidder.

I live and work in the Caribbean; my family tree is rooted in the sugar cane plantations of Barbados. I feel connected to the younger generation of regional image makers who seek a hybrid expression which gives new form to our experience.

I am committed to creating visual narratives that implore society to look within itself and to expose contradiction that, if left to prevailing market trends, would go unchallenged. Through reflection and expression, artists can offer fresh landscapes that challenge myths, erode barriers, and create a forum for dialogue.

Born: 1963, St. Michael, Barbados

Education: Mobility Programme, Studio Art Centre International, Italy, 1984–1985; B.F.A., Maryland Institute, College of Art, Baltimore, 1986; M.F.A., Mason Gross School of Visual Arts, Rutgers, The State University of New Jersey, New Brunswick, 1989

Lives: St. Joseph, Barbados

Putting on My Blackness
1987
Oil on canvas
48 x 60 in.
Courtesy of the artist

The Things We Worship
1992
Acrylic on wood
67 x 95 in. (open)
Courtesy of the artist
(facing page, front shown closed; see pp. 2, 3, and 94)

David Gall

Before I am an artist I am a human being. I think it is important to understand this because being an artist is a function of my humanity: it serves to help me comprehend, demonstrate, and transform my humanity. Too often I think we forget that fact and get carried away by our role as artists, skewing it out of a healthy relationship with other aspects of our self. It is my intuitions of the experiences of the Caribbean person that form the content of my work, and which characterizes it as Caribbean. This will differ from artist to artist, since like any other artist anywhere, we are subject to different motivations, are of different backgrounds, and integrate into our work different influences; or if similar influences, integrate them differently. To look for a Caribbean style through superficial examination of forms would be to limit us to stereotypes and partial truths. . . . If the United States is overshadowed by white founding fathers and grand notions of democracy, Caribbean people are mobilized by death and rebirth, the Middle Passage and triumph over the attempts to belittle our humanity. That is a central characteristic of the Caribbean experience.

If the artist is to fulfill his/her role properly in the Caribbean he/she cannot be content with the definitions and institutions that we have inherited from colonial powers. We have to redefine these institutions to suit ourselves. That is a more important task than just painting and exhibiting. It is also more difficult. That is what, among other things, I hope my life and work will help to bring into clearer focus.

Born: 1952, Bridgetown, Barbados

Education: B.F.A., Visva Bharati University, 1973–1978; M.F.A., Maharaja Sahajirao University of Baroda, 1978–1980; University of the West Indies, 1990–1991; currently pursuing Ph.D. in art education at Pennsylvania State University

Lives: University Park, Pennsylvania

Paradise with Anubis
1985
Oil on canvas
56 x 36 in.
Courtesy of The National Cultural Foundation of Barbados

Gwen Knight

I was born in Barbados and moved with my family to the United States when I was seven. My memories of the Caribbean are the blue sea, the scent of flowers, and the warm sun. These things make me feel Caribbean, and I hope they are symbolic in my paintings.

Different kinds of art have intrigued me and given pleasure and inspiration. I would say West African art has influenced me because it is powerful and mystical. [I am attracted to] Asian drawings for their linear beauty and economy of means, and the Impressionist school for its use of color and its subtleness.

[In describing my artistic philosophy, I suggest you] follow your vision and observe, observe, observe. Do works about the things you have experienced and your feelings about them; use your strengths. If you draw well, use drawing. If you are a colorist, use that skill. Whatever you do best, use that, then work on your weaknesses.

Born: 1913, Bridgetown, Barbados

Education: Howard University School of Fine Arts, Washington, D.C., 1931–1933; New School for Social Research, New York City, 1960–1966; Skowhegan School of Painting and Sculpture, Skowhegan, Maine, 1968–1970

Lives: Seattle, Washington

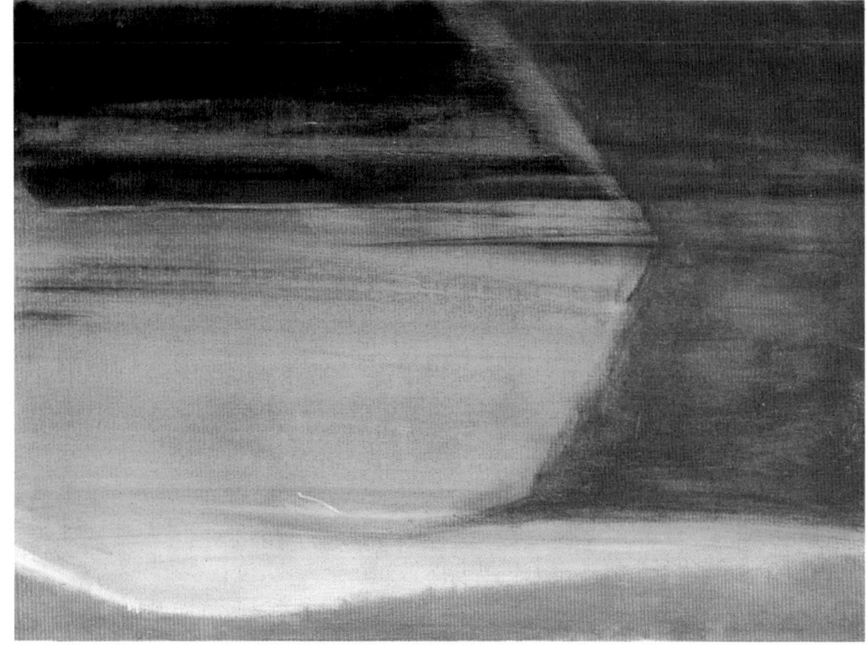

Seascape
1987
Oil on canvas
30 x 42 in.
Courtesy of Hampton University Museum

Robes
1987
Oil on canvas
42 x 30 in.
Courtesy of The St. Paul Companies, St. Paul, Minnesota
(facing page)

G.KNIGHT.L

Ras Akyem Ramsay

Art is an act of magic: an intuitive response to a primal/ancestral imperative; a passionate compulsive urge to create or destroy. . . .

Born: 1953, Bridgetown, Barbados

Education: Edna Manley School of Visual Arts, Kingston, Jamaica, 1979–1983

Lives: St. Michael, Barbados

Gethsemane I
1992
Oil on canvas
72 x 54 in.
Courtesy of Jim and Judy Taylor

Gethsemane II
1992
Oil on canvas
48 x 36 in.
Courtesy of Allisandra Cummins
(facing page)

Bendel Hydes

My work employs the language of biomorphic abstraction to explore ways in which nature and culture interact, reflecting on both the rational and ritualistic concerns of perceiving these opposites. Through a vocabulary of semifigurative shapes and symbols, issues such as isolation, vulnerability, survival, and the character of place traverse the boundary between physical abstraction and emotional reality in my paintings, forming the narrative that binds the work together.

I am interested in meaning that depends on context and in visual signifiers that resonate the nature of experience through that context. In this way, the language of my work is strongly influenced by my roots in the Caribbean, reflecting on the mix of African, European, and seafaring traditions that informed my early experience.

The mind and memory of my work is in the process. Whether it is sculpting and mixing paint with another substance or applying continuous washes and drips of color over another, I aim to question the aesthetics of the materials I use. In my early work these included sand, thatch fiber, and found objects, which allowed me to question the seemingly hidden impulses that lay behind the fundamental instincts of a very isolated and underdeveloped island society. In my later work this has given way to a scraping or washing away of color and form, as intense scrutinizing is paid to the gesture.

Born: 1952, Grand Cayman, Cayman Islands

Education: Liverpool College of Art, England, 1971–1972; Canterbury College of Art, England, 1972–1974; B.A., Clark University, Worcester, Massachusetts, 1976

Lives: New York City

Afternoon in Boca
1989
Oil on canvas
66 x 74 in.
Courtesy of the artist

Gulf Stream
1989
Oil on canvas
38 x 68 in.
Courtesy of John E. Hurlstone
(facing page)

Luis Cruz Azaceta

[The major influences on my art] date back to Goya—his work made me realize the power that a work of art can exercise on a person, socially, politically, and aesthetically. Later, the German Expressionists, especially Max Beckman, [were influential] for their abundance of humanism. And in terms of contemporary artists is Peter Saul, for his satirical bombardment on a passive society.

[How does my art identify itself as Caribbean?] Sunny, breezy days, beautiful beaches, palm trees, sounds of boots, sirens, starry nights, dictator's terror, fear, tortures, executions, carnivals, graves—all moving together with laughter, screams, and joy to the rhythms of merengues and cha cha cha to an unmarked pit.

My concern is with humanity. I want to confront the viewer with life and what we are doing to each other. And although we try to manicure reality—to make it like Hollywood—it is actually very brutal. In my work I present the victim; that is my theme: human cruelties. I hope to awaken a sense of compassion.

Born: 1942, Havana, Cuba

Education: School of Visual Arts, New York City, 1969

Lives: New Orleans, Louisiana

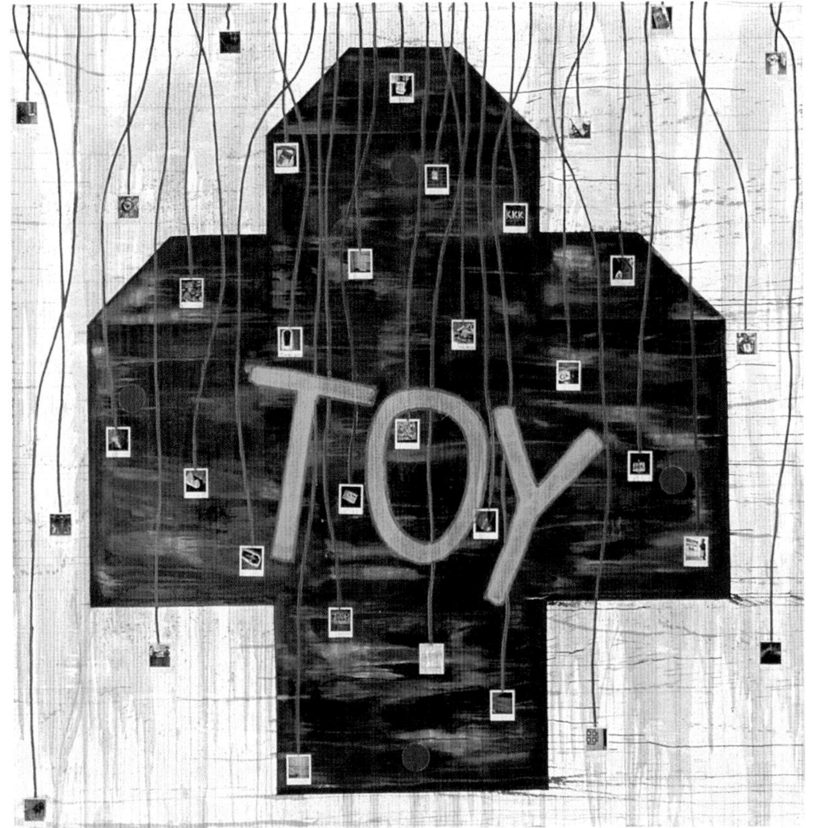

Toy
1994
Acrylic on canvas and Polaroids
120 x 120 in.
Courtesy of the artist and Frumkin/Adams Gallery, New York

Terror
1994
Acrylic on canvas and Polaroids
94 1/2 x 76 1/4 in.
Courtesy of the artist and Frumkin/Adams Gallery, New York
(facing page)

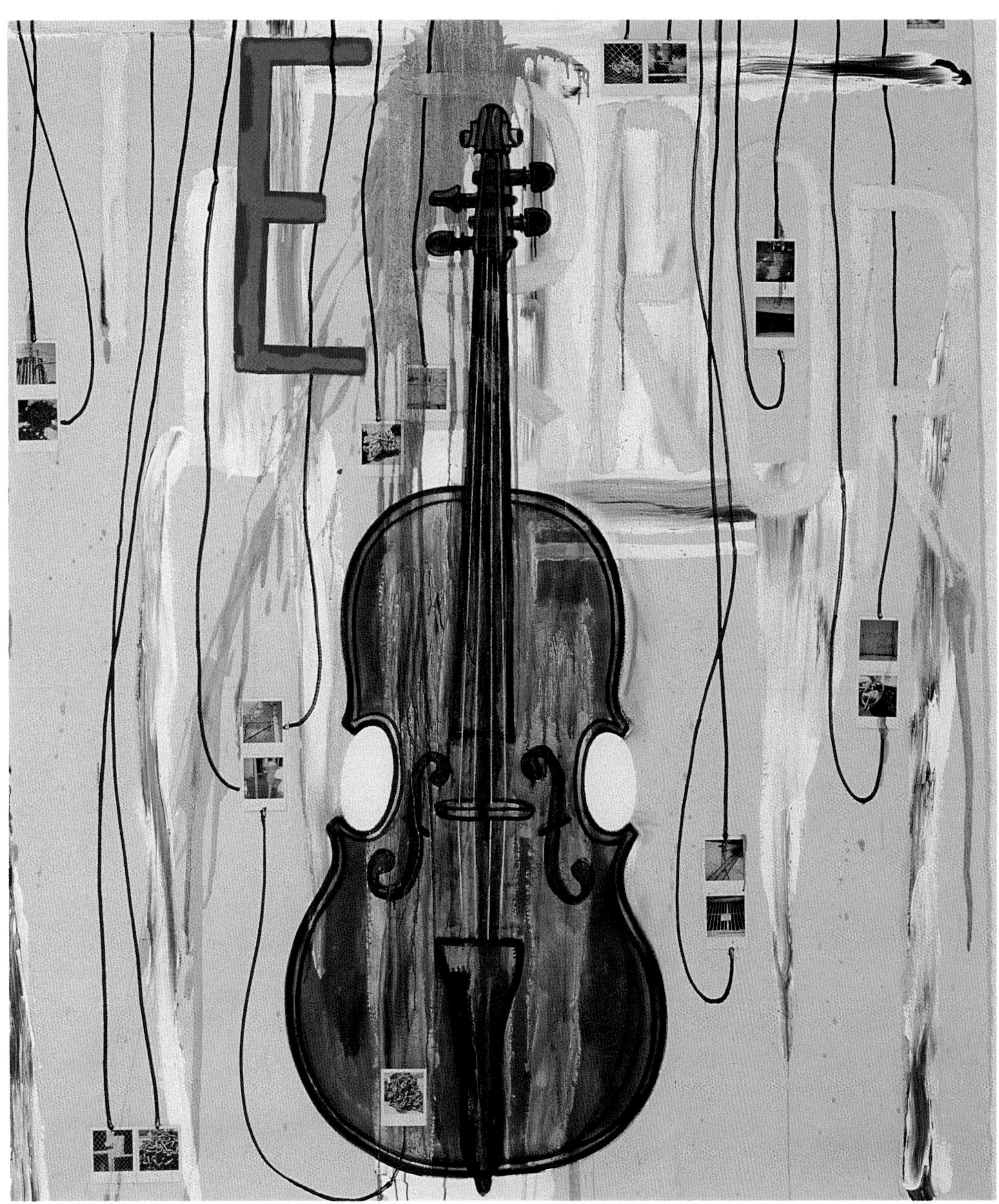

José Bedia

I feel that there are elements that contain a force at the level of a universal symbol, which is useful since Cuban iconography is rather poor. With this in mind I have studied Afro-Cuban art which forms a part of our ancestral roots. I am not like Picasso, for example, who in order to understand African art had to buy ritual masks and to visit museums devoted to the subject. I am part of this culture and I can assimilate all I need from it. . . .

My work is the result of a very personal interpretation of the primitive world in general. I believe that there are still many useful things, not only from the art of a specific culture, but from "all" the diverse manifestations and productions of those cultures which have been designated as "primitive," that we can assimilate with great benefit to the enrichment of our own cultural heritage. . . .

Born: 1959, Havana, Cuba

Education: School of Art of San Alejandro, Havana, 1976; Superior Institute of Art, Havana, 1981

Lives: Miami, Florida

Lembo brazo fuerte
1993
Acrylic and oil stick on canvas
83 x 170 in.
Courtesy of Frumkin/Adams Gallery, New York

S. Silvestre (St. Sylvester)
1993
Acrylic on canvas
108 x 67 1/2 in.
Courtesy of Mr. and Mrs. Andreu Pietri
(facing page)

Mujer de poder (Woman of Power)
1993
Acrylic, chain, leather hide, and canvas
82 1/2 x 78 1/2 in.
Courtesy of Bacardi Art Foundation
(see page 1)

gurunfinda
OSAIN
S.S. SILVESTRE
sindaula ndundu YAMBAKA
BUTANSEKE

María Magdalena Campos-Pons

I do not think my art identifies itself as Caribbean or Latin American or black. I do believe there are issues and specific bodies of concepts or information that have a particular historical or geographical appeal. If one of these entities is embodied in my work it might become distinct in the content of a work produced perhaps by a Norwegian, for instance, but besides this specifically my aesthetic concerns . . . function beyond geographical, ethnic, or class borders.

I definitely believe that it is reductionist and dangerous to base a definition of art or art production upon the parameters of location or race. The Caribbean waters share more similarities than differences with the rest of the ocean. This is also true of the works of art produced and nurtured in the Caribbean and the rest of the [world].

There are many artists to whom I owe respect and inspiration, and of course I may have stolen something from one or two of them. Literature, film, and music are very often a great source of inspiration, as well as African art, Western art, Mesoamerican art, and Cuban vernacular iconography. Early on the Cuban painter Antonio Vidal gave me words of encouragement, confidence, and trust.

As an artist I am a communicator. Form and content have equal value in my work. I am on a path with the goal to search for beauty and spread it as I encounter it.

Born: 1959, Matanzas, Cuba

Education: National School of Art, Havana, 1980; Higher Institute of Art (ISA), Havana, 1985; Massachusetts College of Art, Boston, 1988

Lives: Jamaica Plain, Massachusetts

La verdad no mata (The Truth Doesn't Kill You)
1992
Mixed media, wood, marble, and glass
118 x 78 x 11 in.
Courtesy of the artist

LA VERDAD NO MATA

Tomás Esson

My recent life has been punctuated by many significant changes. After living in Cuba for twenty-seven years, I came to live in the United States of America, "defecting to the enemy." I lived in Miami for three years and learned other facets of being Cuban. Then I came to New York, realizing that was a gift of God.

One of the most significant changes was the collision with the forces of the art market. In the context where I became an artist in Cuba, the existence of this market was ignored or underestimated. Only in the last four years have I realized that many artistic manifestations molding my artistic growth were generated by the powerful moves of the art market. Reacting to what the market demands and maintaining my integrity has been a great challenge. Having the possibility to see up close the masterpieces I had only known from printed reproductions and understanding the nuances of texture and color of the originals has also been a major influence.

The fact that I was born in Cuba and that I have Cuban Jamaican roots doesn't identify me automatically with Caribbean issues. I am more concerned with concepts involving the highest levels of art, . . . issues of the visual arts that concern artists in every corner of the world. . . . I do not want to be only the object matter in this experiment. I want to be also in the lab.

Born: 1963, Havana, Cuba

Education: Academia de Artes Plásticas San Alejandro, Havana, 1982; Instituto Superior de Arte, Havana, 1987

Lives: New York City

Dos deseos (Two Wishes)
1991
Oil on canvas
59 1/2 x 132 in.
Courtesy of Peter Menendez, Miami

Mala puntería (Bad Aim)
1991
Oil on canvas
77 x 57 in.
Courtesy of Porter Randall Gallery and Galeria Ramis Barquet
(facing page)

Lia Galletti

I have only been influenced by my father, an artist himself, who paints day in and day out. Then I learned about work myself, experimenting until there was no end, and developed my own technique.

My art is Caribbean in that it reflects my own spirit. I'm romantic, colorful, playful, and splashy. Like water.

My two paintings in this exhibition best express my artistic philosophy: "Kiss the sky and smell the roses: this bud's for you."

Born: 1943, Havana, Cuba

Education: Self-taught artist

Lives: Washington, D.C.

Kiss in the Sky
1993
Mixed technique on canvas
60 x 53 in.
Courtesy of the artist

Smell the Roses
1993
Mixed technique on canvas
60 x 53 in.
Courtesy of the artist
(facing page)

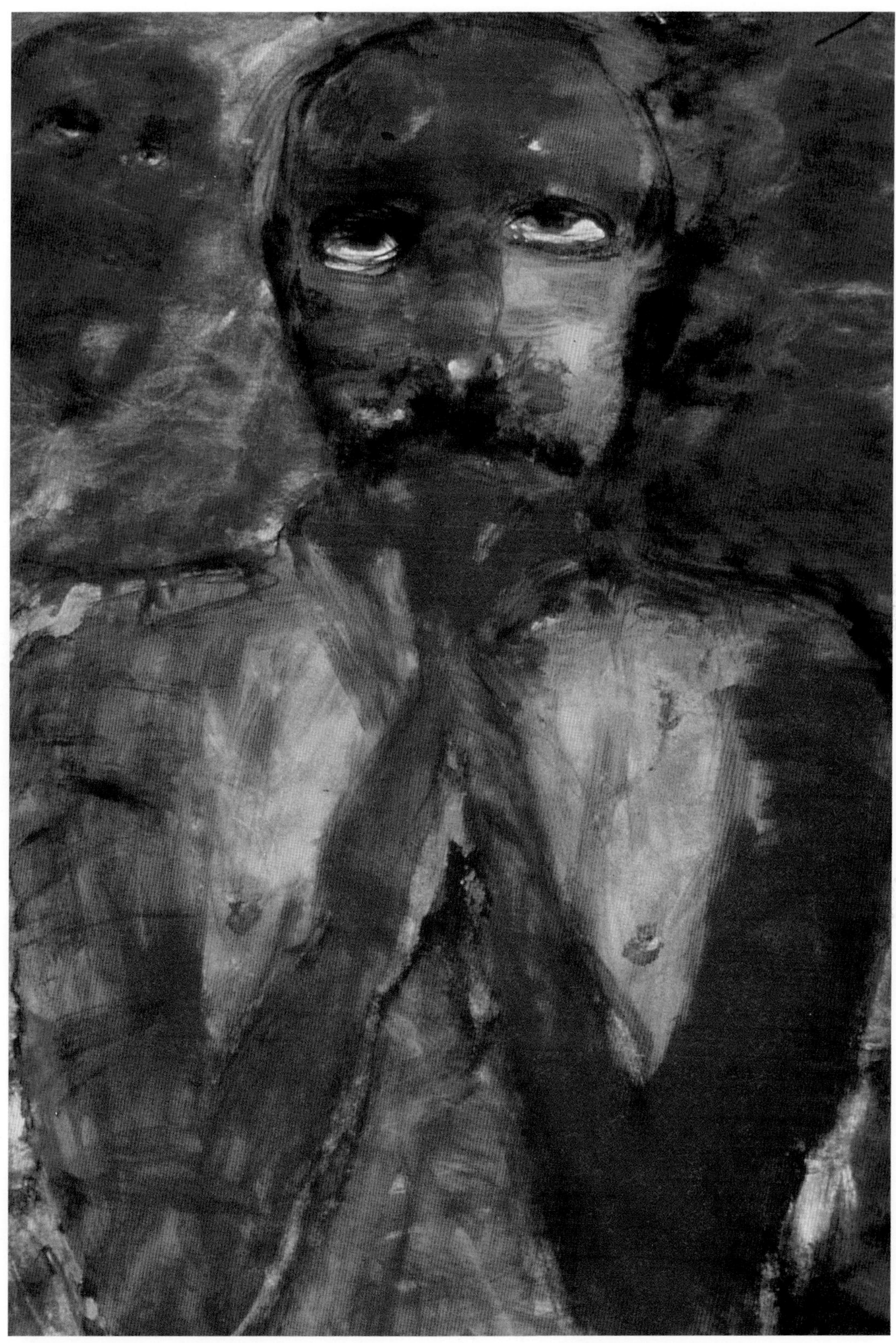

Wifredo Lam

[Wifredo] Lam's relationship with the New York School and the postwar School of Paris was multifaceted and probably more seminal than has been perceived until now. His cultivation of a totemic and mythic metamorphic imagery during the early 1940s was contemporaneous with that of the Abstract Expressionists. He distinguished himself from the Surrealists by expressing an intention that was about exploring the unity of nature rather than deconstructing it. —*Lowery Stokes Sims, 1992*

"Why do you paint?" I asked Wifredo Lam. He replied, "It's a way of communicating between human beings. Just one of the ways one can try to explain with full liberty. Some will do it with music, others with literature; I, with painting."

Who inspired him? Who encouraged him? "It was not my family! It was my godmother, Mantonica Wilson, who felt sure that I possessed the magical strength that she recognized within herself. I was inspired by all the reproductions of works from Africa, Asia, van Gogh, Gauguin, also classical artists such as Leonardo da Vinci." — *Herbert Gentry, 1981*

Born: 1902, Sagua La Grande, Cuba

Education: Academia San Alejandro, Havana, 1918–1923

Died: 1982

Exodo (Exodus)
1948
Oil on burlap
48 x 60 in.
Courtesy of The Howard University
Gallery of Art, Washington, D.C.

José García Cordero

José García Cordero has chosen impossible images, a game in which the relationship with nature is conceived as a dialectical absurdity, where objects and animals exorcise the memory of time. Within the atmosphere the artist strives to create, each element introduces a mixture of the logical and the illogical, from which the main theme derives. The geographical, cultural, and linguistic bipolarity of García Cordero, who divides his time between Paris and Santo Domingo, influences language and painting, traveling across the echoes of several images, balanced between wisdom and instinct. However, he does not belong to that visual and philosophical "magical identity" present in Latin American art for several years. He has joined, on the other hand, an independent, figurative movement, a crossroads of diverse ideas related to surrealism, fantasy, and New Realism. . . .

If the artist has been able to retain the passionate intensity of a Gauguin, the spatial symphony of a Matisse, or the expressive escapism of a Van Gogh in his work, it is also within the tradition of Mexican realism (one remembers Diego Rivera in the organic twisting of his tortured trees) that he has rediscovered the spirit of the medieval bestiary, even more hallucinatory and grotesque than that of Bosch. . . .

His realism adds intensity to an extraordinarily physical quality; one feels the strength of a perfect relationship between design and painting. [He] pursues a coherent symbolical and pictorial search, while he fathoms the abyss of ridicule and nonsense. —*Christine Frerot*

Born: 1951, Santiago, Dominican Republic

Education: University of Santo Domingo, 1970–1976; atelier of the painter Hernández Ortega, Santo Domingo, 1972–1973; Université Paris VIII, 1976–1980

Lives: Santo Domingo, Dominican Republic, and Paris, France

Las palmas de Morel (Morel's Palm Trees)
1994
Acrylic on canvas
68 x 60 in.
Courtesy of Lyle O. Reitzel-Arte Contemporaneo

José Perdomo

In Perdomo's work one can find a metaphorical will that acts like a living organism. The basic function of this technique is not to allow influenced tastes to dominate his doings. His paintings are extremely well conceived in their theoretical aspect. However, in them, formal procedures are transformed into instruments that are visible to the [naked] eye but, in reality, are not the intended expression. He goes beyond the limits of the genius in order to reach [the essential]. . . . The painter reaches his goals without escaping the traditional form of the art. In this way he extracts the poetical potential that surrounds the work and transforms it into images that border with reality as well as [verisimilitude]. This technique reminds us of don Ramón del Valle Inclán when he asserted, "Nothing is as is, rather as how it is remembered." —*José Antonio Pérez Ruiz*

Born: 1943, Santo Domingo, Dominican Republic

Education: National School of Fine Arts, Santo Domingo, 1961–1965; in the ateliers of Paul Giudicelli, 1961–1963, and Gilberto Hernández Ortega, 1963–1965; Pratt Graphics, New York City, 1968–1970

Lives: Santo Domingo, Dominican Republic

El mundo mágico de JOP
(The Magic World of JOP)
1992
Mixed media
70 x 114 in.
Courtesy of the Art Museum of the Americas, Organization of American States, Washington, D.C.
(not shown)

El mundo mágico de JOP
(The Magic World of JOP)
1994
Oil and paintstick on canvas
70 x 70 in.
Courtesy of the artist

Genaro Phillips

The two major influences on my art are Wifredo Lam and Marc Chagall. My art identifies itself as Caribbean by the profundity of the subject or theme and the utilization of the images that identify our culture. My personal philosophy is focused and directed to communicate myself with others and at the same time to give others the opportunity to disclose to me the arts that they were sometimes wishing to express and to identify with themselves.

My Sub-Conscious
1989
Acrylic on canvas
40 x 60 in.
Courtesy of the artist

Tropic I
1989
Acrylic on canvas
40 x 30 in.
Courtesy of Jacob Aybar
(facing page)

Tropic II
1989
Acrylic on canvas
40 x 36 in.
Courtesy of the artist
(see p. 18)

Born: 1955, Santo Domingo, Dominican Republic

Education: Universidad Auónoma de Santo Domingo; National School of Fine Arts, Santo Domingo

Lives: New York City

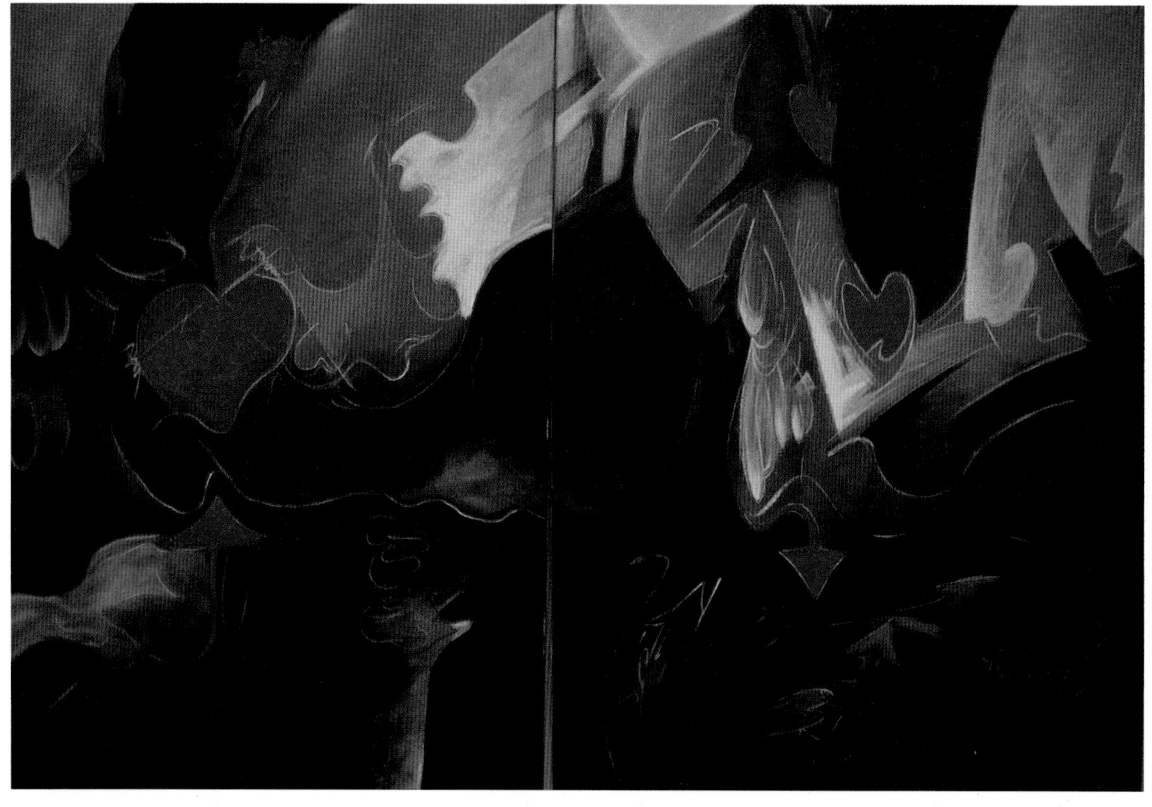

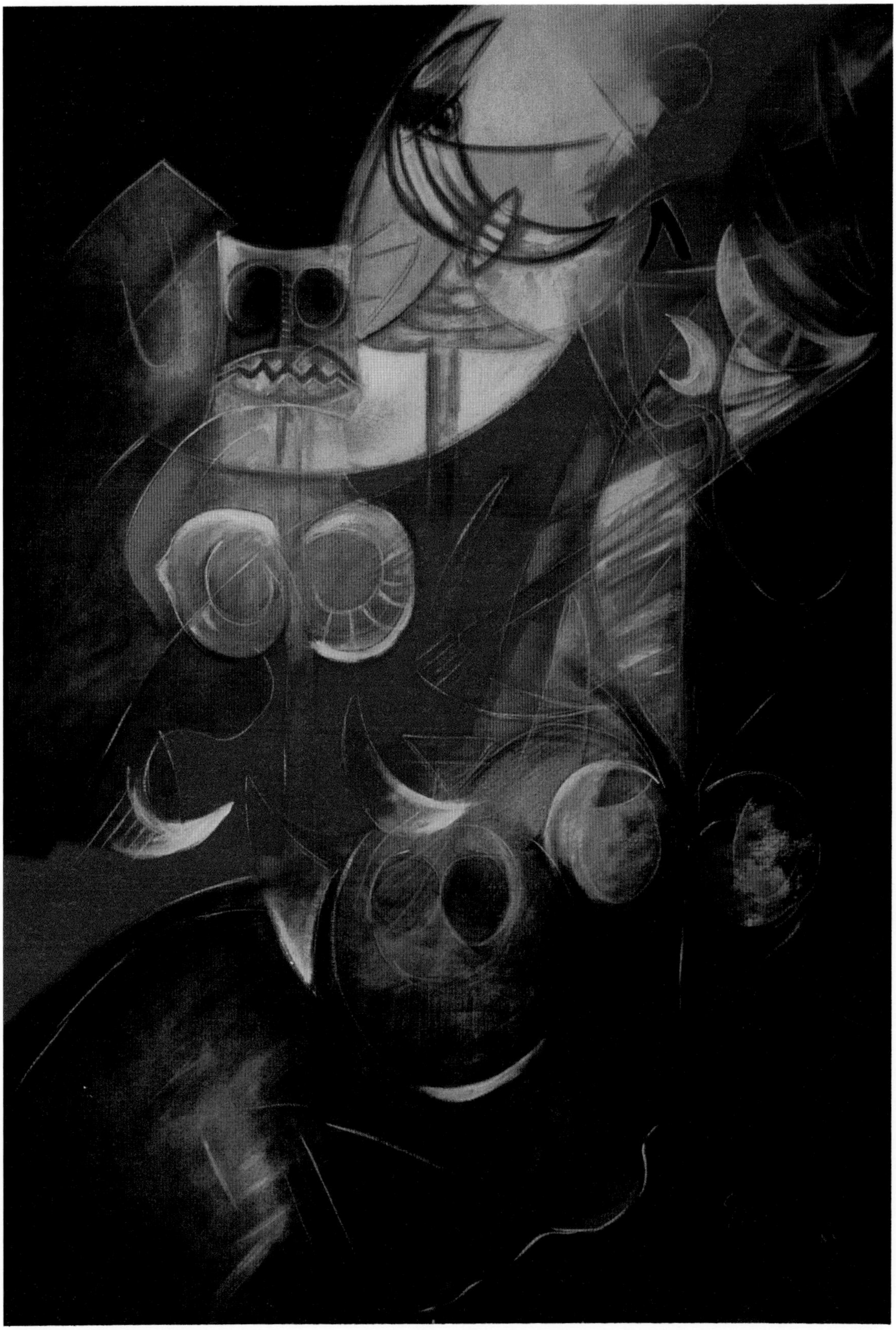

Inés Tolentino

In my works I can distinguish three types of influences. . . . I always bear in mind the works of Goya, particularly "The Caprices," Tapies, Bacon, Dubuffet, Rauschenberg, and Jasper Johns. Pop art especially attracts me. I like its sense of critics, of game, of humor. Among the literary influences are the Dominican poet Pedro Mir, Cuban writer Alejo Carpentier, and the Colombian Gabriel Garcia Marquez—very Caribbean all. They act through their texts in the background of my creations. And last, I must say that I am under my own influence, where my childhood fears and uncertainties are still prevailing.

If I dared describe my artistic philosophy, I [would say] that in my works I try to define the meaning of living. . . . With a fully positive attitude, I wish to eliminate the superfluous, anything which distracts and confuses us, so to be able to offer each spectator his own story of my work: that one of the individual self which becomes the universal self, traveler of time and space.

A Caribbean identity appears in my work without an imposing will to show it. . . . My Caribbean is a magic mixture of sun and shadow, of sacred and profane elements, of the desire of feasts and secular misfortunes.

Born: 1962, Santo Domingo, Dominican Republic

Education: National School of Fine Arts, Santo Domingo; Ecole Nationale Supérieure des Beaux-Arts (ENSBA), Paris; University of Paris I, Sorbonne

Lives: Paris, France

Las desventuras de los amos (Misfortunes of the Masters)
1992
Acrylic on canvas
46 1/2 x 36 3/4 in.
Courtesy of the Art Museum of the Americas, Organization of American States, Washington, D.C.

Los caminos del infortunio (The Roads of Misfortune)
1992
Acrylic on canvas
51 x 38 in.
Courtesy of the artist
(facing page)

Frank Bowling

Born: 1936, Bartica, Essequibo, Guyana

Education: Slade School of Arts, London University, and Royal College of Art, London, 1959–1962

Lives: Brooklyn, New York, and London, England

Jamsahibwall
1990
Acrylic on canvas
74 x 140 in. (7 panels)
Courtesy of Camille Love Gallery, Atlanta, Georgia

Karl Broodhagen

My largest piece of sculpture is an eight-foot figure of a slave in revolt on the Emancipation Monument at St. Barnabas Roundabout in Barbados. I am interested in people. I specialize in portraiture. In my carvings *Benin Head,* I am fascinated by slanting eyes. I set out to make a piece with slanting eyes and pouting lips. I had cut much too deep across the eyes, which made the piece look like a Benin head. I named it so.

My approach to my work has always been and is "sincerity and hard work."

Born: 1909, Georgetown, Guyana

Education: Goldsmith's College, South East London, 1952–1954; otherwise self-taught artist

Lives: St. Michael, Barbados

Benin Head
1971
Ebony and wood
22 1/2 x 10 1/4 x 11 1/2 in.
Courtesy of Indrani and David Gall

Dudley Charles

My work is an expression of events and images encountered in my life, reflections of the multicultural, multiracial society that comprises Guyanese society. Most of the subjects I paint are drawn from the diversity of folklore, and over the years I have developed a mythopoetic expression of this, what we call in Guyana "a cook-up." The dominant influence in terms of these myths and folkloric figures is African; these influences are common in the African culture of many other Caribbean countries. . . . The language I use and the mere fact I'm a painter makes them and their expression universal.

My art is influenced by the art of the world, and because I am self-taught there are really no specific influences that have affected me. Many of my early paintings were compared to the work of the great Cuban master Wifredo Lam, but I was making my images that way long before I saw [his work] or became aware of him. I suppose it's more the spirit of the work, because we all draw from the same well of repressed ancestral memories. I conceptualize the expression of these folkloric images in illusion; consequently I superimpose images to get that feeling of movement in the paintings. I paste paper, cut up and reassemble the canvas, mix rice paper with acrylic gel. I also use papier-mâché to help create a collage feeling. I use anything I can get my hands on to make the painting look like I feel.

Born: 1945, Georgetown, Guyana

Education: Self-taught artist

Lives: Hyattsville, Maryland

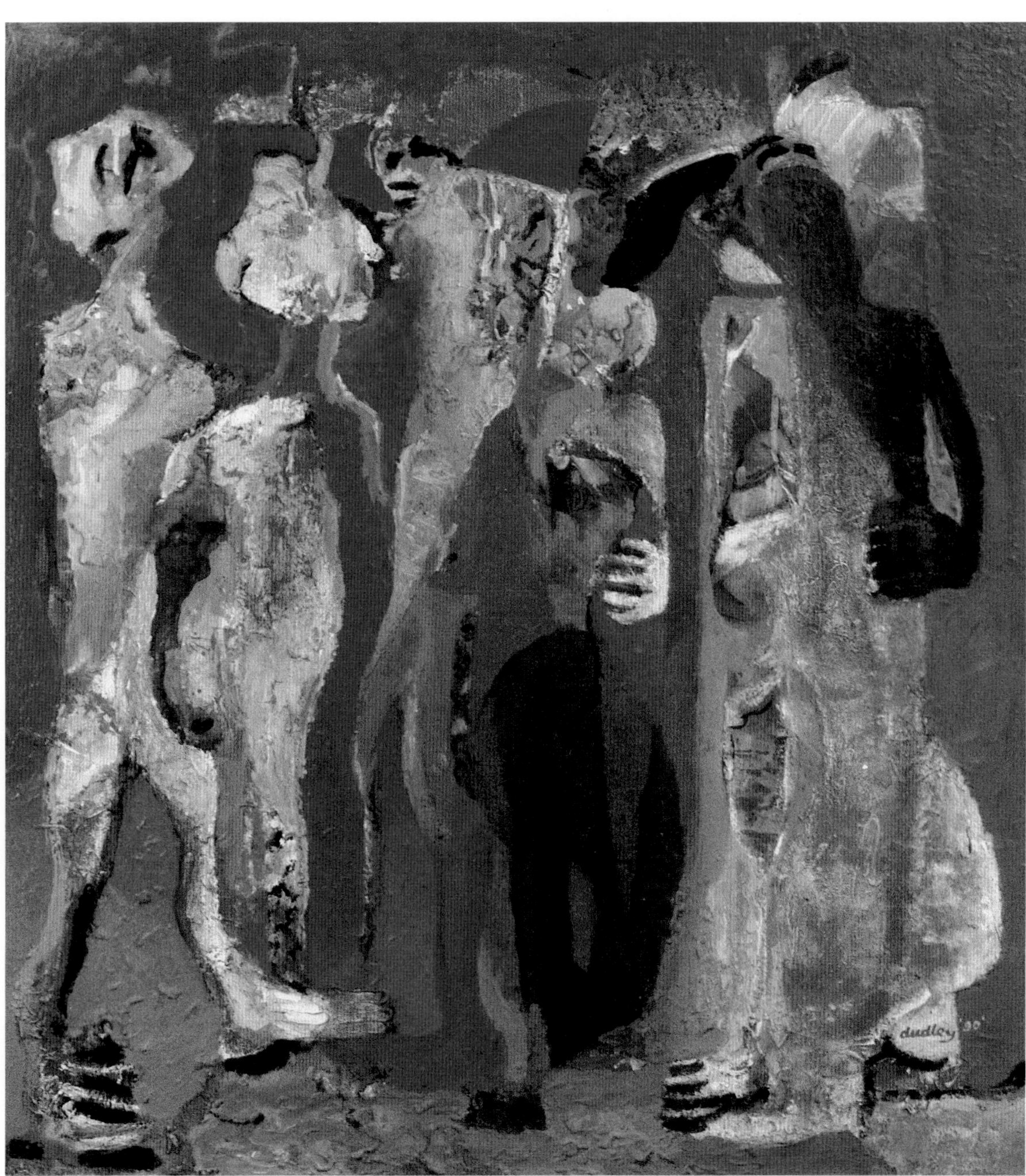

Forest Lights
1991
Acrylic on canvas
27 x 49 in.
Courtesy of Richards' Collection
(facing page and cover, detail)

Queh Queh Peoples
1990
Acrylic on canvas
36 x 33 in.
Courtesy of Richards' Collection

Stanley Greaves

The continuing direction of my work has been an investigation into the relationship between intellect and imagination. The processes by which they combine to transform the experiences of the psyche with those of the world of phenomenon is totally fascinating. For this reason the ambiguities of dreams and the revelations of mythological drama have been extremely instructive to me when dealing with products of the imagination. The focus of my work is more of an allegorical nature as opposed to the formalistic concerns of abstract art. In addition it is an investigation from a fundamentalist position, seeking to establish the harmonics of things and events at a symbolic level.

Dali and Ernst, my very early influences, were, in a conceptual and non-stylistic sense, later replaced by Magritte and Chirico, whose metaphysical concerns related to what I was attempting. In recent years the Latin American artists Tamayo, A. Morales, and Lam, among others, caught my attention. As "New World" people we share common historical, transformation, and existential experiences. Titian and Ingres also contribute to my experiments with the human figure.

Pursuit of the "avant garde," "the cutting edge," in today's jargon has become meaningless. The need to shock is no longer a necessity. Today's world has found more devastating ways of achieving this. Artists need to re-affirm the spirit of endeavor of humanity's artistic past in seeking to establish comparative performance levels of distinction.

Born: 1934, Georgetown, Guyana

Education: Working People's Art Class, 1946–1951; University of Newcastle-upon-Tyne, England, 1962–1968, B.A. Honours Degree, Fine Art, 1967, Diploma in Education, 1968; Howard University, Washington, D.C., Fulbright Scholarship, 1979–1980, M.A. Fine Art, 1980

Lives: St. Michael, Barbados

Channa Man
1978
Oil on cotton on panel
37 x 48 in.
Courtesy of The Dorothy Taitt Foundation, Guyana

The Hatman
1992
Acrylics on canvas scroll with mahogany batons
44 3/4 x 32 3/4 in.
Courtesy of the artist
(facing page)

Gregory A. Henry

Through my sculpture and paintings I try to reach an inner truth through images and materials that are common to humanity. I have always been interested in storytelling, usually referring to my childhood memories in order to create visual images that commune with the viewer on many levels. I feel that my interest in storytelling through my art stems from conversations with my elders in Guyana. They often spoke in parables, using metaphors when discussing everyday occurrences. When I would ask them what did they mean, they would always answer, "You'll know in time." This intrigued me. I was also interested in how things function. If it was a new toy that you wound up and watched run, I wanted to find out how it worked. If it was a chicken laying an egg, I wanted to know how that was. This curiosity for mechanics and how nature works and the parables that my elders shared fascinated me as a youth.

Born: 1961, Essequibo, Guyana

Education: B.F.A., Ohio University, Athens, Ohio, 1985; M.F.A., Rhinehart School of Sculpture, Maryland Institute, College of Art, Baltimore, 1987

Lives: Hampton, Virginia

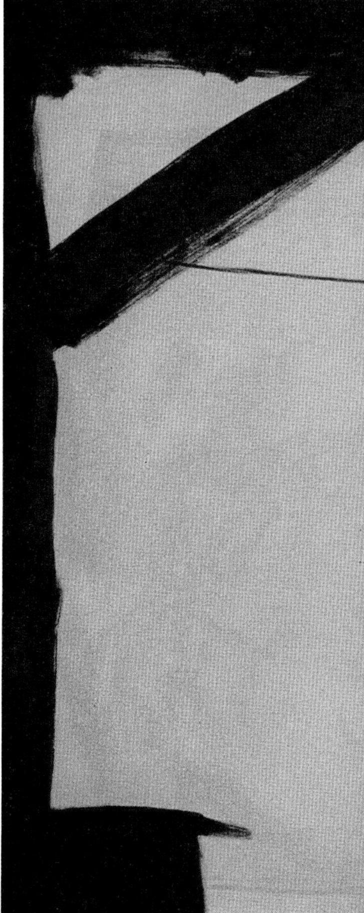

Fetching Water
1990
Oil on canvas
32 1/2 x 64 3/4 in.
Courtesy of the artist

Philippe Dodard

Philippe Dodard initially came out of the Poto-Mitan School of Tiga, one of Haiti's most respected contemporary, avant-garde artists and the founder of l'Ecole du Soleil. Dodard came to real prominence as a member of Port-au-Prince's "School of Beauty," [which included] such prominent artists as Bernard Séjourné, Jean-René Jérôme, Jean-Claude Legagneur, and Simil. . . . [They] celebrated spirituality and beauty, especially the beauty of women, over the mundane. The style adopted by these painters was characterized by swooping, curving lines and brushstrokes, swan-like necks, and long, graceful limbs and bodies . . . beautiful mask-like tranquil faces, a rich, sensuous, otherworldly use of color, a precise depiction of form, and dream-like landscapes. —*Quincy Troupe, 1990*

The Magic Wedding: The goddess Erzulie is meeting with the force of war asking for peace. Together they are holding a kind of flag that represents the Caribbean and also symbolizes fertility. *Open the Gate:* It is a cry from the goddess of love to have the embargo lifted from Haiti. Her face is closed in a small window and the god of death is standing before her. —*Philippe Dodard, 1995*

Born: 1954, Port-au-Prince, Haiti

Education: Ecole d'Art Poto-Mitan, 1970; Collège Roger Anglade, 1973; Académie des Beaux-Arts, 1973; Ecole Internationale de Bordeaux, 1978

Lives: Port-au-Prince, Haiti

The Magic Wedding
1993
Acrylic on canvas
72 x 72 in.
Courtesy of The Sanford A. Rubenstein Collection, Wesley Hills, New York

Open the Gate
ca. 1994
Acrylic on canvas, ink on paper
60 x 48 in.
Courtesy of The Sanford A. Rubenstein Collection, Wesley Hills, New York
(facing page)

Edouard Duval Carrié

There is no doubt that the evolution of my work is linked to what can be loosely referred to as "Haitian art." What can be considered truly Haitian? Haiti was PanAfricanist before this term was ever coined in reference to political movements in Africa, i.e., the deportation of African people on a continental scale for the slave trade. The diversity of the African mosaic was partially reconstructed on a small island that was a fraction of the size of the mother continent. Added to this African microcosm are the Europeans who organized this forced migration, all forming an impossible cocktail, which, as we know, erupted in a quite singular revolution. This model is a recurrent one in the Caribbean, with slight variations making the area a melting pot.

A sense of rootlessness generally exists in the area. On a political level, leaders in the region have had to contend with this vacuum by forging an unsuccessful sense of national unity. We are relatively free of roots and traditions, fundamental elements that we daily try to reconstruct for ourselves through a constant recreation of our myths, values, and aspirations. The tools used for this vast enterprise are as numerous as they are diverse. A recurrent one for the region is definitely appropriation. We reevaluate all information beached on our shores and adapt its content to our own ends. Our memories are fragmented recollections that do not follow the rigorous linear readings of history. Our reality is a reconstruction made of such disparate elements and materials that we are in a perpetual state of wonder, pondering about the collapse, but there is a strong dose of poetry in this, which I try to capture in my work.

Born: 1954, Port-au-Prince, Haiti

Education: Ecole Nationale Supérieure des Beaux Arts, Paris; B.A., University of Loyola, Montreal, Quebec; supplementary studies at McGill University and the University of Montreal, Quebec

Lives: Miami Beach, Florida

Les Trois Petits Anges (Three Small Angels)
1990
Oil on canvas
55 x 55 in.
Courtesy of The Sanford A. Rubenstein Collection, Wesley Hills, New York

Danse de la Mort (Dance of Death)
1993
Oil on canvas
55 x 55 in.
Courtesy of The Mireille Chancy Gonzalez Collection
(facing page)

Andre Juste

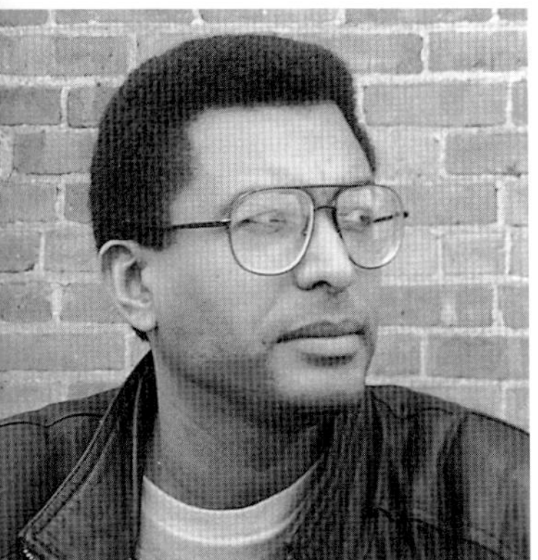

One major influence on my art has been modernist American art of the 1950s and 1960s, particularly the all-over approach of some of the Abstract Expressionists, their bold, large-scale format, and, more importantly, the rigorous or "tight" method of the Minimalists. (I have eschewed, however, the latter's reductivism and "purity.") I've imbibed the expressive quality, that is, the energy or "fire" found in Pollock and filtered it through the rational, factual, and physically objective lens of some of the Minimalists. Thus to a considerable degree I am a formalist, but one who has been burdened with rather elemental ideas, such as death, power, and salvation.

Moreover, my formalism is inflected by my socio-cultural memory, stemming from my Haitian background. My memory undermines to some degree the would-be "universality" of my formalism and impregnates it with a certain local or regional flavor. Such a flavor, I believe, manifests itself through my use of color—the type seen, for instance, in Haiti's Tap-Tap trucks—and choice of subject matter as well as through the numinous quality found in many of my works. It is particularly in this sense that my art identifies itself with the Caribbean.

Born: 1956, Port-au-Prince, Haiti

Education: B.A. English Literature and Art, Brooklyn College, City University of New York (CUNY), 1979; M.F.A. Painting, Brooklyn College, CUNY, 1983

Lives: Peekskill, New York

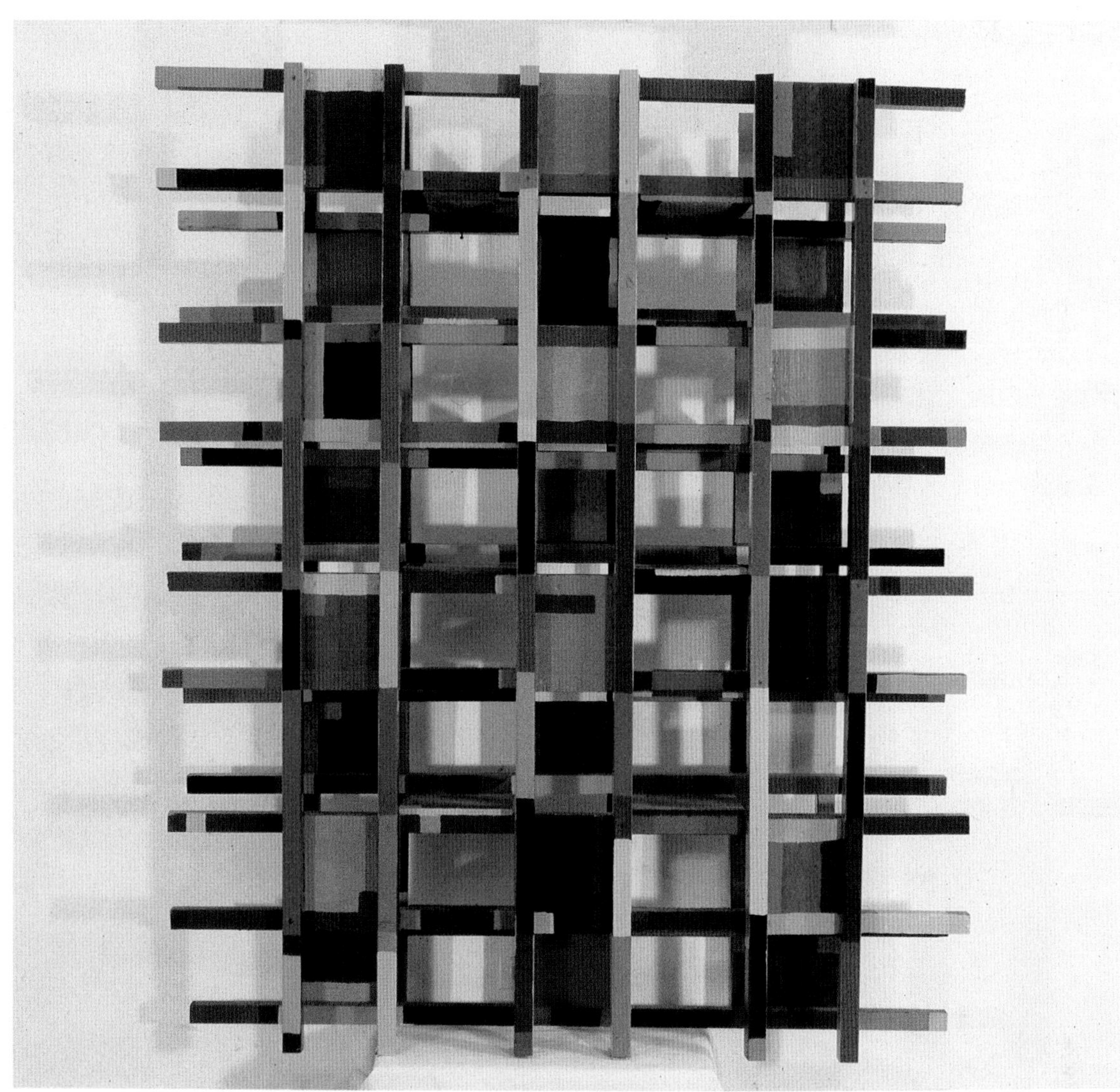

Early Hangings
1989
Latex on plywood
52 x 120 x 4 in.
Courtesy of the artist
(facing page)

Prospect
1986
Enamel and wood
74 x 63 x 13 in.
Courtesy of the artist

Jean Claude Rigaud

I find my sources in the sculpture of Archipenko, Brancusi, Henry Moore, and Calder. Like many contemporary artists, I am as concerned with space as I am with form, and I understand the manner in which modern sculptors have used form or line to enclose space rather than creating solid mass standing in space. The open areas become an integral part of the composition, to be given equal importance with the enclosing line or form. This has been one of the most important departures from classical sculpture taken by artists in this century. My sculpture evokes an architectonic concept and the forms are basically geometric.

I do not have a preconceived idea; as the sculpture proceeds, the subject reveals itself. When I hold one piece of metal in my hand, I instinctively know where the next piece should go. When all the parts work well together, I feel the sculpture is complete. This intuition is based on solid experience and discipline. I understand structure, without which no sculpture can stand, either literally or figuratively.

I like the fact that my work appeals to a broad spectrum of people. Its very approachability is part of what I am looking for: the chance to reach out and make contact with the spectator.

Born: 1945, Port-au-Prince, Haiti

Education: B.F.A., National University of Mexico, Mexico City, 1965–1968; New York City Community College, New York, 1970–1972; Teachers College, Columbia University, New York, 1974–1978; University of Miami, Florida, 1982–1984

Lives: Miami, Florida

Construction #5
1993
Steel
35 x 11 x 14 in.
Courtesy of Mr. and Mrs. Daniel Lopez

Guitar Player
1993
Steel
33 1/2 x 17 x 10 in.
Courtesy of Mr. and Mrs. Miguel Rodrigo-Mazure
(facing page)

Bernard Séjourné

Bernard Séjourné was one of Haiti's most gifted contemporary artists and was the founder of the "School of Beauty," which gives honor to women. He showed an interest in art at an early age and was influenced no doubt by his uncle Maurice Borno, who was a founding member of the Centre d'Art and was among the pioneers of modern art in Haiti.

After study abroad, Séjourné returned to Haiti, becoming one of the country's most important modern painters and sculptors. He created the art for the 1986 label of Chateau Mouton Rothschild, the famous premier Cru Bordeaux wine. Among other artists who created art for these labels have been Picasso, Dalí, Chagall, and Miró. Séjourné was the first black and West Indian to have been chosen for this honor. —*Audreon Bratton, 1995*

Born: 1947, Port-au-Prince, Haiti

Education: Academy of Fine Arts, Port-au-Prince; Jamaican School of Fine Arts and Crafts, Kingston; Art Students League, New York; American Art School, New York

Died: 1994

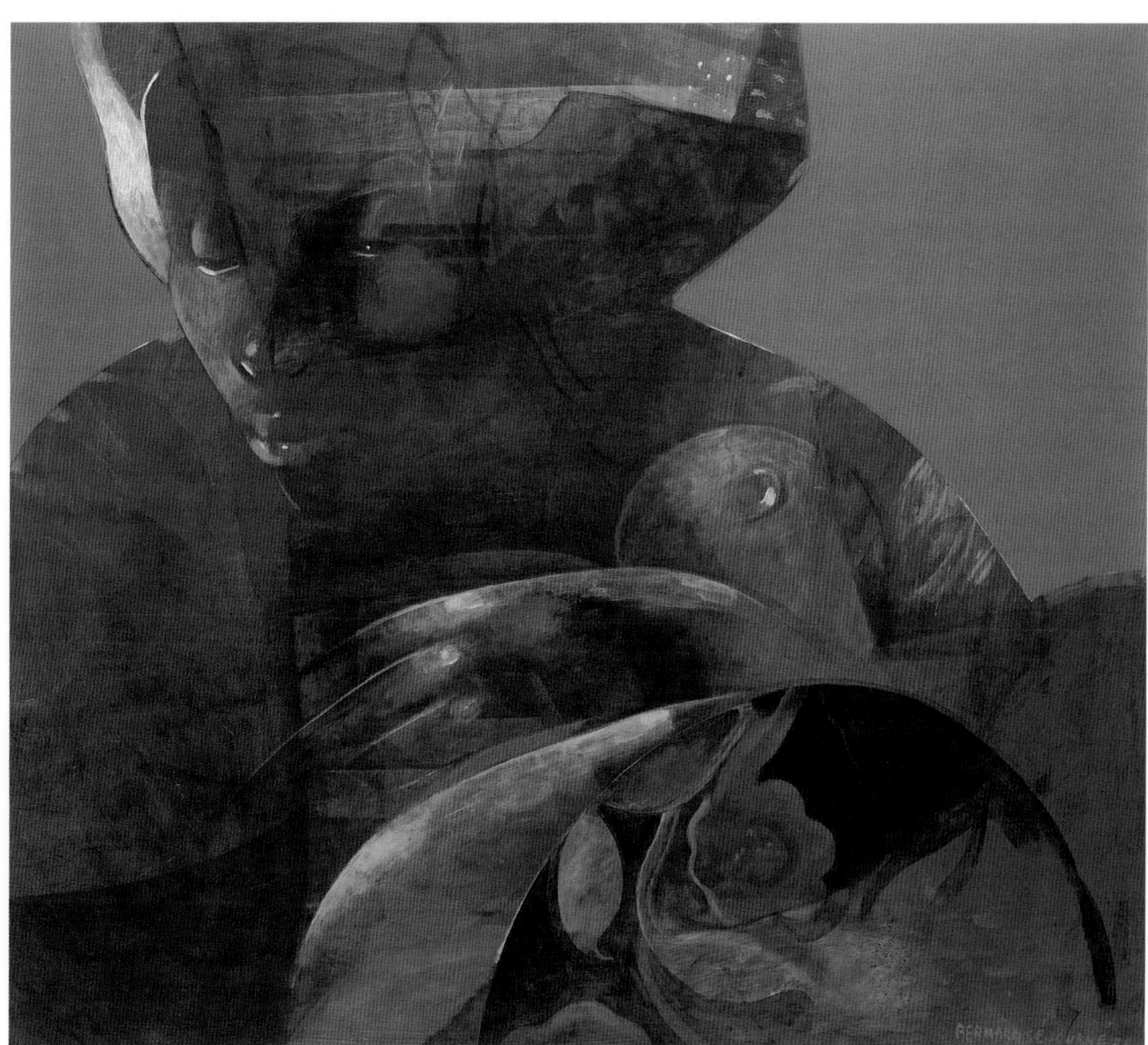

Mother and Child
1978
Acrylic on masonite
33 3/4 x 39 in.
Courtesy of Audreon Bratton

Luce Turnier

[Luce Turnier] came from her native Jacmel while still very young to begin her studies. In 1944 she entered the Centre d'Art as a student, and by 1946 she participated in an exhibition organized by UNESCO at the Museum of Modern Art, Paris. Recipient of two Rockefeller Foundation scholarships, she studied at the Art Students League, New York. She received a scholarship from the French Government to study at the Grande Chaumière in Paris in the early 1950s. She traveled back and forth from Haiti to the United States to Europe, always maintaining her connection to the Centre d'Art.
— *Michel Philippe Lerebours*

Born: 1924, Jacmel, Haiti

Education: Centre d'Art, 1944; Art Students League, New York City; Grande Chaumière, Paris

Died: 1994

Jean-Pierre
1990
Oil on composition board
28 1/2 x 24 in.
Courtesy of Mae Gabriel Haitian Art

David Boxer

My preparation as an artist has been limited almost exclusively to the study of the history of art and a great deal of looking at art, and it is this, a quite intensive involvement with the art of Europe, of Africa, and of the New World, which has been the key element in the development of my work.

I feel that where the "language" of my art is concerned, my work is very much a part of the so-called mainstream Western tradition. Yet by virtue of much of its content, the ideas with which I wrestle, my art is definitely Jamaican and Caribbean. Racial hybridization and cultural pluralism, the results of a particular colonial history, are not only key molding forces of my art, but have become the essence, the substance of much of my iconography as well.

My art, manifested in a whole variety of media (found objects, assemblage, installation, painting, collage), is not regulated by any overt philosophical stance. Creating art is for me a way of thinking, of ordering, or at least of assembling thoughts, of ruminating, of remembering, of dreaming, of cherishing, of "dispelling the furies." In short, it is an ongoing visual diary of the thoughts and memories, the fears and drives, of one twentieth-century man who lives through a life on one small, complex, disturbing Caribbean island.

Born: 1946, St. Andrew, Jamaica

Education: A.B. History of Art, Cornell University, Ithaca, New York, 1969; M.A. (1972), Ph.D. (1975), Johns Hopkins University, Baltimore, Maryland

Lives: Kingston, Jamaica

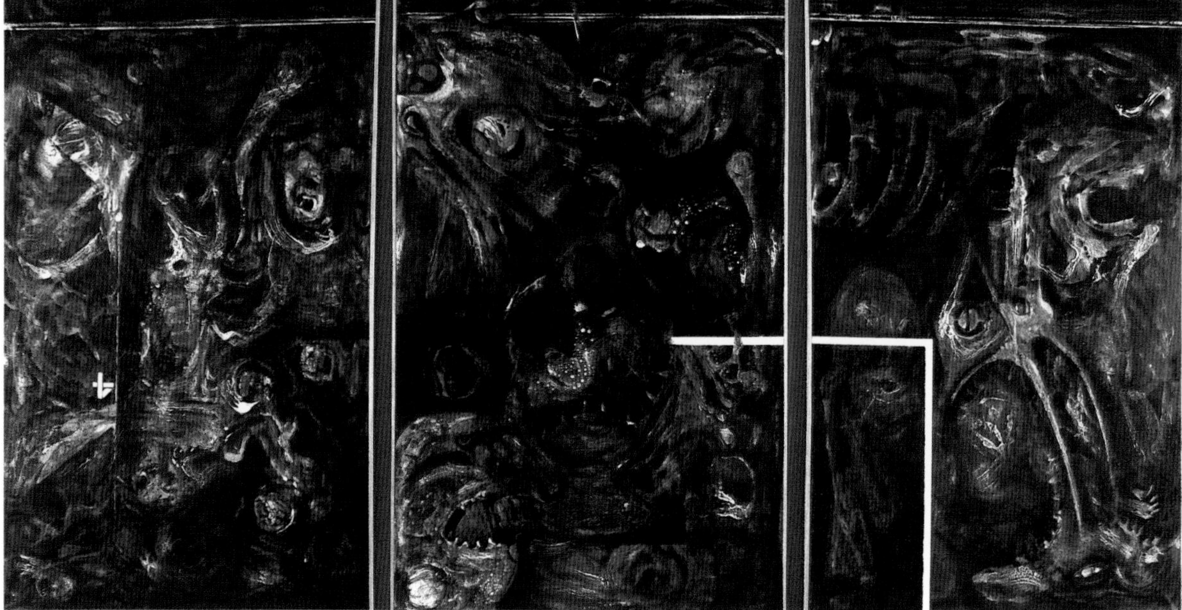

Passage
1977
Mixed media on canvas
49 x 93 in. (three panels)
Courtesy of the A.D. Scott Collection, National Gallery of Jamaica
(facing page)

Pieta
1984
Mixed media on canvas
71 3/4 x 48 in.
Courtesy of the National Gallery of Jamaica

Eric Cadien

Eric Cadien has been described by David Boxer as "a highly charged classicist or a 'cool' expressionist." Cadien's work indeed combines classical restraint and a disciplined sense of structure with the visual language and thematic concerns of modern expressionism. This duality can be attributed to the artist's personality as well as to his educational background. Although Cadien is now best known as a painter, he was initially trained as a sculptor. This background endowed him with a strong plastic sense and a disciplined approach to the formal aspects of his work which is visible even in his most lyrical paintings. As a result of these apparent contradictions, the work of this prolific and versatile Jamaican artist defies easy categorization.

In Eric Cadien's work we see a strong awareness of the work of European and North American modern masters like Picasso, Henry Moore and Giacometti, Willem De Kooning and the artists of the Cobra group—Karel Appel, Corneille and Asger Jorn in particular. Yet Cadien's work is also highly individual and distinctly Jamaican in character. Although he is younger than Jamaican artists like Karl Parboosingh, Eugene Hyde, Winston Patrick, Kofi Kayiga, Milton George or David Boxer, he shares many of the artistic interests of that generation, in the first place a strong commitment to modernism. His work is also akin to that of younger Jamaican artists such as Robert Cookhorne ("African") and Stanford Watson. In fact, Cadien's work illustrates the continuity in the course of Jamaican art while he can be seen as a presursor of recent developments.

—Veerle Poupeye-Rammelaere, 1992

Born: 1954, Trelawny, Jamaica

Education: Kingston College; Jamaica School of Art (now the Edna Manley School for the Visual Arts) 1975; Ontario College of Art, Canada

Died: 1993

Figures in Composition
1992
Acrylic on canvas
15 1/2 x 11 1/2 in.
Courtesy of Janice L. Galbraith

Margaret Chen

In 1981 I began a series of seventeen wall pieces entitled "Steppe." Assembling and glueing, building layer upon layer, scraping, scoring, carving to an inner compulsion that propelled me to work now furiously and spontaneously, at other times slowly and repetitively. That whole process became not only an exploration of the passage of time but also of my roots—an imaginary subterranean journey beneath the Steppes of Asia, of life that was no more and of what remained, accumulating, layer upon layer, vague shadows, nebulous shapes.

It is in hindsight that I became aware of a correspondence and cyclic quality about my work. The "Cross-Section" series, begun in 1988, seems to be a natural progression from the earlier "Steppe" series. The cracked and abraded surfaces continue to be "the imprint and the emblem of passing time."

Born: 1951, St. Catherine, Jamaica

Education: Diploma in Sculpture, Jamaica School of Art, 1976; B.F.A. (1984), M.F.A. (1986), York University, North York, Ontario

Lives: Kingston, Jamaica

Steppe IX
1982
Mixed media on plywood
82 1/2 x 109 1/2 in.
Courtesy of the National Gallery of Jamaica

Albert Chong

The concept of the Thrones for the Ancestors first surfaced in my work in 1981 . . . but did not appear again until 1987. . . . The [first] Throne was a discarded chair that I covered with codfish skin. Codfish assumed a place of importance in my diet as I was a Jamaican living abroad, concerned with maintaining a national identity separate from the mainstream. Cooking the food I grew up with seemed a way of connecting with the past. Salted cod from Newfoundland is an integral ingredient of the Jamaican national dish and was readily available in my neighborhood. On Sundays when I would cook it, I would separate the skin carefully from the flesh. Eventually books, boxes, a walking stick, and the chair were covered with the codfish skin. . . .

The Throne series are found chairs that are embellished and dedicated to ancestral and other spirit forces. [The chairs also refer to] shrines and altars on which to make offerings to elemental forces and to the gods and deities of Africa as they manifested themselves in the new world. Individually, they are used to generate images that refer to the attributes of African gods that made the transition to the "New World" via the consciousness of their devotees who arrived on the shores of the Americas in chains.

Born: 1958, Kingston, Jamaica

Education: B.F.A., Honors, School of Visual Arts, New York, 1981; M.F.A., University of California, San Diego, 1991

Lives: Boulder, Colorado

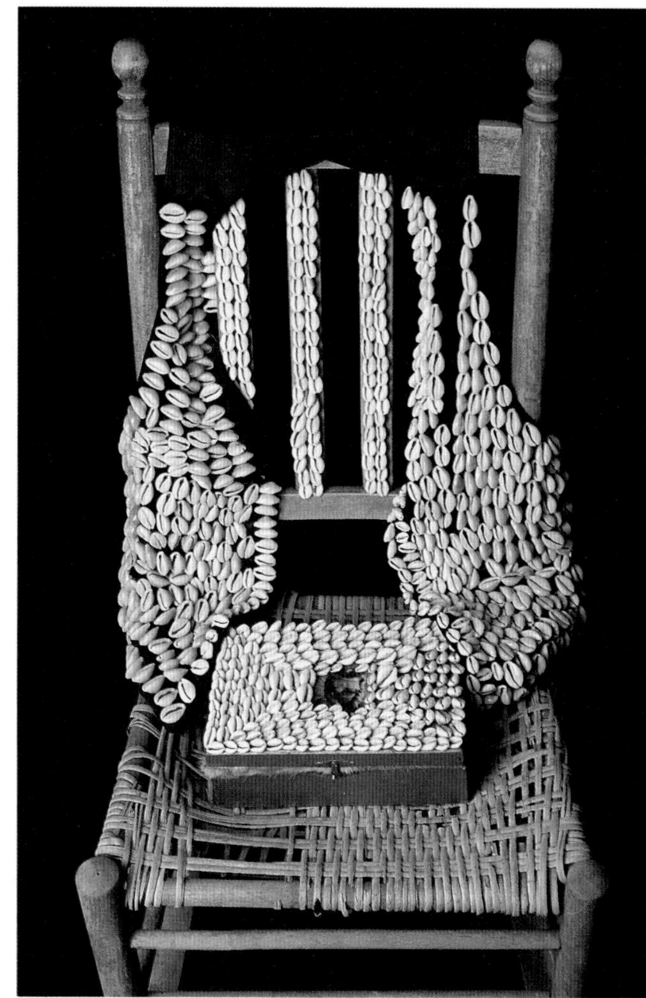

The Cowrie Rocker with Vest, Cowrie Box, and Codfish Book
1994
Chair, shells, codfish skin
34 x 24 x 18 in.
Courtesy of Porter Randall Gallery, La Jolla, California

Codfish Throne with Joshua Tree Spines
1991
Codfish skin, wood, Joshua tree spines
34 x 17 x 16 in.
Courtesy of Porter Randall Gallery, La Jolla, California
(facing page)

Karl "Jerry" Craig

Art to me is the gift to the human race by which man/woman can bear his/her soul and express his/her true inner self. It is the peak of the pyramid of human intelligence. Art is also the greatest universal form of communication because it relies on the visual, the tactile, the spiritual, the emotional, and the inspirational—therefore it crosses all barriers of Race, Religion, and Languages. It has the power to link mankind.

There is no doubt that one's environment coupled with retentions and contemporary cultures of the Caribbean has a direct influence on the works produced.

The rich heritage of the many races, their retentions and cultures have fused to form the people of the Caribbean and together with the great natural beauty of the Islands, have had a direct influence on the artists of the region. It has given us a great wealth of inspiration from which to draw in the creation of the versatility of Caribbean art.

Born: 1936, Montego Bay, Jamaica

Education: Cornwall College, Montego Bay, Jamaica, 1947–1952; St. Martin's School of Art, London, 1953–1957; Maryland Institute, College of Art, Baltimore, 1980–1981

Lives: Kingston, Jamaica, and Miramar, Florida

Islands
1992
Mixed media
51 x 37 in.
Courtesy of the Art Museum of the Americas, Organization of American States, Washington, D.C.

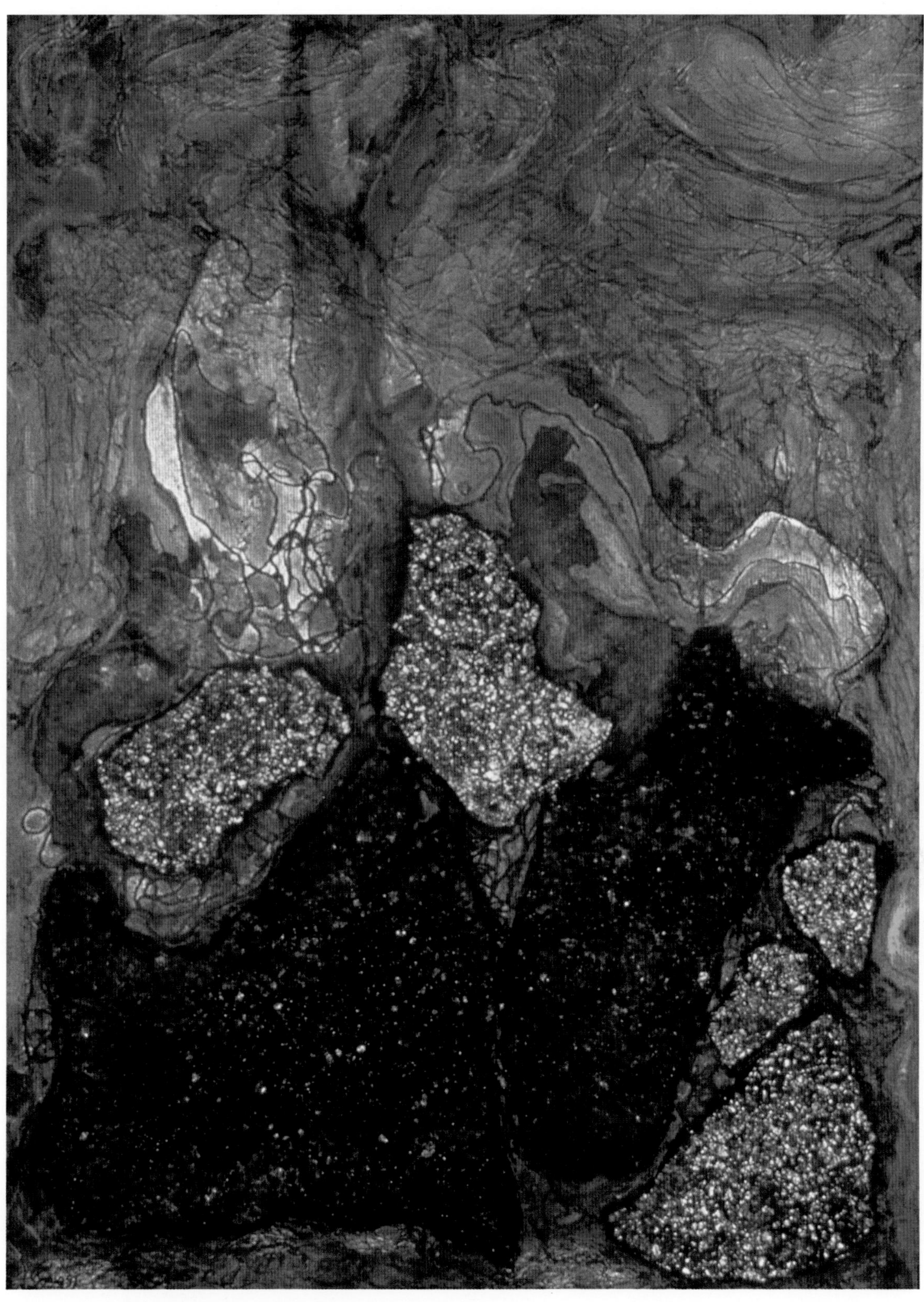

Christopher Gonzalez

Ogotemmeli, symbolized in *The Sage,* was a wise man of the peasant-warrior Dogon tribe in Africa. In his discussions with [the author Marcel] Griaule, Ogotemmeli revealed his tribe's philosophy of the primary importance of the individual and his relationship to society, the universe, and the Divine. This man's words struck a spiritual cord in [me] and created a strong bond of kinship.

It quenched a certain, deep-down, spiritual thirst. It awakened an "ancientcy" that I have always felt in my being. Ogotemmeli—sage, priest, elder, warrior, hunter—expressed "Nommo," "vital force," "creative word," and it became one within me. . . . Since *Sage Ogo,* my works have been dominated by sagehood, so much that critics have said I see myself as a prophet and am presumptuous enough to think I've been specially sent by God. I do accept the fact that I am a unique child of God who loves and worships Him. I also accept the fact that we are all children of God, unique in our individuality and possessing the essence of the sage, with the ability to foretell the future, to heal, to communicate beyond physical limitations. We are evidence of God's greatest miracle in the world.

Born: 1943, Kingston, Jamaica

Education: B.F.A. (1963), Jamaican School of Art, Kingston; M.F.A. (1972), California College of Arts and Craft

Lives: St. Ann, Jamaica

The Tree of Life
(Second version)
1984–1985
Mahogany
23 1/2 x 18 x 21 in.
Courtesy of The Wallace Campbell Collection (on extended loan to the National Gallery of Jamaica)

The Sage
n.d.
Wood
78 x 36 x 4 in.
Courtesy of Mrs. Victoria Durant-Gonzalez
(facing page)

Peter Wayne Lewis

What informs my visual vocabulary is my diverse cultural background, which has its roots in the country of my birth, Jamaica, West Indies. . . . A distinct African, English-Jamaican, subsequently American tradition, and newly discovered Jewish history cannot be denied in my psychological make-up and is undeniably influential in my art making process. . . .

To re-awaken my particular humanity, I am exploring the primitive subconscious mind from the dawn of time through the vehicle of painting. It is a spiritual covenant between me and the higher forces that make up the fabric of time. I want to transcend my limited self of the flesh and work towards my spiritual rejuvenation. This choice of painting the unknown quotient, hopefully, will lead to some sort of residue which holds something of permanent value. My work is about exploring universal layers of life and serves as a comment on the human condition. The arenas of human activity represented in my paintings are birthing, sacrifice, hunting, sex, death, and nature.

I strive only to present reflections of my collective inner world and share some time and space in which individuals find their own answers and inspiration. They are not to inform, but to transform, for they live and die by your gaze.

Born: 1953, Kingston, Jamaica

Education: B.A. Painting (1976), M.A. Painting (1979), San Jose State University, California

Lives: Hoboken, New Jersey

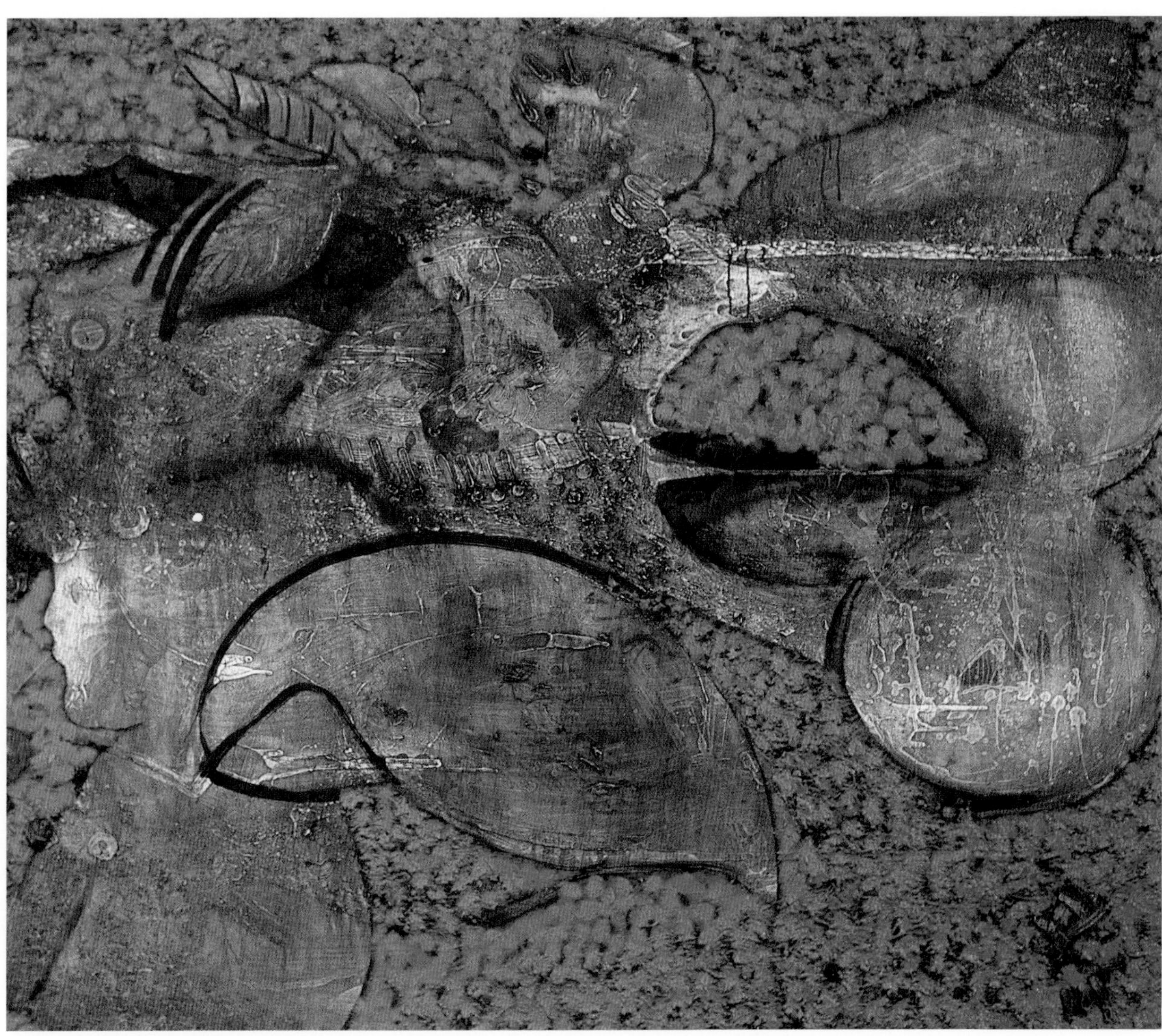

Exterior
1991
Oil on canvas
48 x 66 in.
Courtesy of Mr. Bruce M. Cohen and Ms. Ramona M. Vipperman

Mystic Night
1991
Oil on canvas
54 x 72 in.
Courtesy of the artist
(facing page)

Edna Manley

She was a great and courageous artist who took risks investing in the talents of the young from all walks of life. She understood the artist's need to have total command over inner landscapes. . . . As a sculptor chiseling away at her mahogany and Guatemalan redwood Edna Manley come to learn that the artist is in constant dialogue with her material which now resists the vision the artist has for it, now complies, when the carver's route goes not too much against the grain, finding in the end that harmony of form and feeling, shape and substance. — *Rex Nettleford, 1987*

Born: 1900, Yorkshire, England

Education: Regents Street Polytechnic, London, 1918; St. Martin's School of Art, London, 1919

Died: 1987

The Diggers
1936
Mahogany
37 1/2 x 22 x 1 1/2 in.
Courtesy of the National Gallery of Jamaica

Alvin Marriott

Born: 1902, Essex Hall, St. Andrew, Jamaica

Education: Camberwell School of Art, London, 1940's; self-taught

Died: 1992

Head
1939
Mahogany
18 x 8 x 7 in.
Courtesy of the National Gallery of Jamaica

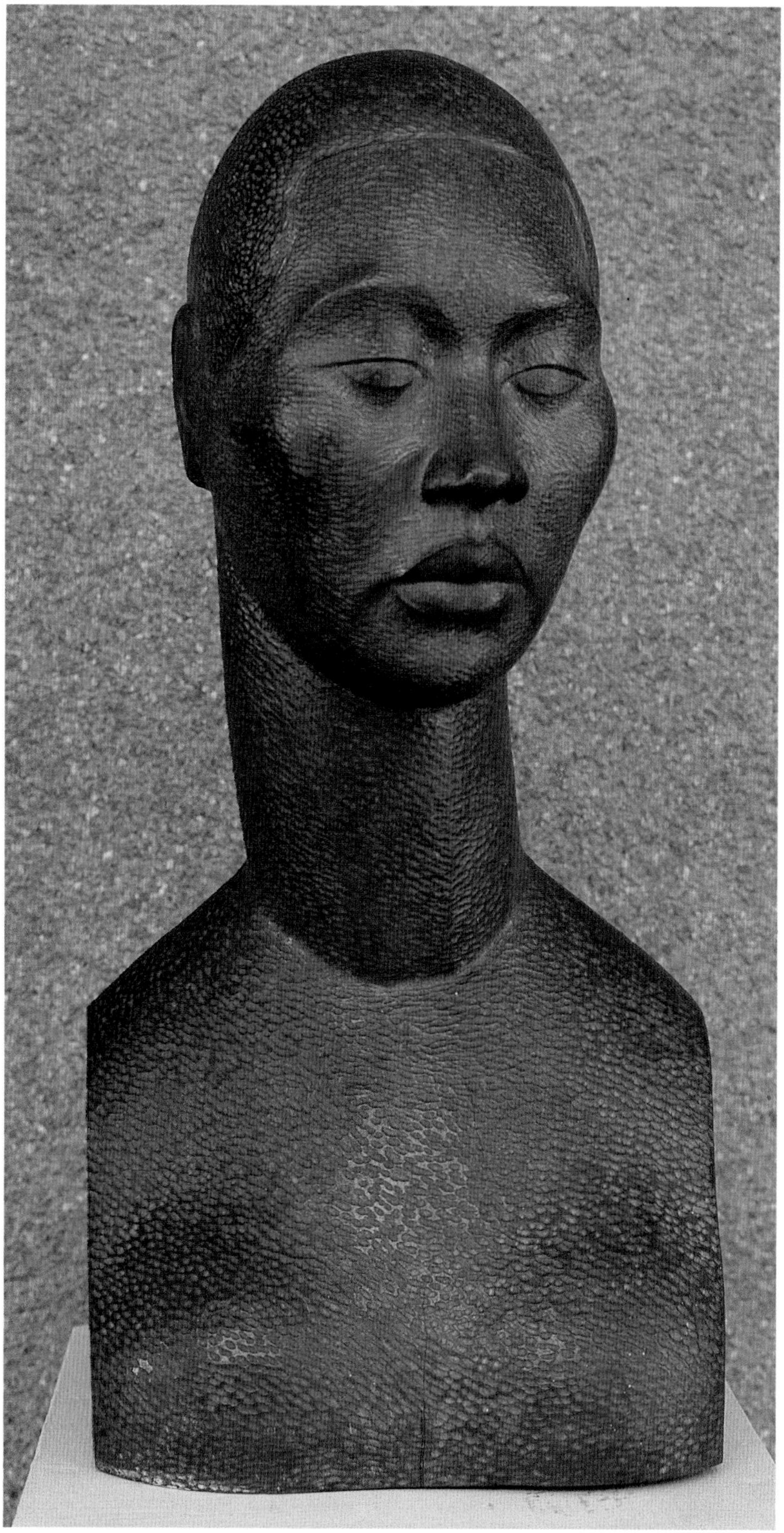

Boysie
1962
Oak
21 x 13 x 9 1/2 in.
Courtesy of the A.D. Scott Collection, National Gallery of Jamaica
(facing page)

Michael M. Milton

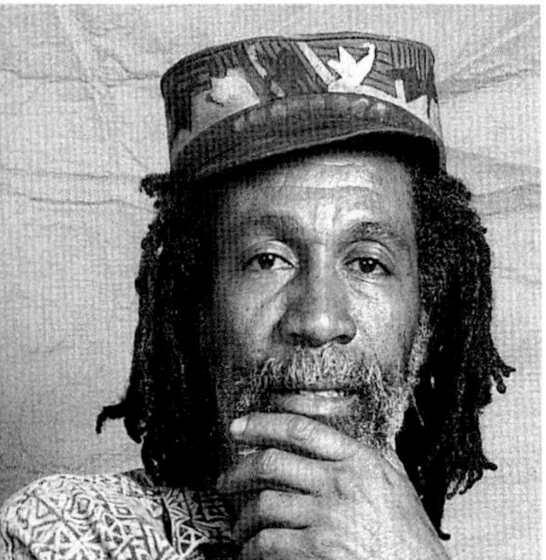

I have made sculptural forms with two strong beliefs that extend from my living in Jamaica. First, I am concerned with the recycling of materials. Being from a place where materials are scarce and expensive, . . . we lived by the code "waste not, want not." Whatever a person needs, that person builds. From living in a big American city, I have found endless supplies of free and interesting materials.

Second, the idea that forms have the power to suggest [influences] . . . the forms I assemble. These forms develop from the supply of materials on hand. Since my method of working is mostly one of construction and addition, I work towards deciding "when it is enough," . . . the poetic charge of finding the end. This notion of forms with powers is implicit in many African cultures. Art created with that kind of intention carries the work beyond [its materials and] how it was made. My influence here is from the mask and the many aspects of tribal architecture.

Born: 1949, Kingston, Jamaica

Education: Art Students League, New York, 1969; B.F.A., School of Visual Arts, New York, 1977; M.F.A., Colorado University, Boulder, 1995

Lives: Boulder, Colorado

Kore Abbrassinia
1992
Wood, oil, copper, leather
84 x 24 x 24 in.
Courtesy of the artist
(right)

C Sharp Minor
1990
Wood and copper
108 x 38 x 15 in.
Courtesy of Myrella Moses
(far right)

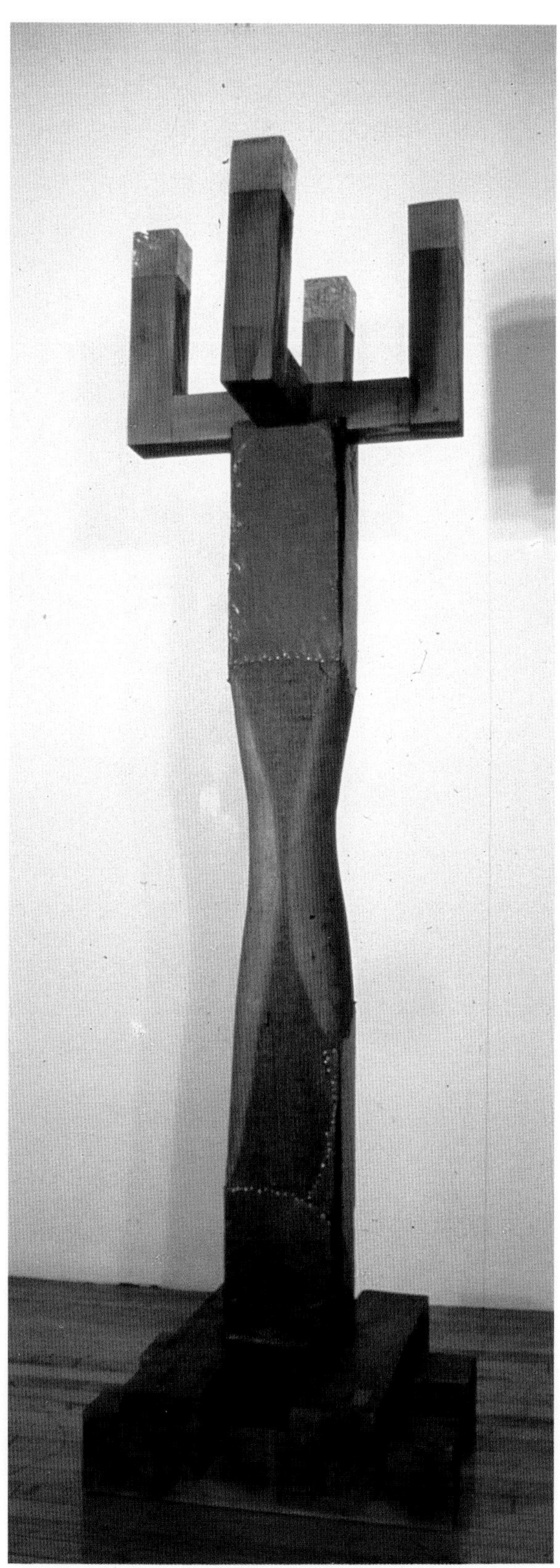

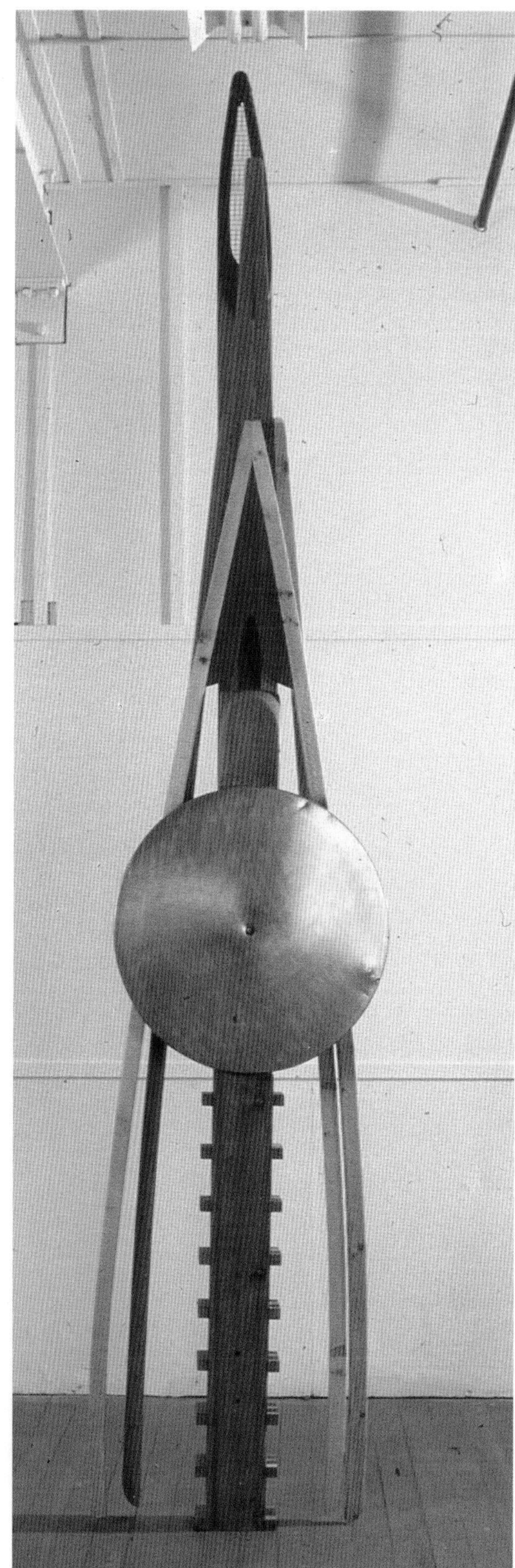

Ronald Moody

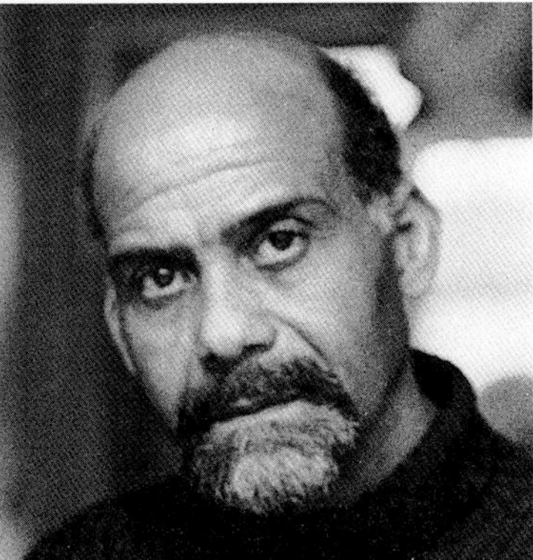

Of the wood sculptures, the head of Richard St. Barbe Baker, the colossal head, *Tacet,* and the huddled squatting figure of *The Onlooker* are memorable. In these days, when more and more artists lean away from the rigours of carving [and toward] the more ingratiating medium of clay, an artist who will commit himself to forms imaginatively projected into the unhewn wood is to be respected. —*Ray Watkinson, 1960*

Born: 1900, Kingston, Jamaica

Education: Calabar College, Jamaica; Kings College, London University

Died: 1984

The Onlooker
1959
Teak
25 5/8 x 12 5/8 x 15 in.
Collection of the artist, courtesy of Cynthia Moody

Keith Morrison

My ideas on art are a mixture of my experiences in the Caribbean and worldwide. I do not try to authenticate these experiences, but to evolve from them a personal lexicon of myths and images which become the stage for my own artistic world. My art is about love, hate, death, and humor, all in conflict. I want to express the full-range of life which I have experienced, with all its truths and contradictions. I want to create paintings which have the epic sweep of novels, which tell stories, allude to history, and which contain the substance of drama, sometimes comic, sometimes tragic, but always portrayed in a poetic way. However, I try to retain a consciousness of the physical art of painting as the guiding psychological presence in my work, by revealing the visceral quality of the pigment I paint with, and by making marks, images, and gestures which interrelate abstractly, even as in other ways they may be more specific. Thus my paintings are not reality; they are paintings, visual images which convey a range of emotion and thought in a philosophical way.

Born: 1942, Linstead, Jamaica

Education: University of Chicago, 1959–1963; B.F.A. (1963), M.F.A. (1965), Art Institute of Chicago; DePaul University, Chicago, 1965–1967; Loyola University, Chicago, 1967

Lives: San Francisco, California

Tombstones
1991
Oil on canvas
62 x 72 in.
Courtesy of the artist

Stafford Schliefer

I think much of my expressionist material reflects an energetic, kinetic, sometimes seemingly frivolous vitality of the most somber subject matter. For example, in the Caribbean mind the Carnival dancer becomes the expressionist symbolism of abandonment of physical restraint, which is usually associated with paternal, everyday behavior and the "well-bred" classes. On Carnival day the tables are turned: a symbolic "gesturing" of sexual freedom is indulged and has perhaps, or would, offend the sensibilities of relatively "somber" or "serious" Eurocentric views. Thusly, the festival vibration may seem lewd and/or disgusting to some moralists or sociologists, but is seen on the lighter side by others as good fun and for laughter of the most genuine kind—the truly ethnoculturally unpretentious.

I am a painter motivated strongly by the concept of "art for art's sake." An artist should express what is really felt. . . . The condition of "feeling" is, of course, associated with "seeing"; the transposition of what is "felt" or "seen" depends on responses relating to the subjective subconscious to be satisfactorily effective. If the basic rules of balancing color, composition, and space are ignored, my product diminishes by an equivalent degree. . . .

Born: 1939, Kingston, Jamaica

Education: Self-taught artist

Lives: St. Andrew, Jamaica

Carnival Dance
1992
Oil on canvas
33 x 24 in.
Courtesy of the artist

Osmond Watson

As an Afro-Caribbean man who resides in the Caribbean and who is faced with Caribbean problems, my philosophy on art is simple. My aim is to glorify Black people through my work with the hope that it will uplift the masses of the region, giving dignity and self-respect where it is needed and to make people more aware of their own beauty. Having said that, it stands to reason that there's no reason for Afro-Caribbean artists to imitate the goings-on of Europe and America, which is not to say that their efforts should not be appreciated and respected. My images of women are either Madonnas, Magdalenes, or Rasta princesses. The men are either Rasta priests, Christ images, or people engaged in everyday activities depicting some form of Afro-Caribbean folklore. My heritage is so rich in folklore there is no fear of exhausting one's chosen material during one's lifetime. An added plus is the constant source of inspiration of national hero Marcus Garvey, whose work is a must for every conscious Black man and freedom fighter. Unfortunately, not all people of African heritage think along these lines, despite the common experience, which means that my views are not overly popular, but be that as it may, I will continue to work to the best of my ability, knowing full well my effort is the best that I am capable of at any given moment in time. It is also my gift to my people and hopefully the world. Enjoy.

Born: 1934, Kingston, Jamaica

Education: Junior Centre Art Classes, 1947–1952; Jamaica School of Art and Craft, 1952–1958; St. Martin's School of Art, London, 1962–1965

Lives: St. Andrew, Jamaica

Peace and Love
1969
Oil on hardboard
17 x 11 1/2 in.
Courtesy of the National Gallery of Jamaica

Revival Kingdom
1969
Wood
54 x 22 x 1 1/2 in.
Courtesy of the National Gallery of Jamaica
(facing page)

Myrna Báez

The major influences on my art have been the Spanish painter Juan Genovés, at the time I was studying at the Academie San Fernando in Madrid, and later, in Puerto Rico, my fellow artists José Antonio Torres Martinó and Lorenzo Homar. During the 1970s, when I spent a year at the Pratt Graphic Center in New York, I became familiar with the paintings, on raw canvas, of the artists of the New York School, an experience which was to change both my graphic work and my painting.

As someone born in Puerto Rico, I have lived and painted things that have to do with Puerto Rico during all my artistic life. I respond to visual effects. Landscapes, people, and interiors are my themes. Light and the way it affects color in the tropics, creating a very special ambience, is a protagonist in my compositions. Color, which is all-pervasive in the tropics, is a strong characteristic of my art.

The elements that appear in my work speak a Caribbean idiom: windows are open, curtains are moved by gentle breezes, and the vegetation is familiar to those of us who have lived in these islands: crotons, palm trees, and mangroves are given pride of place. . . . I try to confront people with their own surroundings, and to present an unaccustomed version of reality. In an attempt to present the observer with his own image, I try to jolt him into viewing things differently.

Born: 1931, San Juan, Puerto Rico

Education: B.S., University of Puerto Rico, 1951; M.A., Royal Academy of San Fernando, Madrid, 1951–1957

Lives: San Juan, Puerto Rico

Retrato de un sueño
(Portrait of a Dream)
1988–1990
Oil on canvas
48 x 58 in.
Courtesy of Galeria Botello, San Juan, Puerto Rico

Entre cortinas (Between Curtains)
1993
Oil on canvas
40 x 54 in.
Courtesy of Galeria Botello, San Juan, Puerto Rico
(facing page)

Diógenes Ballester

The earliest influences on my art were my family, my community, and the natural wonders of the south of Puerto Rico. When I was a boy, my father taught me to make kites and *vejigante* masks and to mix paint. The santos, totems, dolls, and masks on my mother's, aunt's, and grandmother's altars were powerful, magical spirit images to my child's eyes, as were the organic sea forms that crept and washed up on the shores of La Playa. These oneiric images have always found their way to my canvases, whether as realistic aspects, parts of surreal picture stories, or abstractions.

The legacy of my ancestry inclines me toward a method of blending images and ideas with spiritual and emotional expressions. For me it is the lyrical beauty from such syncretic power that gives profound meaning to the notion of harmony. The flow of images and their sensibility connect. This compels me to discover the totality in the painting, to use the chromatic quality and the textural surface, to blend ideas and images into a diverse although unified whole, to capture the flowing and the ethereal quality of spiritual energy.

I synthesize in my paintings various strands of my particular cultural legacy, cohere them into my world view, and project them into my paintings. The narrative abstraction of figures, symbols, and forms which manifest themselves on the canvases upon which I work tell of the Puerto Rican integration of the Afro-Caribbean spiritual knowing that has sustained and nourished my people. This knowing is my source of inspiration, language, and power.

Born: 1956, La Playa de Ponce, Puerto Rico

Education: B.F.A. (1978), Catholic University of Puerto Rico, Ponce; M.F.A. (1986), University of Wisconsin-Madison

Lives: New York City and La Playa de Ponce, Puerto Rico

Reminder of the Spirit
1987–1993
Encaustic on linen
50 x 62 in.
Courtesy of the artist
(facing page)

Magic of the Patchouli II
1993
Encaustic on linen
78 x 48 in.
Courtesy of the artist

María de Mater O'Neill

[María de Mater] O'Neill's *Autorretrato VIII* (1988), from her late 1980s cycle of self-portraits, is a playful reinterpretation of Myrna Báez's *Mujer desnuda frente al espejo.* In contrast to Báez's muted colors and large estranged solitary, dream-like interiors, O'Neill's rendering bursts into an exuberant display of vivid colors and the proliferation of erotically charged icons and enigmatic signs. While Báez's *Mujer desnuda* evokes silence and stillness, *Autorretrato VIII* conveys a noisy flurry of dynamism laced with violence. Oscillating between play and belligerence, this self-portrait seems to be an exercise in unleashed tension, as the mirror image kicks a hole through the bright yellow contemplative figure.
—Ivette Romero-Cesáreo

Born: 1960, San Juan, Puerto Rico

Education: B.F.A., The Cooper Union School of Arts and Science, New York City, 1984

Lives: Miramar, Puerto Rico

Autorretrato VIII
1988
Acrylic, oil stick, oils, and gouache on canvas
76 x 62 in.
Courtesy of the Museum of Contemporary Art of Puerto Rico

CORRECT

Arnaldo Roche Rabell

There [is] a big, huge world inside of me that I decided to investigate. The search led to myself—I tried to visualize how people see me and how I see other people. . . . I decided I had to get out of myself, to relate an inside reality to an outside reality. I decided to do it in a different way from academic artists—who related to the world through their eyes, through looking and translating what they see to paper. I decided just to relate to the world in a physical way. . . .

My intention is to touch people in an emotional and in a physical way. I put them under canvas or paper, and I trace them with my hands, just as I find them. I do not use professional models, but friends—people whom I know or get to know, people who will cooperate with me because they respect me and care for me and for what I am doing. And I give them back my respect and consideration through doing a piece of artwork with them.

Born: 1955, Santurce, Puerto Rico

Education: University of Puerto Rico, 1974–1978; B.F.A. (1982), M.F.A. (1984), School of the Art Institute of Chicago

Lives: Santurce, Puerto Rico

De pronto un eclipse
(Suddenly an Eclipse)
1994
Oil on linen
78 x 78 in.
Courtesy of Galeria Botello, San Juan, Puerto Rico

La sabiduría de la loca
(The Wisdom of the Madwoman)
1991
Oil on canvas
78 x 78 in.
Courtesy of Private Collection, Galeria Botello, San Juan, Puerto Rico
(see p. 4)

Nelson Santiago

My earliest influences in art were the Impressionists. As my works became more of a personal interpretation, I recognized the influence of contemporaries such as Carlos Alfonso and Arnaldo Roche Rabell. The energy of their canvases and the language of their symbols have guided me through my transition. The dichotomy of my background (Puerto Rican) with its American cultural influence is a strong force in my interpretations on the canvas. Yet I feel that my work identifies itself as Caribbean through naive symbols, narrative, color, and my personal view of myself as a "Boricua." My philosophy of art is a synthesis of all naive, outsider, and academic studies transcribed through a personal filter, such as myself.

Born: 1946, Cayey, Puerto Rico

Education: V.P.R., Puerto Rico, 1964–1967; Art Students League, New York City, 1969; Torpedo Factory Art League, Alexandria, Virginia, 1983–1985; Northern Virginia Community College, 1986–1988; Miami Dade Community College, 1988–1989; B.F.A., F.I.U., Florida, 1991–1993

Lives: Miami, Florida

Fantasy of Symbols
1993
Mixed media on canvas
48 x 48 in.
Courtesy of the artist

Crouched Man
1993
Mixed media on canvas
65 x 45 in.
Courtesy of the artist
(facing page)

Juan Carlos Toca

Born: 1966, Rio Piedras, Puerto Rico

Education: Robert Morgan Vocational Technical Institute; Miami Dade Community College

Lives: Miami, Florida

I CREATE

Life abounds me.

I breathe

I see

I touch

I feel

Emotions are stimulated. Inspiration initiated.

I create

Colors, forms, and textures excite me. They become a permanent reminder of who I am.

I am a facilitator

A mirror of time to be appreciated.

I am Toca

Birds of Paradise
1993
Copper
48 x 36 x 36 in.
Courtesy of the artist

Ademola Olugebefola

Simply put, my artistic and life philosophy are one and the same. Everything in the universe is interconnected. There are different levels of active and inert energy in all things, whether it be the color deposited in the paper towels used to wipe my brushes, a glass or plastic fragment found in the street, dried soil from a house plant, or a cowrie shell: they all are used in one form or another and play a significant role in the completed work.

My mind and hands are instruments of higher forces in the universe, therefore I am but a conduit in the circular time continuum. In this solar system we exist in "there is nothing new under the sun," so I believe much of my work is informed with solar biological equations, ancestral power, and metaphysical energy beyond conscious thought or imagination. The viewer or "participant" then becomes an integral part of the reason for the very existence of the work. While I believe the finished object—regardless of medium—has a "life" independent of intellectual cognizance, its supreme purpose is to engage the human senses. For it is only then that my ultimate objective—to reach past the frontal lobes of the mind—and hopefully discover the "oneness" of our humanity is possible.

Born: 1941, Charlotte Amalie, St. Thomas

Education: High School of Fashion Industries, New York; Fashion Institute of Technology, New York; Weusi Academy of Arts and Studies, New York; Bob Blackburn Printmaking Atelier

Lives: New York City

Pyramidical Journey II
1990
Oil, shells, and mixed media
22 1/2 x 17 in.
Courtesy of Grinnell Fine Art Collection

Pyramidical Journey I
1990
Mixed media
22 1/2 x 17 in.
Courtesy of Grinnell Fine Art Collection
(facing page)

Claude Fiddler

Over the past twenty years, Mr. Fiddler's images are symbolic of the pain and blood of African people during the voyage from their homeland into the Americas.

In his travels throughout the United States and Europe, there have been influences that changed the way he now views those images. These changes are due to cultural differences and learning that one can be isolated because of skin color, language, or ancestral descent.

Mr. Fiddler considers life—and all that is associated with it—to be an enigma. "We, as human animals, have been forever cast in the darkness in search of light . . . in search of truth. In reality, all we would like is to know, who we really are; where are we from; and where are we going? Thus . . . I paint." Some of his greatest influences have not been other painters. He has gathered influences from writers such as Derek Walcott, Birago Diop, Mampele, Aimé Césaire, and Uanhenga Xitu. — *the artist*

Born: 1946, Parkhill, St. Vincent

Education: Queens Royal College, Port of Spain, 1965–1968; University of South Florida, Tampa, 1975–1979

Lives: Los Angeles, California

Jack-o-Lantern
Ca. 1994
Oil on canvas
48 x 48 in.
Courtesy of the artist

Firebird
1992
Oil on canvas
60 x 48 in.
Courtesy of the artist
(facing page)

Francisco Cabral

My sculptures were brought into existence in an atmosphere void of limitations, such as language, race, religion, political, or ideological beliefs. . . . I consider this art to transcend visionary speculation. I was born and grew up in the Caribbean, which is made up of French, Spanish, English, and Dutch speaking people, descendants of Spanish, African, Indian, and European settlers, and to a great extent [the Caribbean] represents the world. Hence, I believe my works speak to all the peoples of the world. The works speak with a Caribbean accent derived from a history of colonialism founded on policies of exploitation, slavery, and indentureship, a people deprived of any sense of identity, and it is for these reasons I believe my work has a Caribbean soul. . . .

The individual characteristic of my work derives from the fundamental truth that all of mankind is equal, and the objective is to obliterate all the scars made by political viruses, creating an inoculation against the spread of bitterness and hatred, by expanding the consciousness [and] to live with dignity and pride, justifying one's existence on the face of the earth.

Born: 1949, Port of Spain, Trinidad

Education: Self-taught artist

Lives: Miami, Florida

Zebra Crossing
1989
Wood and steel
126 x 35 x 32 in.
Courtesy of the artist

Horse Power
1989
Mixed media and car parts
40 x 36 x 96 in.
Courtesy of the artist
(facing page)

LeRoy Clarke

I have always believed that "in my father's house, there are many mansions" to be the wisdom of the creation. Its pure form. History can attempt to describe the attempt by others to completely obliterate my house and its people, to the extent that my 'African Mansion' endures as senseless hieroglyphs that lead to a nowhere in memory. . .

My self-imposed duty is to re-chart its ruin, to piece it together from its beginning, to utter the cypher. Eye am El Tucuche, the new Artist, warrior painter-poet, who claims neither name or roof: who will sacrifice child or field; who will utter words like nails stripped from my fingers, each a burning testimony of larva. . . I know nothing else. Can a mango bear an orange?

My art is Obeah. El Tucuche is an Obeahman.

Born: 1938, Port of Spain, Trinidad

Education: Self-taught artist

Lives: Port of Spain, Trinidad

Apotheosis of El Tucuche
1989
Oil on canvas
90 x 60 in.
Courtesy of the artist
(facing page)

Full Moon in Aripo
1988
Oil on canvas
68 x 97 in.
Courtesy of the artist

Pantheon
1992
Oil on canvas
69 x 85 in.
Courtesy of the artist
(see p. 48)

Christopher Cozier

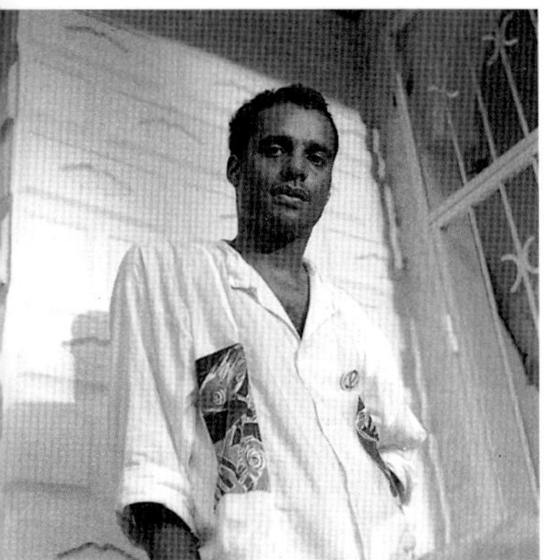

Looking at our idea of painting, there is an irony when one considers that the vigor of our experience and landscape are preserved within 18 x 24 inch glass containers, reconstructed with nineteenth-century European pictorial devices, which are propagated as our most appropriate. . . . The end result is that within a preserved condition there is a preserved convention. . . . There has been a serious dissatisfaction with the existing context and its expectations. This has caused a number of younger artists to investigate other media and situations that are more about responding to how our public space has been transformed. For me, it has been television because television was given to us at Independence in 1962 to usher us into the "modern world" (?). This means that I am the first television generation as well as the first to be schooled under national development policies of the "Rising Nation." So, we went from *The Wind in the Willows* to "Bonanza."

Born: 1959, Port of Spain, Trinidad

Education: J.S. Donaldson Technical Institute, Port of Spain, 1977–1980; B.F.A., The Maryland Institute, College of Art, Baltimore, 1983–1986; Studio Art Centers International, Florence, Italy, 1985; M.F.A., Mason Gross School of the Arts, Rutgers University, New Brunswick, New Jersey, 1986–1988

Lives: Diego Martin, Trinidad

Blue Night
1994
Mixed media on wood
60 x 144 in.
Courtesy of the artist

God
made
me
ALWAYS
ATTENTION

Kenwyn Crichlow

I am a product of the Caribbean with its complex and many-layered history and culture. Coming out of such a region with such a complex temper, a region capable of extreme visual surprises and a region with the widest spectrum of the shades of humanity, I attempt to reflect in my paintings the brown of our earth, the blue-gold of our sky, the aquamarine of our sea, the whiteness of our sand, and the tantalizing exuberance of our people.

Born: 1951, San Fernando, Trinidad

Education: Mausica Teachers' College, 1970–1972; Goldsmith's College, University of London, 1974–1978; University of the West Indies, Kingston, Jamaica, 1992

Lives: St. Augustine, Trinidad

Blue Epic: Silence
1989
Mixed media on canvas
53 1/2 x 59 1/2 in.
Courtesy of the artist

Shastri Maharaj

My artwork proposes to be representative of a Caribbean iconography. In so doing I use my Eurocentric and North American indoctrination of art as a foundation.

A fascination for the mythology of ancient worlds provides greater purpose and meaning for the justification of my visual content. In time I expect that I will approach my artworks with the unpolluted attitude and manner that prevailed in areas of the world that have been untouched by the white man's sensibility.

Born: 1953, Siparia, Trinidad

Education: Naparima Colelge, San Fernando, Trinidad, 1965–1970; Valsayn Teacher's College, 1979–1981; B.F.A., University of Manitoba, Winnipeg, 1982–1985; M.A., University of the West Indies, Trinidad, 1989–1990

Lives: Chaguanas, Trinidad

The Love Letter
1985
Acrylic on canvas
33 x 47 in.
Courtesy of the artist

Wendy M. Nanan

Some Notes on Idyllic Marriage

An Amerindian statue *La Divina Pastora* is worshipped by both Hindus and Catholics in Trinidad at a Catholic church. The hierarchies of both religions disapprove of the mixing of faiths, but this makes no difference to people of all races who share in common a love of idols and rituals in worship. They willingly accommodate the crossover of the cultures.

In this piece La Divina is handed a garland or marriage knot by Krishna. He is teasingly seductive; she is shocked. Both expressions are true to their real images. Perhaps she is shocked by the strangeness of his color and form. . . . We as people merge in Trinidad, accepting the richness of our differences when not separated by the politics of power.

My influences are not from the world of academia but rather from the layers of visual and life experiences of an island society. We can only create as a reaction to the things which make us as we are, and in doing so try to understand the forces which make us artisans of a particular time and space. The images may be Caribbean—temples, bananas, shells, flowers—yet the themes are the quests of people anywhere, anytime—female power and sexuality, time, birth, death and regeneration, politics, and the exploration of the personal animus.

Born: 1955, Port of Spain, Trinidad

Education: B.F.A., Wolverhampton Polytechnic, England, 1979

Lives: Port of Spain, Trinidad

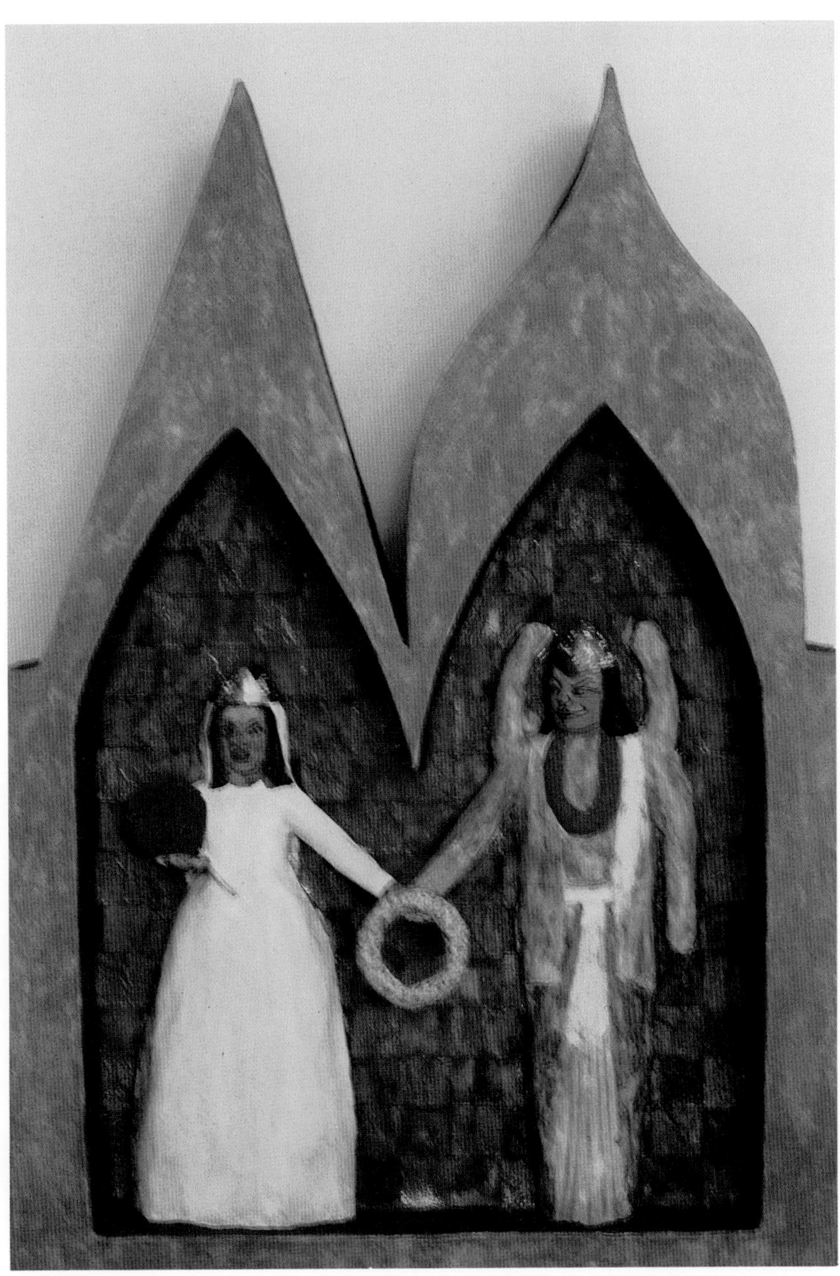

Idyllic Marriage
1989
Mixed media
21 x 14 1/2 x 3 1/4 in.
Courtesy of the artist

Shengé Ka Pharaoh

The images that occupy the paintings of Shengé Ka Pharaoh represent a world of ancestral spirits. Art for Pharaoh is an act of releasing a spirit world which dwells both within people and natural materials. Painting becomes a means of transmitting the presence and power of the invisible, a communicating vessel that holds a flash of recognition between the living and the dead. . . .

Pharaoh's engagement with painting can be seen as a commitment to reinvesting the making of images with cultural practices of spiritual possession. The repetition of figures and forms throughout his work suggests a virtual pictorial transposition of a sensory mode of perception and non-cognitive way towards knowledge. At times, the images appear as virtual gestures made through an immediate bodily contact with the surface of the painting. The circular forms and continuous lines that define and weave together a mosaic of faces or bodies pulse like the rhythms of Afro-Caribbean music, the music of Ska, Reggae, and Calypso. The paintings serve as a kind of visual corollary to the incantational chants or movements of dancers who become possessed by the sound of music. Each form aspires towards generating forces of energy for transformation and change.

—*Charles Merewether, 1991*

Born: 1955, Maraval, Trinidad

Education: Self-taught artist

Lives: New York City

Spirits of the Night
1991–1994
Mixed media on canvas
72 x 68 in.
Courtesy of Todd and Kimberly Kay

Omra
1992–1994
Mixed media on canvas
80 x 81 in.
Courtesy of Todd and Kimberly Kay
(facing page)

Selected Exhibitions of Participating Artists

Ademola Olugebefola

Individual

1991 "25 Year Retrospective of a Virgin Island Artist," Ft. Frederik Museum, Frederiksted, St. Croix
"Legacy/Future," Edith Barrett Gallery, Syracuse University, Utica, New York

1989 "Metaphysical Excursions Harlem Roots," Design Masters Intergroup Galleries, New York City

1986 "New/Ancient Visions," Automation House Gallery, New York City

1978 "New Works on Paper: Corrugated Music," Grinnell Gallery, New York City

Group

1992 "Celebrating African Identity: Icons and Politics of Representation, An International Exhibition," A Space Gallery, Toronto

1990 "Voices Expressing What Is: An Exhibition Against Racism," Westbeth Gallery, New York City

1989 "Black Art, Ancestral Legacy," Dallas Museum of Art, Texas (traveling exhibition)

1988 "Master and Pupils II: The Education of the Black Artist," Jamaica Art Center, Queens, New York

1986 "Art Census USA," Philadelphia Academy of the Fine Arts, Pennsylvania

1985 "Since the Harlem Renaissance," Bucknell University Gallery, Lewisburg, Pennsylvania (traveling exhibition)

1981 CARIFESTA, 4th International Caribbean Festival of the Arts, Barbados

Luis Cruz Azaceta

Individual

1995 "Made on Tchoupitoulas," Sylvia Schmidt Gallery, New Orleans

1994 "Luis Cruz Azaceta: Street Life in America, A Man Caught Between Two Cultures," La Raza/Galeria Posada, Sacramento
"HELL: Luis Cruz Azaceta Selected Works from 1978–93," The Alternative Museum, New York City

1993 "New Paintings from the New Orleans Series," Frumkin/Adams Gallery, New York City
"Crossing," Fredric Snitzer Gallery, Coral Gables
"Biting the Edge," Contemporary Art Center, New Orleans

1992 "Day Without Art," Rhode Island School of Design Museum, Providence

1991 "Obras Selectas: Trayectoria," Galeria Botello, Hato Rey, Puerto Rico

1990 "Luis Cruz Azaceta: The AIDS Epidemic Series," The John and Mable Ringling Museum of Art, Sarasota (traveling exhibition)

Group

1995 "New Orleans Contemporary Artists," La Serre, Lyonnaise de Banque, St. Etienne, France
"Cuba: La Isla Posible," Centro de Cultura de arte contemporaneo, Barcelona, Spain
"1995 New Orleans Triennial," New Orleans Museum of Art, Louisiana
"Civil Rights Now," Southeastern Center of Contemporary Art (SECCA), Winston-Salem (traveling exhibition)

1994 "In Common: Luis Cruz Azaceta, José Bedia, Sandy Winters," Fredric Snitzer Gallery, Coral Gables

1993 "43rd Biennial of Contemporary American Painting," The Corcoran Gallery of Art, Washington, D.C.
"Cuban Artists of the 20th Century," Museum of Art, Fort Lauderdale
"Azaceta, Bedia and Roche," Frumkin/Adams Gallery, New York City

1992 "Latin American Artists of the 20th Century," organized by the Museum of Modern Art, New York City (traveling exhibition)

1989 "Hispanic Art in the United States: Thirty Contemporary Painters and Sculptors," Museum of Fine Arts, Houston (traveling exhibition)

Diógenes Ballester

Individual

1993 "Spiritual Celebration," Museo de Las Americas, Old San Juan, Puerto Rico

1991 "Abstraction of Portraits and Allegories," Catholic University of Puerto Rico, Ponce

1990 "Vulnerability," Interchurch Center Art Gallery, New York City

1989 "Volition," Taller Boricua Gallery, New York City

1986 "Diógenes Ballester: Exhibition in Salute to the VII San Juan Biennial of Latin American and Caribbean Biennial of Printmaking," Multiple Insurance Galleries, Hato Rey, Puerto Rico
"The Struggle," Art Gallery, University of Wisconsin-Madison

1983 "Diógenes Ballester," Puerto Rican Athenaeum Gallery, Old San Juan, Puerto Rico

Group

1993 "The 6th International Biennial of Print and Drawing Exhibit: 1993" R.O.C., Taipei Fine Arts Museum, Taiwan
"Another Perspective: Selections from the Permanent Collection," The Bronx Museum for the Arts, New York
"X Biennial of Latin American and Caribbean Printmaking," Museo del Arsenal La Puntilla, Old San Juan, Puerto Rico

1992 "Recent Acquisitions," Museo del Barrio, New York City

1991 "The South of the World: The Other Contemporary Art," Marsala Museum of Contemporary Art, Italy (also shown in Palermo)

1990 "American Drawing Biennial II," Muscarelle Museum of Arts, College of William and Mary, Williamsburg, Virginia
"A Pure Ancient Spirit," Longwood Art Gallery, Bronx, New York

1989 "International Print Biennial Varna '89," Varna, Bulgaria

José Bedia

Individual

1995 "Mundele Quiere Saber" (White Person Wants to Know), Fredric Snitzer Gallery, Coral Gables

1994 "José Bedia: De Donde Vengo," organized by the Institute of Contemporary Art, University of Pennsylvania, Philadelphia (traveling exhibition)
"Casi Todo Lo Que Es Mio," Fredric Snitzer Gallery, Coral Gables
"José Bedia," Frumkin/Adams Gallery, New York City (also in 1992 and 1991)

1993 "Fabula," Galeria Fernando Quintana, Bogota, Columbia

1991 "Los Presagios," IV Bienal de La Havana, Cuba

Group

1994 "Heroes and Heroines: From Myth to Reality," New Jersey Center for the Visual Arts, Summit
"Points of Interest/Points of Departure," John Berggruen Gallery, San Francisco
"In Common: Luis Cruz Azaceta, José Bedia, Sandy Winters," Fredric Snitzer Gallery, Coral Gables

1993 "Cuban Artists of the 20th Century," Museum of Art, Fort Lauderdale, Florida
"Face of the Gods: Art and Altars of Africa and the African Americas," Museum of African Art, New York City (traveling exhibition)
"Azaceta, Bedia and Roche," Frumkin/Adams Gallery, New York City

1992 "Latin American Artists of the 20th Century," organized by the Museum of Modern Art, New York City (traveling exhibition)
"Migrations: Latin American Art and the Modernist Imagination," Museum of Art, Rhode Island School of Design, Providence

1991 "El Corazon Sangrante/The Bleeding Heart," organized by The Institute of Contemporary Art, Boston (traveling exhibition)

Frank Bowling

Individual

1995 The Cut Gallery, Waterloo, London
AFTU/Bill Hodges Gallery, New York

1993 National Academy of Sciences, Washington, D.C.

1991 Wilmer Jennings at Kenkeleba Gallery, New York

1989 Tibor de Nagy Gallery, New York (also in 1986, 1983, 1982, 1980, 1979, and 1976)
"Bowling through the Decade," The Royal West of England Academy, Bristol, and University Art Gallery, Reading, England

1988 Municipal Art Gallery, Limerick, Ireland
Crawford Art Gallery, Cork, Ireland

1978 "Frank Bowling Retrospective," Polytechnic Art Gallery, Newcastle-upon-Tyne

Group

1994 "Dimensions of Guyana," Camille Love Gallery, Atlanta
"Gala," Brenau University, Gainesville, Georgia

1993 "Landscape as Metaphor: The Transcendental Vision," Fitchburg Museum, Massachusetts (traveling exhibition)

1992 "A/Cross Currents, Synthesis in African American Abstract

Painting," Dakar Biennale, Senegal

1991 "Affinities in Paint," Crane Gallery, London
"In Search of Freedom: African American Abstract Painting 1945–75," Kenkeleba Gallery, New York City (traveling exhibition)

1989 "The Other Story: Afro-Asian Artists in Post-War Britain," Hayward Gallery, London (traveling exhibition)

David Boxer

Individual

1990 "In Situ III: Small Works," The Artist's Studio, Kingston

1988 "In Situ II: Some Persistent Themes," The Artist's Studio, Kingston

1985 "In Situ I," The Artist's Studio, Kingston

1984 "Works on Paper," Frame Centre Gallery, Kingston

1979 Museum of Modern Art of Latin America, Washington, D.C.

Group

1995 1st Johannesburg Biennale, Johannesburg, South Africa

1994 "Arawak Vibrations: Homage to the Jamaican Taíno," National Gallery of Jamaica, Kingston

1992 1st Biennial of Caribbean and Central American Painting, Santo Domingo
"1492/1992 Un Nouveau Regard Sur Les Caraibes," Espace Carpeaux, Courbevoie, France (traveling exhibition)

1990 "Tribute to Jamaica and Puerto Rico," Fondo del Sol Gallery, Washington, D.C.

1987 "Recent Works: David Boxer, Eric Cadien, Robert Cookhorne," Mutual Life Gallery, Kingston

1986 Wifredo Lam Bienale, Havana, Cuba

Ras Ishi Butcher

Group

1994 5th Havana Bienale, Wifredo Lam Centre, Cuba
Preview Exhibition of Santo Domingo Biennial of Painting, Barbados Museum

1993 "Homage to Indigenous People," Pelican Art Gallery
"Carib Art: Contemporary Art from the Caribbean," International Trade Centre, Curacao, The Netherlands Antilles (traveling exhibition)
First Caribbean and Central American Biennial of Painting, Museum of the Americas, Washington, D.C.

1992 "Caribbean and Central American Biennial of Painting," Santo Domingo
"Caribbean Artists Today," Florence, Italy

1991 Caribbean Exhibition, Drexel University, Philadelphia

1990 Barbados Exhibition, Museum of Modern Art of Latin America, Washington, D.C.
International Exhibition, Palais de Congres, Montreal

Francisco Cabral

Individual

1993 Aquarela Galleries, Port of Spain

1992 Museo Arte Moderno, Santo Domingo
Arts Pavilion, "Expo 92," Seville

1991 Royal Victoria Institute (National Museum), Port of Spain
Glasgow Arts Centre, Scotland

1990 Napier Polytechnic, Edinburgh
Crawford Arts Centre, St. Andrews, Scotland

1989 Gallery 1.2.3.4, Port of Spain (also in 1986)

Group

1995 Otro Pais Escalas Africanas, Fundacion "La Caixa," Palma de Mallorca, Spain

1994 Otro Pais Escalas Africanas, Centro Atiantico de Arte Moderno, Las Palmas de Gran Canaria, Spain

1991 Fourth Bienale, National Museum of Fine Arts, Havana

1989 Third Bienale, National Museum of Fine Arts, Havana

1988 Caribbean Invitational, National Gallery of Jamaica, Kingston

Eric Cadien

Individual

1992 Mutual Life Gallery, Kingston, Jamaica (also in 1988, 1987, 1986, and 1985)

1980 Diplomat Gallery, Kingston

1977 Bolivar Gallery, Kingston (also in 1976)

Group

1992 "1492/1992 Un Nouveau Regard Sur Les Caraibes," Espace Carpeaux, Courbevoie, France (traveling exhibition)
"Jamaica to Brooklyn 1992," Salena Gallery, Brooklyn, New York

1991 "Eric Cadien, Gene Pearson," Malraux Gallery, Los Angeles
"Out of Many One People," Virginia Miller Art Gallery, Coral Gables, Florida

1989 "Eric Cadien, Cecil Cooper, Richard Fatta," Contemporary Art Centre, Kingston

1987 "David Boxer, Eric Cadien, Robert 'African' Cookhorne," Mutual Life Gallery, Kingston

María Magdalena Campos-Pons

Individual

1994 "History of People who Were Not Heroes," Bunting Institute of Radcliffe

College, Cambridge, Massachusetts
1993 "Let Me Tell You," INTAR, Latin America Gallery, New York City
"Racially Inscribed Body," Akin Gallery, Boston
1992 "Como el Cuerop de un Homber es un Arbol . . . / How the Body of a Person is a Tree. . .," Gallery La Centrale/Powerhouse, Montreal
1991 "Sangre Negra/Black Blood," Gallery Burning, Montreal
"A Woman at the Border/Una Mujer en la Frontera," SOHO 20 Gallery, New York City

Group

1995 "Latin-American Women Artists, 1915–1995," Milwaukee Art Museum, Wisconsin (traveling exhibition)
"Witness," Leonard and Bina Ellen Art Gallery, Montreal
"Cuba: La Isla Posible," Centro de Cultura de arte contemporaneo, Barcelona, Spain
"Human Nature," New Museum of Contemporary Art, New York City
1994 "Rejoining the Spiritual: The Land in Latin American Art," The Maryland Institute, College of Art, Baltimore
"Transcending the Borders of Memory," Norton Gallery and School of Art, West Palm Beach
1993 "Trade Routes," The New Museum of Contemporary Art, New York City
1992 "Ways to See: New Art from Massachusetts," Institute of Contemporary Art, Boston
"The Year of the White Bear," Walker Center for the Arts, Minneapolis
1991 IV Bienale de La Havana, National Museum of Fine Arts, Cuba
"El Corazon Sangrante/The Bleeding Heart," organized by The Institute of Contemporary Art, Boston (traveling exhibition)

Dudley Charles

Individual

1993 Skoto Gallery for Contemporary African Art, Soho, New York
1992 Kallon Gallery, Stanford, Connecticut
1990 Watermark/Cargo Gallery, Kingston, New York
1989 Guyana Embassy, Washington, D.C.
1988 Guyana National Museum, Georgetown

Group

1992 Eleventh Caribbean Arts and Humanities Festival, Medgar Evans College, Brooklyn, New York
1991 "Art of Guyana: Celebrating Twenty-five Years of Independence," Martin Luther King Memorial Library, Washington, D.C.
1989 "Art from Guyana: Painter and Sculptor," Eudora Welty Library, Jackson, Mississippi
1988 "Abstract Attitudes: Contemporary Guyanese Artists in America," Gallery 843, Brooklyn, New York
1987 Roots and Culture Art Gallery, Georgetown, Guyana

Margaret Chen

Individual

1990 "Cross Section," Upstairs Downstairs Gallery, Kingston
1986 "Pentimento," IDA Gallery, York University, North York, Ontario
1984 "Temporal Vessel," York University, North York, Ontario

Group

1994 "Arawak Vibrations: Homage to the Jamaican Taíno," National Gallery of Jamaica, Kingston
"Contemporary Works," Frame Centre Gallery, Kingston
Santo Domingo Biennial of Painting, Galerie de Arte Moderno, Santo Domingo (also in 1992)
"Annual National Exhibition," National Gallery of Jamaica, Kingston (also in 1993, 1992, 1991, 1990, and 1988)
1992 "Jamaica to Brooklyn 1992," Salena Gallery, Brooklyn, New York
"1492/1992 Un Nouveau Regard Sur Les Caraibes," Espace Carpeaux, Courbevoie, France (traveling exhibition)
1991 "Aspects VIII: 8 Jamaican Avant Garde Artists," National Gallery of Jamaica, Kingston

Albert Chong

Individual

1995 "Albert Chong: Photographs from Ancestral Dialogues," Cleveland Museum of Art, Ohio
"Selections: Photographs by Albert Chong," Artscene, Lamar Community College, Lamar, Colorado
1994 "Yard: A Jamaican Portrait," Chelsea Galleries, Kingston
"Yin/Yang, Us/Them," La Torre de Tejuana, Mexico, InSite 94
"Albert Chong: Works from Ancestral Dialogues," Ansel Adams Center for Photography
1991 "Homecoming: New Photography," Chelsea Galleries, Kingston

Group

1995 "Africus," 1st Johannesburg Biennial, Johannesburg, South Africa

“Still/Life: The Body as Object in Contemporary Photography,” Americas Society Art Gallery, New York City
1994 “Imagining Families: Images and Voices,” National Museum of African Art, Smithsonian Institution, Washington, D.C.
5th Havana Bienale, Wifredo Lam Centre, National Museum of Fine Arts, Cuba
1993 “Inside the Black Experience,” Union Gallery, University of Arizona, Tucson
“Ritos en Vivo” (Living Rites), Carla Stellweg Latin American and Contemporary Art, New York City
1992 “Jamaica to Brooklyn 1992,” Salena Gallery, Brooklyn, New York
“Images and Objects,” Porter Randall Gallery, La Jolla, California
1991 “The Pleasures and Terrors of Domestic Comfort,” Museum of Modern Art, New York (traveling exhibition)
1990 “The Decade Show,” The New Museum of Contemporary Art, New York City

José García Cordero

Individual

1994 “Gardens of Delirium,” Lumbreras-Fisher Fine Art, Coral Gables
Art Miami ‘94, Miami Beach
1993 “García Cordero and his extramodern friends,” Museum of Modern Art, Santo Domingo
“Still Life,” Galería Atelier Gazcue, Santo Domingo
1992 Galerie Municipal, Vitry-sur-Seine
1991 Museum “La Puntilla,” San Juan
Espace “Dilema,” Paris (also in 1990, 1989, and 1988)
Galería de la Casa del Teatro, Santo Domingo (also in 1990)

Group

1993 Javier Lumbreras Fine Art, Coral Gables, Florida
1992 Biennial of Visual Arts, Santo Domingo (also in 1990, 1983, and 1979)
1991 “Novembre a Vitry,” Vitry-sur-Seine
1987 “Coltar,” Pont-Aven (also in 1986)

Christopher Cozier

Individual

1994 “Blue Soap” (video installation), Aquarela Galeries, Port of Spain
1992 “Analysis of a Tamarind Rod” (performance), Crossover Design, Port of Spain
“New Works,” Aquarela Galeries, Port of Spain
“Conversation with a Shirt Jac about Art” (performance), Barbados Museum and Historical Society, Bridgetown

Group

1994 Second Biennial of Painting of the Caribbean and Central America, Museum of Modern Art, Santo Domingo
5th Havana Bienale, Cuba
1992 “Alternative Expressions,” CARIFESTA 5, Port of Spain
“1492/1992 Un Nouveau Regard Sur Les Caraibes,” Espace Carpeaux, Courbevoie, France (traveling exhibition)
1988 “From Myth and Experience: Three Caribbean Artists,” Gallery Caribe, Philadelphia

Jerry “Karl” Craig

Individual

1992 Studio Exhibition, Tankerville Avenue, Kingston
1991 Museum of Modern Art of Latin America, Washington, D.C.
1990 Gallery des Artistes, West Palm Beach, Florida
1986 Frame Centre Gallery, Kingston

Group

1994 “The Forerunners,” Mutual Life 150th Anniversary, Mutual Life Gallery, Kingston
1993 “Four Jamaican Artists,” Frame Centre Gallery, Kingston
1992 Biennial of Latin American and Caribbean Visual Arts, Santo Domingo
1991 “50 Masters of Latin America and the Caribbean,” Nagoya Museum, Japan
“Jamaican Abstracts,” Galerie Malraux, Los Angeles
1990 “Jamaican Light,” Chelsea Gallery, Kingston

Kenwyn Crichlow

Individual

1992 “The Blue Epic,” St. George’s, Grenada
1991 “The Blue Epic,” Gallery 1.2.3.4., Port of Spain
1989 I.F.A. Gallery, Bonn
1986 Commonwealth Institute, London

Group

1992 CARIFESTA, Gallery 1.2.3.4., Port of Spain
“Contemporary Art in Trinidad,” October Gallery, London
Bienal of Caribbean Art, Museo del Arte Moderno, Santo Domingo

Annalee Davis

Individual

1990 “Woman-Scream Niche,” Barbados Museum, Bridgetown
1989 “I Wish You Would Hair Me,” Mason Gross School of Visual Arts, Rutgers, State

University of New Jersey, New Brunswick
1988 Caribbean Invitational I, National Gallery of Jamaica, Kingston

Group

1994 22nd Bienal Internacional de Sao Paulo, Brazil
2nd Bienal of Caribbean and Latin America, Museo de Arte Moderno, Santo Domingo
IV Bienal Internacional de Pintura, Cuenca, Ecuador
Festival International de la Peinture, Chateau-Musée Grimaldi, Cagnes-sur-Mer, France
1993 "Carib Art: Contemporary Art from the Caribbean," International Trade Centre, Curacao, The Netherlands Antilles (traveling exhibition)
1992 "Biennial of Painting of the Caribbean and Central America," Museo de Arte Moderno, Santo Domingo
"Art over Sugar," Vaucluse Sugar Cane Factory, Barbados
"1492/1992 Un Nouveau Regard Sur Les Caraibes," Espace Carpeaux, Courbevoie, France (traveling exhibition)
1991 "The Circle and the Abyss," South Gallery, Rutgers, State University of New Jersey, New Brunswick

Philippe Dodard

Individual

1994 "Soir d'encrier," Heim America, Fisher Island, Florida, with Galerie Marassa
1993 "The Spirit in Haiti," Gallery Lakaye, Los Angeles
1992 Art Miami '92, Miami, Florida
1990 "Mask, Mirror, and Totem," Margareth Porter Public Relations, New York City

Group

1995 "Haitian Contemporary Art," Centre Wifredo Lam, Havana
"Bridging Continent: Connecting African and Latin American Art," Aldo Castillo Gallery, Chicago
1994 IV Bienal Internacional de Pintura, Cuenca, Ecuador
1993 "500 Years After: Caribbean and Central American Painting," Art Museum of the Americas, Washington, D.C.
"Carib Art: Contemporary Art from the Caribbean," International Trade Centre, Curacao, The Netherlands Antilles (traveling exhibition)
1992 CARIFESTA V, Port of Spain
"Biennial of Painting of the Caribbean and Central America," Museo de Arte Moderno, Santo Domingo
1991 "Visions III" (with Tiga and Ronald Mevs), Galerie Armand and Galerie Marassa, Paris
1990 Design Center of the Americas, Dania, Florida

Edouard Duval Carrié

Individual

1994 "Le Jardin Sauvage," Fernando Quintana Gallery, Bogota, Columbia
Porter Randall Gallery, San Diego
1993 Installation of 23 sculptures and 3 murals in temple of the Dagbo Hou Non, highest spiritual leader in Ouidah, Benin, for first Vaudoun Cultures Festival
1991 Malraux Gallery, Los Angeles
Galerie Armand, Paris

Group

1995 "Trees" (project director), Ground Level Gallery, South Florida Art Center, Miami Beach
1994 "La Foret Sacrée," installation at Organization of American States, Washington, D.C., to celebrate anniversary of new Haitian constitution
"After Nature," Center of Contemporary Art, Miami
"Pinturerias: El Arte del Arte Taurino," Fundacion Cultural Artension, Palacio de Bellas Artes, Mexico
1993 "Storytelling: Narrative in Latin American Art," COCA, Miami
Gallery Gutierrez Fine Arts, Miami Beach
"La Peintres Marron," Chateau des Ducs de Bretagne, Nantes
1992 "Schwarze Freiheit im Dialog," project for Culture Cooperation and the Galerie der Handwerskammer, Hamburg, Germany
"Paris Connections," Bomani Gallery, San Francisco
1990 Ecole des Beaux Arts, Lille, France
Lemoyne-Owens College and Shelby State University, Memphis
Galerie Nationale, Dakar, Senegal

Tomás Esson

Individual

1993 "Chá-Chá-Chá," Galeria Ramis Barquet at Art Cologne Internationaler Kunstmarkt
"A Tarro Partido III," Fredric Snitzer Gallery, Coral Gables
1991 "¡Que Calor!" Fredric Snitzer Gallery, Coral Gables
1988 "A Tarro Partido II," Centro de Arte 23 y 12, Havana (exhibition censured and closed by authorities)
"ESSONSISEHACE," Instituto Superior de Arte, Havana

1987	"A Tarro Partido," Museo Provincial de Villa Clara, Santa Clara, Cuba

Group

1995	"Cuba: La Isla Posible," Centre de Cultura Contemporánia de Barcelona, Spain
	"Premio Marco 1994," Museo de Arte Contemporaneo de Monterrey, Mexico
1993	"Bad Aim," Porter Randall Gallery, La Jolla
	"Prospect 93," Kunsthalle, Frankfurt, Germany
	"4 Cubans Today," Iturralde Gallery, Los Angeles
1992	"Aquì Arte Hispano en Orlando," City Hall, Orlando
	"Cuatro Que Se Fueron," Osuna Gallery, Washington, D.C.
1991	"De Cubaanse Renaissance," Maatschappij Arti et Amicitiae, Amsterdam (artist removed from exhibition under pressure from Communist government of Cuba)

Claude Fiddler

Individual

1994	Edison Community College, Ft. Meyers, Florida
1993	Off the Wall of Time Fine Art Gallery, Los Angeles
1992	Malraux Gallery, Los Angeles
1986	Eitharong Gallery, Orlando

Group

1995	Tampa Museum of Art, Florida
1994	University of Houston, Texas
	San Francisco State University, California
1993	Wadsworth Atheneum, Hartford, Connecticut
1992	Florida Gulf Coast Art Center, Belleaire
1991	Hampton Museum of Art, Virginia

Lia Galletti

Individual

1994	"Legal Eyes," Miami
1993	"Footprints," RIU Pan American Ocean Resort, Miami Beach
	"Orisha," Frame Centre Gallery, Kingston
	"The White Hand" and "Polka-Dot Heart" (installations), Washington, D.C.
1992	"Ego Works" (installation), Coral Gables, Florida

Group

1993	"The Cards are on the Table," Florida International University, Miami
	"In the Eyes of the Beholder," Miami-Dade Public Library System, Miami
1992	Darmay Art Gallery, San José, Costa Rica
	Vatican Biennial, Buenos Aires, Argentina
	"Genesis: 3 Artists for AIDS Benefit," Center for the Fine Arts, Miami
1991	"Rostros en Miami," Memphis Gallery, Miami
1987	"Cuban Artists in North America," National Library of Canada, Ottawa
	"Contemporary Cuban Art," Metropolitan Museum of Coral Gables

Christopher Gonzalez

Individual

1995	Mutual Life Gallery, Kingston (also in 1991, 1989, 1986, and 1983)
1988	Frame Centre Gallery, Kingston

Group

1989	"Reunion," Bay Gallery, Montego Bay
1985	"Jamaican Art 1922–1982," organized by the Smithsonian Institution Traveling Exhibition Service (SITES), Washington, D.C., and the National Gallery of Jamaica, Kingston (traveling exhibition)
	Upstairs Downstairs Gallery, Kingston
1980	Chi-Wara Gallery, Atlanta

Stanley Greaves

Has exhibited extensively in Guyana (1950–1985) and in Barbados (1987 to present day). Work also exhibited in Venezuela, Canada, the United States, the United Kingdom, and France. Has participated in Biennials held in Brazil, Colombia, Cuba, and the Dominican Republic, as well as CARIFESTA exhibitions in Guyana, Jamaica, Cuba, Barbados, and Trinidad.

Gregory A. Henry

Individual

1995	"Fancy Yard Series," Medical College of Virginia
1994	"Synthesis: Paintings and Sculpture by Greg Henry," Hampton University Museum, Virginia
1993	Roanoke Museum of Art, Virginia
1992	Pungo Art Gallery, Virginia Beach
1991	Meredith Art Gallery, Virginia State University
1990	Virginia Beach Center for the Arts, Virginia Beach

Group

1995	"Eight Paths to a Journey," organized by the Virginia Museum of Fine Arts, Richmond (traveling exhibition)
1994	Mabey Art Gallery, Richmond, Virginia (also in 1993)
	On the Hill Gallery, Yorktown, Virginia
1993	"New Regional Paintings II," Moody Art Gallery, University of Alabama
1991	Jamaica Arts Center, Jamaica, Queens, New York
	"Artists Who Teach," Charles Taylor Art Center, Hampton, Virginia
	"Dimensions of African Americans," Open Space

Gallery, Yorktown Art Center, Virginia

1990 "Next Generation: Southern Black Aesthetics," organized by the Southeastern Center of Contemporary Art (SECCA), Winston-Salem, North Carolina (traveling exhibition)

"Trends and Traditions in Modern Art," University of Virginia, Charlottesville

Bendel Hydes

Individual

1995 "Homage to Cayos Miskitos," National Cultural Foundation, Cayman Islands

1991 Clark University, Worcester, Massachusetts

1990 "Bendel Hydes Offshore," Bettal Gallery, New York City

1986 "New Paintings," Commonwealth Institute, London

"New Paintings," Cayman National Theatre, Cayman Islands

Group

1995 CARIFESTA VI, Caribbean Festival of the Arts, Port of Spain

"Carib Art," Harquail Cultural Center, Cayman Islands (traveling exhibition)

1994 "Caribbean and Central American Painting Today," Museo de Las Americas, San Juan

"Spellbound," Blondies Contemporary Art, New York City

Sound Shore Gallery, Stamford, Connecticut

1993 "500 Years After: Caribbean and Central American Painting," Art Museum of the Americas, Washington, D.C.

"Carib Art: Contemporary Art from the Caribbean," International Trade Centre, Curacao, The Netherlands Antilles (traveling exhibition)

1992 "Abstract Art in the 90's: Where is it at? Where is it going?" Sound Shore Gallery, Stamford, Connecticut

"First Caribbean and Latin American Bienale of Painting," Museo de Arte Moderno, Santo Domingo

"Caymanian Art," National Museum of the Cayman Islands, Grand Cayman

1991 "Emerging Artists," Kenkeleba Gallery, New York City

"The South of the World: The Other Contemporary Art," Marsala Museum of Contemporary Art, Italy (also shown in Palermo)

1990 "22nd National Painting Exhibition," Washington and Jefferson College, Washington, Pennsylvania

Andre Juste

Individual

1994 "Double Vision," Westchester Community College, Valhalla, New York

1992 "Builders of Gods: New Relief Paintings," The Atrium at RAE Park, Peekskill, New York

"Public Execution," Jan Peek Square, Peekskill, New York

"Weaving a Metaphor: Collages and Drawings," Temple Israel of Northern Westchester, Croton, New York

1990 "Seven Works: Large Scale Relief Paintings," The Atrium at RAE Park, Peekskill, New York

Group

1994 "In Search of the Spirit," Hastings Gallery, Hastings, New York

"Spells and Incantations," Deitrich Contemporary Art, New York City

1993 "Americans All: Conversations Between Cultures," Reader's Digest, Chappaqua, New York

1991 "The South of the World: The Other Contemporary Art," Marsala Museum of Contemporary Art, Italy (also shown in Palermo)

1990 "Cardinal Points and Points Between," Kenkeleba Gallery, New York City

"Artist in the Market Place," The Bronx Museum of the Arts, Bronx, New York

Gwen Knight

Individual

1994 Francine Seders Gallery, Seattle (also in 1987 and 1977)

1988 Virginia Lacy Jones Gallery, Atlanta University Center, Georgia

Group

1995 "Women Across the Arts," Washington State Convention and Trade Center, Seattle

"Richness in Diversity," SAFECO, Seattle

1994 "Contemporary African American Artists," The St. Paul Companies, St. Paul, Minnesota

1993 "African American Eclectic," Security Pacific Gallery, Seattle

"Significant Others: Artist Wives of Artists," Kraushaar Galleries, New York

1992 "It Figures, The Human Image in Art," Index Gallery, Clark College, Vancouver, Washington

1991 "Please and Thank Yous, True Stories," Galleria Potatohead, Seattle (traveling exhibition)

1990 "Works on Paper and Canvas: Multi-Cultural Perspectives," Washington State Capital Museum, Olympia

Peter Wayne Lewis

Individual

1995 "Blue Swan Suite Paintings," Rosenberg + Kaufman Fine Art, New York City
"Black Swan Suite Paintings," Frederick Spratt Gallery, San Jose

1994 "Sumerian Farewell Paintings," Frederick Spratt Gallery, San Jose

1993 "Stammtisch Paintings," Kunst/Raum, Stuttgart
"Koto Cycle Works," A & M Art Gallery, Chiba, Japan

1992 "Paintings," Kunsthaus Ostbayern, Viechtach, Germany
"Paintings," d.p. Fong and Spratt Galleries, San Jose

1990 "Works on Paper," Kunsthaus Ostbayern, Viechtach, Germany

Group

1994 Biennial of Caribbean and Latin American Painting, Museo de Arte Moderno, Santo Domingo
"Exhibition to Honor Dr. Maya Angelou," National Arts Club, New York City

1993 "The Tenth Summer," Stephen Rosenberg Gallery, New York City
"Bay Area Prints," Amerika Haus Stuttgart, Germany

1992 Walter/McBean Gallery, San Francisco Art Institute

1991 "Peter Lewis, Bert Yarborough and Far Field Artists," Toyota Corporation, Toyota, Japan
"Pacific Rim Art Now, 1991," Otaru Municipal Art Museum, Sapporo

1990 "Art Document '90 in Hokkaido," Hokkaido Museum of Modern Art, Sapporo
"Positive Actions/Visual Aid," The Institute for Contemporary Art, New York City

Ronald Moody

Individual

1961 "Ronald Moody," Woodstock Gallery, London

1960 "Ronald Moody: Sculpture," Woodstock Gallery, London

1950 "The Works of Ronald Moody," Galerie Apollinaire, London

1946 "Sculpture by Ronald C. Moody," Arcade Gallery, London

Group

1965 Society of Portrait Sculptors 13th Annual Exhibition, London (participated in nearly all of the Society's annual exhibitions since 1954)

1964 "The Portrait in the Round," Society of Portrait Sculptors, London

1963 Royal Academy of Arts 195th Summer Exhibition, London

1962 National Society 29th Show at the Royal Institute Galleries, London

1960 "Festival of West Indian Art and Craft," Leicestershire Museums and Art Gallery, England

1959 Kensington Artists 8th Annual Exhibition (participated in its annual exhibitions since 1953)

Keith Morrison

Individual

1991 Brody's Gallery, Washington, D.C. (also in 1987)

1990 Alternative Museum, New York City
Fondo del Sol Gallery, Washington, D.C.

Group

1994 "Free Within Ourselves," National Museum of American Art, Smithsonian Institution, Washington, D.C.
"Post-Colonial California," San Francisco State University
Parrish Gallery, Washington, D.C.

1993 Brandywine Graphic Workshop, Philadelphia
Cavin-Morris Gallery, New York City

1992 Isobel Neal Gallery, Chicago
Museum of Modern Art, Monterrey, Mexico

1991 "Artists of Conscience," Alternative Museum, New York City
"Myth and Magic in the Americas: The Eighties," Museum of Modern Art, Monterrey, Mexico

1989 "The Blues Aesthetics," Washington Project for the Arts, Washington, D.C.
"Art by Americans and Brazilians of African Descent," California Afro-American Museum, Los Angeles

José Perdomo

Individual

1993 "José Perdomo," Praxis Arte Internacional, Santo Domingo

1991 "José Perdomo y una exposicion de signos memorables," Sala de Arte y Cultura, Universidad Autonoma de Santo Domingo

1990 "Homenaje a los Hijos del Sol," Galería Nacional de Arte Moderno, Santo Domingo
"La Búsqueda del Origen Perdido," Fundación Internacional de Arte, Galería Praxis, Lima, Peru

1989 "Trópico 87–89," Museo de las Casas Reales, Casa de Bastida, Santo Domingo

1988 "Serie Trópico," Fundación Internacional de Arte Praxis, Galería Praxis, Lima

1987 "José Perdomo 20 años de pintura," Instituto Dominicano de Cultura Hispánica y Galería Boinayel Muestra Antológica, Santo Domingo

Shengé Ka Pharoah

Individual

1991 Galeria Ramis Barquet, Monterrey, Mexico
Vrej Baghoomian Gallery, New York City (also in 1990 and 1989)

1987 Turske Whitney, Los Angeles

1986 Tirske and Turske, Zurich

Group

1994 Lower East Side Museum, New York City

1993 Carl Hammer Gallery, Chicago

1992 "Emerging Latin American Artists," Carla Stellweg Latin American and Contemporary Art, New York City
"Uncommon Ground: 23 Latin American Artists," College Art Gallery, State University of New York (SUNY), New Paltz

1991 "Myth and Magic in the Americas: The Eighties," Museum of Contemporary Art, Monterrey

Genaro Phillips

Individual

1988 "Tropica y Jungla," Arawak Art Gallery, Santo Domingo

1987 "Reminiscencias Tropicales," International University of Puerto Rico, San Juan

1985 "Cuando la Noche Cae Sobre los Ingenios y los Bueyes Desaparecen" (When the Night Falls on the Sugar Mills and the Oxen Disappear), Museum of Royal Houses, Santo Domingo
"En Torno al Folclor" (About Folklore), National University of Pedro Henriquez Urena, Santo Domingo

Group

1989 "Primer Festival de Las Artes Plásticas" (First Festival of Fine Arts), Gallery of Modern Art, Santo Domingo

1988 "100 Años de la Pintura Dominicana," Museum of Royal Houses, Santo Domingo

1986 "Exposición de Miniaturas, Inauguración Galeria '80" (Exhibition of Miniatures, Inauguration of Gallery '80), Gallery of Art '80, Santo Domingo
"Exposición Colective an Higüey," Art Gallery Higüey, Higüey, Dominican Republic

1985 "Exposición por la Paz" (Exhibition for Peace), National Library, Santo Domingo
"Exposición Año de la Juventud" (Year of the Youth Exhibition), National Archives, Santo Domingo

1984 "Exposición Genración '80, Un Paso Más" (Generation '80, One More Step), Institute of Spanish Culture, Santo Domingo

Ras Akyem Ramsay

Group

1994 2nd Bienale of Painting, Santo Domingo
5th Havana Bienal, Cuba
"Contemporary Art of Our Environment," Ministry of Foreign Affairs, Barbados

1993 "Xamayca Triangular Workshop," Portland, Jamaica
"Carib Art: Contemporary Art from the Caribbean," International Trade Centre, Curacao, The Netherlands Antilles (traveling exhibition)

1992 1st Bienale of Latin American and Caribbean Painting, Santo Domingo
"Art over Sugar," Vaucluse Sugar Cane Factory, Barbados

1990 Art Museum of the Americas, Organization of American States, Washington, D.C.

1989 3rd Bienale of Latin American/African and Caribbean Painting, Wifredo Lam Centre, Havana
"Vexx" (with Ras Ishi Butcher), Queen's Park Gallery, Barbados

1988 "Two" (with Ras Ishi Butcher), Gallery Caribe, Philadelphia

Jean Claude Rigaud

Individual

1993 Corbino Gallery, Sarasota, Florida

1992 Miami International Art Exposition 1992, Miami Beach Convention Center

1990 Gallery Caribe, Fort Lauderdale

1989 Fredric Snitzer Gallery, Coral Gables

1988 Gallery Max, Kane Concourse, Bay Harbor Islands, Florida

Group

1994 "The 2nd Fujisankei Biennale," Hakone Open Air Museum, Tokyo

1993 "International Outdoor Sculpture Exhibition," Art on Brickell, Miami

1992 "Couleurs Magiques," Musée de La Commanderie D'Unet, Paris

1991 "Hort 33," Museum of Art, Fort Lauderdale
"Rediscovering the Americas," Bacardi Art Gallery, Miami

1989 "Hort 31," Museum of Art, Fort Lauderdale

Arnaldo Roche Rabell

Individual

1995 "Arnaldo Roche-Rabell," Museo de Arte Moderno, Mexico

1994 "El Legado–The Legacy," Frumkin/Adams Gallery, New York City
Galeria Botello, Hato Rey, Puerto Rico (also in 1993, 1992, 1991, and 1989)

1993 "Arnaldo Roche-Rabell: Fuegos," Museo de Arte

Contemporaneo de Puerto Rico, Santurce
"Arnaldo Roche Rabell: Art and Revelation," Museo de Arte Contemporaneo, San Juan
Frumkin/Adams Gallery, New York City (also in 1991 and 1990)

1992 "Arnaldo Roche: The First Ten Years," Museo de Arte Contemporaneo, Monterrey, Mexico
Sette Gallery, Scottsdale, Arizona (also in 1991 and 1989)

1991 "Raptos," Museum Casa Roig, Humacao, Puerto Rico
"Illuminaciones," Galeria Arte Actual Mexicano, Monterrey

Group

1995 "The Reconstructed Figure," Katonah Museum of Art, New York
Art 1995 Chicago, Navy Pier, Chicago

1994 "American Realism + Figurative Painting," Cline Fine Art Gallery, Santa Fe
"Selections from the Collection," Hirshhorn Museum and Sculpture Garden, Smithsonian Institution, Washington, D.C.

1992 "Latin American Artists of the Twentieth Century," organized by the Museum of Modern Art, New York City (traveling exhibition)
"Face to Face: Self-Portraits of Chicago Artists," Chicago Cultural Center
"Uncommon Ground: Contemporary Latin American Art," Art Gallery, The College at New Paltz, New York

1991 "Cruciformed: Images of the Cross Since 1980," organized by the Cleveland Center for Contemporary Art, Ohio (traveling exhibition)
"Myth and Magic in the Americas: The Eighties," Museum of Contemporary Art, Monterrey, Mexico

1990 "New Art from Puerto Rico," organized by the Museum of Fine Arts, Springfield, Massachusetts (traveling exhibition)
"The Awakening/El Despertar," Discovery Museum, Bridgeport, Connecticut
"New Visions: Carlos Almararaz, Arnaldo Roche Rabell, and Rafael Vadia," Gloria Luria Gallery, Miami

Stafford Schliefer

Group

1991 Malraux Gallery, Los Angeles

1990 "Kunst aus Jamaica," I.F.A. Gallery, Bonn

1988 Caribbean/Brazilian Fine Art, Toronto

1981 "Artists of Arizona: The Black Community," Arizona Bank Galleria, Phoenix

Bernard Séjourné

Individual

1980 Galerie Séjourné, Port-au-Prince (also in 1979, 1978, 1977, and 1976)

1978 Museum of Latin America Arts, Organization of American States, Washington, D.C.

1975 Musée d'Art Haïtien du Collège St. Pierre, Port-au-Prince

Group

1983 Rio Palace Hotel, Rio de Janeiro
Fundaçâo Cultural do Distrito Federal Brasilia, Brasilia

1979 Festival der Weltkulturen, Staatlichen Kunsthalle, Berlin
New Orleans Museum of Art, Louisiana
Milwaukee Art Center, Wisconsin

1978 The Brooklyn Museum, New York
Pépite Galerie, Pétion-Ville, Haiti

1976 CARIFESTA

1975 Museum of Modern Art, Mexico City

Inés Tolentino

Individual

1994 Galerie Botello, Hato Rey, San Juan (also in 1991)

1993 Galerie Carmen Cuenca, Tijuana

1989 Institute of Puerto Rican Culture, San Juan

Group

1994 XIX National Biennial of Visual Art, Santo Domingo
"Femmes artistes dominicaines," Casa Bastidas, Santo Domingo
Salon d'Art Contemporain de Bagneux, France

1993 Selections from the Biennale of Caribbean and Central American Art, Museum of Modern Art of Latin America, Washington, D.C.
"Dominican Art Today," College of Dominican Art, Santo Domingo

1992 "1492/1992 Un Nouveau Regard Sur Les Caraibes," Espace Carpeaux, Courbevoie, France (traveling exhibition)
1st Biennale of Caribbean and Central American Art, Santo Domingo
XVI Concours Nationale E. Leon Jiménes, Santiago

1991 X Biennale of Art, Valparaiso, Chile
"Emerging Art of Latin America," Nagoya, Japan
"Saint Domingue–Paris," Maison de France, Santo Domingo

1990 "Hommage à Van Gogh," Maison de France, Santo Domingo
XIII Concours National E.

Leon Jiménes, Santiago
Nationale Bienale of Visual Arts, Santo Domingo

Luce Turnier

Individual

1994 "Designs, Collages, and Oils," Galerie du Lucernaire, Paris (posthumous)
1991 Galerie de Petit-Pont, Strasbourg
Banque Société, Paris
1984 Pétion-Ville, Haiti
1982 Musée d'Art Haïtien, Port-au-Prince
1980 Randall Gallery, New York City
1979 Art Gallery, Howard University, Washington, D.C.
1978 Galerie Marassa, Pétion-Ville, Haiti
Centre d'Art Haïtien, Port-au-Prince
Galerie Pan Américaine, Pétion-Ville, Haiti

Group

1994 Galerie Antoinette Jean, Paris
1992 Musée d'Art Haïtien, Port-au-Prince
1990 Festival d'Art, Port-au-Prince
1988 "Art Haïtien: Support Papier," Mairie du VIème, Paris
1985 "Masks," Musée d'Art Haïtien, Port-au-Prince

Osmond Watson

Group

1993 "Carib Art: Contemporary Art from the Caribbean," International Trade Centre, Curacao, The Netherlands Antilles (traveling exhibition)
1989 "Black Art/Ancestral Legacy," Dallas Museum of Art, Texas
1985 "Jamaican Art 1922–1982," organized by the Smithsonian Institution Traveling Exhibition Service (SITES), Washington, D.C., and the National Gallery of Jamaica, Kingston (traveling exhibition)
1983 "Remembrance," Commonwealth Institute, London
1981 "Themes and Variations," National Gallery of Jamaica, Kingston
1979 "Contemporary Caribbean Artists/African Expressions," The Bronx Museum of the Arts, Bronx, New York
1978 "The Passion of Christ," National Gallery of Jamaica, Kingston
Week of the Americas, Landmark Bank, Fort Lauderdale
1976 "Five Centuries of Art in Jamaica," National Gallery of Jamaica, Kingston

Glossary

Mary Jane Hewitt

Anancy/Annancy
The trickster spider of folklore in the English-speaking Caribbean who is said to be the New World manifestation of the Ashanti (Ghana) trickster, Anansi.

Benin
An ancient Nigerian (West Africa) kingdom whose stylistic art became world renowned when members of a British naval expedition brought out thousands of objects as war booty in 1897. Benin sculpture, which soon found its way into museum and private collections, holds symbolic sway for people of African descent.

boysie
A Jamaica creole word for son.

bush baby
In Carib mythology, a child of the vessel. The Caribs are noted for their beautiful pottery.

calypso
One of the most popular music forms of Trinidad. Introduced by African slaves, it derived from African praise-songs and songs of derision that had been brought to the Americas in the late eighteenth century. The annual Carnival season provided the main stimulus for the composition and public performance of these topical songs.

Candomble
A genuine African religion transplanted to Brazil where economic, religious, and sexual behavior fuse in a harmonious unity.

chac-chac, shak-shak
A rhythm instrument of African origin, played in Carnival.

Cumfa, Cumfeh
An African religious cult in Guyana.

channa
Highly seasoned chickpeas prepared by roasting or frying. Channa men frequently sell them with hot roasted peanuts from carts or roadside stalls in Trinidad and in other parts of the Caribbean.

cowrie, cowrie shell
A small gastropodous shell once used for coin on the Guinea coast of Africa and in many parts of southern Asia. Also used as art material in traditional and contemporary African art, and in modern and contemporary American art.

creole, creolization
Anyone born or anything grown or produced in the Caribbean or circum-Caribbean. Creolization is the process of becoming a Caribbean person, rather than sustaining a dual nationality.

Diablesse
A Martinique equivalent of *Soucouvant.*

Hosay
A Muslim festival that forms part of the broader celebration of *Muharram,* the first month of the Muslim year. Brought to the Caribbean by East Indians, the Hosay festival unites Hindus, Muslims, and others, and in Trinidad it has developed into a multi-ethnic affair.

indigena
A native-born woman.

Jonkonnu, "John Canoe"
A Jamaican street festival characterized by masked and costumed male dancers depicting characters such as Cowhead, Horsehead, Pitchy Patchy, Devil, Warrior, and Amerindian. Although usually a Christmas—but not a Christian—celebration, it probably emanated from Africa and was syncretized with European elements in the Caribbean.

jouvay
From the French *jour overt* (opening day). A pre-Lenten Carnival celebrated from daybreak to 9:00 a.m.

Kumina, pukkumina, "pocomania"
A religious belief system and rituals which were supposedly submerged in the Maroon communities of the Caribbean during the slave era and emerged in the post-emancipation period (after 1834) when large numbers of Central African "voluntary" immigrants were brought to Jamaica. Elements of creole Christianity are incorporated into it. European observers translated *pukkumina* as "pocomania" (a little crazy) based on their observations of the worship rituals. It is related to other African Caribbean religious expressions in which dance, music, and (spirit) possession are key elements.

limbo dance
With back bent low, pelvis thrust forward, and face looking up, the dancer inches under a low, horizontal pole with flat feet firmly planted on the ground. Called the limbo in Trinidad and *masumba* in the Maroon community of Jamaica. The dancer resembles a human spider.

Loup Garou
A folklore character from Carnival *jouvay.* This demon can take the form of a vampire, but she can be destroyed by sprinkling salt on her skin if she is found in the morning of *jouvay.*

marielito
One of the more than 125,000 Cubans who immigrated to the U.S. during the Mariel boatlift, when American restrictions on Cuban immigration were relaxed between 21 April and 26 September 1980.

Maroon communities
Africans who escaped from their captors and avoided enslavement in the Caribbean, the Guyanas, and Brazil, and retained many of their African traditions.

mas
Abbreviation for masquerade as associated with the Trinidad Carnival.

mestiza
A woman of mixed Spanish and Native American ancestry in Spanish-speaking countries.

n'kondi
Famous Kongo statues into which blades, pins, nails, and wedges have been inserted to represent a vow or legal agreement.

Obeah
Usually regarded as a negative, retaliatory, or punitive practice in the Caribbean. Its practitioners determine whether, according to the circumstance, it is to be used for good or ill.

Papa Bois
A spirit of the forest; a *jouvay* folklore character from Carnival.

Phantom
A *jouvay* folklore character from Carnival who is usually interpreted as a symbol of death or as a ghost.

Ramayana
An East Indian epic recounting the exile of Rama, an incarnation of the god Vishnu, and his long fight against the demonic abductors of his wife Sita.

reggae
A music form that originated in Jamaica in the late 1960s. It is based on *ska,* which emerged from the mass urban population in the 1950s with the combined influences of U.S. pop music, elements of Jamaican traditional music (revival and *pukkumina*), and Rastafarian drumming. Reggae has a heavy four-beat bass rhythm which usually accompanies emotional anti-establishment songs.

Santería
Spanish name for an African Cuban religion. Most of its elements are derived from Yoruba (Nigeria) beliefs and rituals.

Shango
An African Caribbean religion practiced in Trinidad and Tobago and Grenada. Like Cuban *Santería*, most of its elements are derived from Yoruba beliefs and rituals.

soca
Trinidadian soul-calypso music.

Soucouvant
From the French *soucer,* it is part of the *jouvay* of Carnival. The character is based on a folk tale about a bloodsucker who sheds her skin at midnight before flying through the air to attack a victim. She must resume her natural form before daybreak.

tabla
An East Indian hand drum.

Taíno, Tainans
Arawak Amerindians who originated in the region of the Guyanas and Venezuela. They long ago sailed northward and settled on each of the islands of the Antilles, from Trinidad to Cuba.

Vodun, Voudoun, voodoo
The religion of the vast majority of Haitian people. Its metaphysical principles and ritual practices reflect elements of different West African cultures.

wadi, wadis
A river, channel of a river, or a ravine.

zouk
A Martinique word for a place to dance, a party, a lively get-together with music. This form of popular music was developed in the late 1970s in Guadeloupe by Pierre-Edouard Decimus, his brother George, and Jacob Desvarieux, and is based on *mende,* a beat once used by Maroons to signal attack and is now one of the seven *gwoka* (funeral music) rhythms.

Selected Bibliography

Alewitz, Mike. "The Havana Biennial: A Partisan View." *New Art Examiner* 14, pt. 10 (June 1987): 24–27.

Artistas abstractos de Puerto Rico. Exh. cat. Santo Domingo: Galeria de Arte Moderno de Santo Domingo, 1986. In Spanish.

Balderrama, Maria R., ed. *Wifredo Lam and His Contemporaries 1938–1952.* New York: Studio Museum in Harlem, 1992.

Baranik, Rudolf, Luis Camnitzer, Eva Cockcroft, Douglas Crimp, and Lucy R. Lippard. "Cuba Conversation." *Art in America* 75, no. 3 (March 1987): 21–29.

Benson, Legrace. "A Report from Haiti." *Art International* 25, no. 5–6 (May–June 1982): 117–130.

__________. "Kiskeya-lan guinee-Eden: The Utopian Vision in Haitian Painting." Haiti: The Literature and Culture, A Special Issue, part 2. *Callaloo* 15, no. 3 (Summer 1992): 726–735.

Bienal de pintura del Caribe y Centroamerica. Exh. cat. Santo Domingo: Galeria de Arte Moderno, 1992. In Spanish.

Boxer, David. *Edna Manley, Sculptor.* Kingston, Jamaica: National Gallery of Jamaica and Edna Manley Foundation, 1990.

Camnitzer, Luis. *New Art of Cuba.* Austin: University of Texas Press, 1994.

Cervantes, Miguel, Guillermo Olmedo, et al. *Mito y magia en america: los ochenta.* Monterrey, Mexico: Museo de Arte Contemporaneo de Monterrey, 1991. In Spanish.

Christensen, Eleanor Ingalls. *The Art of Haiti.* New York: S.A. Barnes and Company, 1971.

Cockcroft, Eva. "Apolitical Art in Cuba?" *New Art Examiner* 13, no. 4 (December 1985): 34–35.

__________. "Art and Politics: Cuba After the Revolution." *Art in America* 71, no. 11 (December 1983): 35–41.

Cohen, Ronny. "Wifredo Lam" (Galerie Lelong, New York, New York). *Artforum* 29, no. 6 (February 1991): 126–127.

Daniel, Suzanne Garrigues. "The Early Works of Wifredo Lam: 1941–1945." Ph.D. diss., University of Maryland, 1983.

Delgado, Osiris. *Historical Synopsis of the Plastic Arts in Puerto Rico.* San Juan: Gordon, 1979.

Drot, Jean Marie. *L'inconro dei due mondi visto dai pittori di Haiti.* Genova: Edizioni Carte Segrete, 1992. In Italian.

Fouchet, Max-Pol. *Wifredo Lam.* New York: Rizzoli, 1976.

Fusco, Coco. "Drawing New Lines." *The Nation* 247, no. 11 (24 October 1988): 397–401.

Gentry, Herbert. "Wifredo Lam." *International Review of African American Art* 4, no. 4 (1981): p. 8.

Geron, Candido. *Catorce Pintores y Cinco Escultores Dominicanos con Proyeccion Internacional.* Santo Domingo, 1985. In Spanish.

Guzman, Julia M. *Realism and Naturalism in Puerto Rico.* San Juan: Gordon, 1979.

"Haitian Art: A Portfolio of Paintings." Haiti: The Literature and Culture, A Special Issue, part 2. *Callaloo* 15, no. 3 (Summer 1992): 697–707.

Hughes, Robert. "Taking Back His Own Gods" (review of *Wifredo Lam and His Contemporaries 1938–1952,* at Studio Museum, Harlem, New York). *Time* 141, no. 8 (22 February 1993): 68–69.

Kennedy, Jean. "Haitian Art: Inspired by Vodun." *American Visions* 6, no. 3 (June 1991): 14.

_________. "Where Art is Joy: Haitian Art: The First Forty Years." *African Arts* 24, no. 1 (January 1991): 98–100.

Laduke, Betty. "Women and Art in Cuba: 'Feminism is not our issue.'" *Woman's Art Journal* 5, no. 2 (Fall–Winter 1984–1985): 34–40.

Lee, Muna, ed. *Art in Review: Puerto Rico.* San Juan: Gordon, 1979.

Leiris, Nichel, and Lowery S. Sims. *Wifredo Lam.* Paris: Galerie Maeght Lelong, 1986.

Lerebours, Michel Philippe. *Haiti et ses peintres de 1804 a 1980.* 2 vols. Port-au-Prince: Bibliotheque National d'Haiti, 1989. In French.

Leval, Susana Torruella. "Wifredo Lam: Dancing in the Dark." *ARTnews* 93, no. 6 (Summer 1994): 153.

Lippard, Lucy. "Made in the USA: Art from Cuba." *Art in America* 74, pt. 4 (April 1986): 27–35.

MacAdam, Barbara. "Wifredo Lam" (Americas Society, New York, New York). *ARTnews* 92, no. 1 (January 1993): 134.

MacLean, Geoffrey. *Cazabon, An Illustrated Biography of Trinidad's Nineteenth Century Painter.* Port of Spain: Aquerela Galleries, 1986.

_________. *Contemporary Painting—Trinidad and Tobago: LeRoy Clarke, Isaiah James Boodhoo, Kenwyn Crichlow, Embeyo Bahabba.* Port of Spain: October Gallery, 1992.

Merewether, Charles, and Gerardo Mosquera. *Made in Havana: Contemporary Art from Cuba.* Exh. cat. Sydney: Art Gallery of New South Wales, 1988. Part in Spanish.

Merewether, Charles. *Wifredo Lam: A Retrospective of Works on Paper.* New York: Americas Society, 1992.

Mosquera, Gerardo. "Africa in the Art of Latin America." *Art Journal* 51, no. 4 (Winter 1992): 30–39.

Mujica, Barbara. "A Turning Point in Modernism" (Diego Rivera, Joaquin Torres-Garcia, Wifredo Lam, and Roberto Matta). *Americas* 44, no. 2 (March–April 1992): 26–38.

Nessen, Susan. "Crosscurrents of Modernism: Four Latin American Pioneers: Diego Rivera, Joaquin Torres-Garcia, Wifredo Lam, Matta" (Hirshhorn Museum and Sculpture Garden, Washington, D.C.). *Art Journal* 52, no. 2 (Summer 1993): 86–94.

Nunley, John W. "Caribbean Festival Arts: Each and Every Bit of Difference." *African Arts* 22, pt. 3 (May 1989): 68–75.

Pau-Llosa, R. "Landscape and Temporality in Central American and Caribbean Painting." *Art International* 27, pt. 1 (January–March 1984): 28–33.

Peintures Haitiennes. With an introduction by Pierre Monosiet. Paris: Editions Delroisse, n.d. In French.

Presencia Africana en el arte del Caribe. Exh. cat. San Juan: Universidad de Puerto Rico, 1989. In Spanish.

Ramírez, Mari Carmen. *Puerto Rican Painting: Between Past and Present.* Princeton, New Jersey: The Squibb Gallery, 1987.

Rasmussen, Waldo, with Fatima Bercht and Elizabeth Ferrer. *Latin American Artists of the Twentieth Century.* New York: Museum of Modern Art and Harry N. Abrams, Inc., 1993.

Roche Rabell, Arnaldo. *Arnaldo Roche Rabell—Fuegos.* Exh. cat. Santurce: Museo de Arte Contemporaneo de Puerto Rico, Universidad del Sagrado Corazon Santurce, 1993. In Spanish.

Rodman, Selden. *Renaissance in Haiti: Popular Painters in the Black Republic.* New York: Pellegrini and Cudahy, 1948.

__________. *Where Art is Joy: Haitian Art, The First Forty Years.* New York: Ruggles de Latour, 1988.

Sims, Lowery. "In Search of Wifredo Lam." *Arts Magazine* 63, no. 4 (December 1988): 50–56.

__________. "Wifredo Lam: Transpositions of the Surrealist Proposition in the Post-World War II Era." *Arts Magazine* 60, no. 4 (December 1985): 21–25.

Smith, Roberta. "Restraint and Ebullience in Cuban and Colleagues" (review of *Wifredo Lam and His Contemporaries 1938–1952,* at Studio Museum, Harlem, New York). *New York Times* 142 (8 January 1993), Living Arts Pages B3, C3.

Stebich, Ute. *Haitian Art.* New York: Brooklyn Museum and Harry N. Abrams, Inc., 1978.

Straw, Petrine Archer, and Kim Robinson. *Jamaican Art: An Overview, with a Focus on Fifty Artists.* With a foreword by David Boxer. Kingston: Kingston Publishers Ltd., 1990.

"Trinidad and Tobago: A View Through the Arts." *International Review of African American Art* 8, no. 1 (1988).

Tully, Judd. "Cuban Heat Wave." *ARTnews* 93, no. 2 (February 1994): 28.

XIX bienal nacional de artes visuales. Exh. cat. Santo Domingo: Museo de Arte Moderno, 1994. In Spanish.

XVI bienal nacional de artes plasticas. Exh. cat. Santo Domingo: Museo de Arte Moderno, 1984. In Spanish.

Yau, John. "Please Wait by the Coatroom: Wifredo Lam in the Museum of Modern Art." *Arts Magazine* 63, no. 4 (December 1988): 56–60.

Social and Cultural References

Augier, F.R., S.C. Gordon, D.G. Hall, and M. Reckford. *The Making of the West Indies.* London: Longman Caribbean Ltd., 1960.

Brathwaite, Edward. *Contradictory Omens: Cultural Diversity and Integration in the Caribbean.* Mona, Jamaica: Savacou Publications, 1974.

__________. *The Development of Creole Society in Jamaica.* London: Oxford University Press, 1971.

Buhle, Henry, and Paul Buhle, eds. *C.L.R. James's Caribbean.* Durham, North Carolina: Duke University Press, 1992.

Coombs, Orde, ed. *Is Massa Day Dead? Black Moods in the Caribbean.* Garden City, New York: Anchor/Doubleday, 1974.

Cooper, Carolyn. *Noises in the Blood: Orality, Gender and the "Vulgar" Body of Jamaican Popular Culture.* London: MacMillan Press, 1993.

Crahan, Margaret E., and Franklin W. Knight, eds. *Africa and the Caribbean: The Legacies of a Link.* Baltimore: Johns Hopkins University Press, 1979.

Cudjoe, Selwyn R. *Resistance and Caribbean Literature.* Athens, Ohio: Ohio University Press, 1980.

Davis, Stephen. *Reggae Bloodlines: In Search of the Music and Culture of Jamaica.* Garden City, New York: Anchor Press, 1977.

Fagg, John Edwin. *Cuba, Haiti and the Dominican Republic.* Englewood Cliffs, New Jersey: Prentice-Hall, Inc., 1965.

Franco, Jean. *The Modern Culture of Latin America: Society and the Artist.* Rev. ed. Hammondsworth, England: Penguin Books, 1970.

Goldman, Shifra M. *Dimensions of the Americas: Art and Social Change in Latin America and the United States.* Chicago: University of Chicago Press, 1994.

Harris, Wilson. *The Womb of Space: The Cross-Cultural Imagination.* Westport, Connecticut: Greenwood Press, 1983.

Horowitz, Michael M., ed. *Peoples and Cultures of the Caribbean, An Anthropological Reader.* Garden City, New York: Natural History Press, 1971.

Knight, Franklin W. *The Caribbean: The Genesis of a Fragmented Nationalism.* New York: Oxford University Press, 1978.

Kurlansky, Mark. *A Continent of Islands: Searching for the Caribbean Destiny.* Reading, Massachusetts: Addison-Wesley Publishing Co., Inc., 1992.

Lewis, Gordon K. *The Growth of the Modern West Indies.* New York: Monthly Review Press, 1968.

__________. *Main Currents in Caribbean Thought: The Historical Evolution of Caribbean Society in its Ideological Aspects, 1492–1900.* Baltimore: Johns Hopkins University Press, 1983.

Lewis, Samella. *African American Art and Artists.* Berkeley: University of California Press, 1994.

Lowenthal, David. *West Indies Societies.* New York: Oxford University Press, 1972.

McCloy, Shelby T. *The Negro in the French West Indies.* Westport, Connecticut: Negro Universities Press, 1974.

Miller, Jeannette. *Historia de la pintura dominicana/History of Dominican Painting.* Translated by Edison Antigua. Santo Domingo: Amigo del Hogar, 1993.

Nettleford, Rex M. *Caribbean Cultural Identity: The Case of Jamaica.* Kingston, Jamaica: Institute of Jamaica, 1978.

__________. *Identity, Race and Protest in Jamaica.* New York: William Morrow, 1972.

__________. *Inward Stretch, Outward Reach: A Voice from the Caribbean.* Basingstoke: MacMillan Press, 1993.

Rubin, Vera, ed. *Caribbean Studies: A Symposium.* Seattle: University of Washington Press, 1957.

Smith, M.G. *Culture, Race and Class in the Commonwealth Caribbean.* Mona, Jamaica: University of the West Indies, 1984.

__________. *The Plural Society in the British West Indies.* Berkeley: University of California Press, 1974.

Sutton, Constance R., et al., eds. *Caribbean Life in New York City.* New York: Center for Migration Studies of New York, 1994.

Weiss, Rachel, ed. *Being América: Essays on Art, Literature and Identity From Latin America.* Fredonia, New York: White Pine Press, 1991.

Index of Artists

Luis Cruz Azaceta 108
Myrna Báez 178
Diógenes Ballester 180
José Bedia 110
Frank Bowling 128
David Boxer 150
Karl Broodhagen 130
Ras Ishi Butcher 96
Francisco Cabral 194
Eric Cadien 152
María Magdalena Campos-Pons 112
Dudley Charles 132
Margaret Chen 154
Albert Chong 156
LeRoy Clarke 196
José García Cordero 120
Christopher Cozier 198
Karl "Jerry" Craig 158
Kenwyn Crichlow 200
Annalee Davis 98
Philippe Dodard 138
Edouard Duval Carrié 140
Tomás Esson 114
Claude Fiddler 192
David Gall 100
Lia Galletti 116
Christopher Gonzalez 160
Stanley Greaves 134
Gregory A. Henry 136
Bendel Hydes 106
Andre Juste 142
Gwen Knight 102
Wifredo Lam 118
Peter Wayne Lewis 162
Shastri Maharaj 202
Edna Manley 164
Alvin Marriott 166
Michael M. Milton 168
Ronald Moody 170
Keith Morrison 172
Wendy Nanan 204
Ademola Olugebefola 190
María de Mater O'Neill 182
José Perdomo 122
Shengé Ka Pharaoh 206
Genaro Phillips 124
Ras Akyem Ramsay 104
Jean Claude Rigaud 144
Arnaldo Roche Rabell 184
Nelson Santiago 186
Stafford Schliefer 174
Bernard Séjourné 146
Juan Carlos Toca 188
Inés Tolentino 126
Luce Turnier 148
Osmond Watson 176

Photo credits

Page 102, Gwen Knight, by Spike Mafford
Page 106, Jeanne O'Donnell
Page 108, Luis Cruz Azaceta, by Judy Cooper
Page 128, Frank Bowling, by Arlington Weithers
Page 140, Charles Carrié
Page 162, Peter Wayne Lewis, by Oren Slor
Page 164, Brian St. Juste
Page 166, Margaret Bernal
Page 168, Michael M. Milton, by Anderson B. English
Page 170, David Sharkey
Page 172, Keith Morrison, by Jarvis Grant
Page 178, Myrna Báez, by Laura Magruder
Page 184, Arnaldo Roche Rabell, by Johnny Betancourt
Page 190, Ademola Olugebefola, by Pat Davis
Page 196, Richard G. Cook
Page 198, Abigail Hadeed
Photographs of artists on pages 96, 98, 100, 104, 150, 160, 196, 198, and 204 are by Armando Solis.